IAN BROWN

ALREADY IN ME

IAN BROWN - ALREADY IN ME
With And Without The Roses

by Michael O'Connell

A CHROME DREAMS PUBLICATION

First Edition 2006

Published by Chrome Dreams
PO BOX 230, New Malden , Surrey
KT3 6YY, UK

WWW.CHROMEDREAMS.CO.UK

ISBN 1 84240 332 X

Editorial Director   Rob Johnstone
Editor   Cathy Johnstone

Cover design   Sylwia Grzeszczuk
Interior design   Marek Krzysztof Niedziewicz

Front cover photo
Rex

Inside photos
Rex
Live
Redferns
Michael Shepherd
Lancaster Guardian

Record covers courtesy of
Silvertone
Geffen
Revolver
Polydor
DMC

IAN BROWN

ALREADY IN ME

With And Without The Roses

Michael O'Connell

IAN BROWN - ALREADY IN ME
With And Without The Roses

by Michael O'Connell

A CHROME DREAMS PUBLICATION

First Edition 2006

Published by Chrome Dreams
PO BOX 230, New Malden , Surrey
KT3 6YY, UK

WWW.CHROMEDREAMS.CO.UK

ISBN 1 84240 332 X

Editorial Director   Rob Johnstone
Editor   Cathy Johnstone

Cover design   Sylwia Grzeszczuk
Interior design   Marek Krzysztof Niedziewicz

Front cover photo
Rex

Inside photos
Rex
Live
Redferns
Michael Shepherd
Lancaster Guardian

Record covers courtesy of
Silvertone
Geffen
Revolver
Polydor
DMC

A catalogue record for this book is available from the British Library.

Printed and bound in Great Britain by William Clowes Ltd, Beccles, Suffolk

PART ONE

SO YOUNG

PROLOGUE

When the line-up for the 1996 Reading Festival was announced, there was great excitement as people learned that headlining the prestigious Sunday night slot were none other than the Stone Roses. Remarkably, this was the first appearance at a major festival for a band that had become the stuff of legend with their eponymous debut album way back in 1989. For the organisers of the festival it should have represented an important coup; for festival-goers, it could have been a mouth-watering finale. The only problem was that the band presented here in 1996 was very different from the one that had taken the country by storm in 1989.

Ian Brown, John Squire, Mani and Reni is the roll-call of musicians meaning as much to the passionate fans of independent music of the late 80s and early 90s, as John, Paul, George and Ringo did in their time, to Beatles fans. The Stone Roses' first coming revitalised an independent music scene, still recovering from the shock of the Smiths' split in 1986. With their landmark debut, *The Stone Roses,* they had proven themselves as true heirs to the Smiths' long held crown of 'Best English Band'.

Seven years on, at Reading, the band were clinging grimly to their mythic status, despite the fact that, in all the time since, they had released only one follow-up – *Second Coming* – and this to very mixed reviews. More importantly, the names John Squire and Reni were now notably absent from that roll-call.

Reni, their irrepressible genius drummer, had been first to fall by the wayside in May 1995. His breathtaking musicianship had long been a source of inspiration to the band but his departure represented only part of the fall-out surrounding the ill-fated *Second Coming*. Perhaps because there was so much general unrest within the band at the time, the impact of Reni's departure wasn't felt anywhere near as keenly as it should have been. And when John Squire, the Roses' very own guitar hero, followed suit in November of the same year, this should have been recognised as the fatal blow it undoubtedly was. The Stone Roses might have called it a day then and there – certainly the remaining two mem-

9

bers should have thought very seriously before turning up on the Reading bill, under the group's original name.

Yet here were Ian Brown and Mani, with new guitarist, Aziz Ibrahim and drummer Robbie Maddix in tow, holding a press conference backstage at Reading prior to their performance. And, as would later be revealed, at that very moment, Mani was being eyed by Primal Scream with a view to inviting him to be their next bass player. His customary good humour (press-baiting excepted) only served to accentuate Ian Brown as an isolated figure, while each of them in turn, tried vainly to ward off the cynicism of the gathered music press, who were determined to ask about Squire.

While Mani at least tried to communicate enthusiasm for the band, Brown spoke in a resentful tone about the departure of Squire. 'The man hasn't wanted to play with me since 1991' he complained, 'it's hard to know if you've fallen out with someone if they won't talk to you for three years'. He then went on to accuse Squire of being 'on a power trip'. Not the best overture for a gig by a band still bearing the Stone Roses name, and intending to relive their finest moments. According to some accounts, Brown had spent the earlier part of the evening smoking weed – nothing unusual for him – but on this occasion he combined it with a few drinks; this was *very* unusual for him and, if true, undoubtedly affected his mood. And, as many singers would testify, this is a lethal combination before a gig.

American 'Indie Gods' Sonic Youth were billed to precede the Roses at the festival, and as they left the stage it was the turn of what had been the English equivalent, and the ever loyal Roses fans began filtering to the front. Ibrahim, Maddix, keyboard player Nigel Ippinson and, of course, Mani were warmly greeted as they came on and, as they moved confidently into the opening strains of 'I Wanna Be Adored', the first track on the band's classic eponymous album, a new wave of enthusiasm hit the air.

Then, out of the wings came Ian Brown. The tense and tetchy figure at the press conference was now transformed into the swaggering star of old, weaving his way to the middle of the stage, pouting and shadow boxing. For these brief moments his show of defiance in front of a sceptical press made it look as if the band might be vindicated.

Then Brown started singing, leaving the audience visibly reeling in shock. Off-key throughout the first song and every one thereafter, his appalling vocals contributed hugely to the gig quickly sliding into shambles. Some of the audience were seen mimicking Brown, copying his out-of-tune singing and aping his movements that had now become, for want of a better word, embarrassing. No one warmed to the competent but uninspired Ibrahim; people groaned when Maddix tried to inject stadium vibes ("Here we go, here we go, let's see those hands in the air"); John Peel later reported seeing someone in floods of tears. And when a mini-skirted, thigh-length-booted dancer appeared on stage at the end, the pockets of people who had been walking away throughout quickly became an exodus. The Stone Roses, and especially Ian Brown, came off stage with their reputation in tatters.

In the weeks that followed, an announcement of the end of the Stone Roses seemed all but inevitable. Two weeks after the Reading performance, the *NME* reported Mani as having left the band, a rumour which was fiercely denied by the band's management, who insisted that new material and new dates were on their way. This was swiftly contradicted when, on October 29th, it was announced that Mani *was* in fact leaving – to join Primal Scream.

A statement from Ian Brown followed: 'Having spent ten years in the filthiest business in the universe it's a pleasure to announce the end of the Stone Roses. May God bless all who gave us love and support, special thanks to the people of Manchester who sent us on our way. Peace be upon you.'

Ian Brown now stood alone, the only original member of the Stone Roses not to walk away from the band. His former friend and now fierce rival John Squire was already attracting praise for his new outfit, the Seahorses; Reni was happy to be away from the music business altogether, and Mani was welcomed, with open arms, into one of the best bands in Britain. Of all the members of the Stone Roses, it was Ian Brown – the band's perennial spokesman and often brilliant frontman – who seemed to have nowhere to go. But as Mani left, he had a few prophetic words to say about his erstwhile leader.

'Ian's been unfairly savaged,' he commented, 'I know he will have the biggest and loudest laugh some day.'

I

22nd February 1963 was a momentous day in Manchester's music history. The scene was the Oasis café bar on Lloyd Street, in the centre of town. The Oasis opened at 10am for coffee and snacks, closed at 2pm, and then re-opened from 6pm to 2am with DJs and live music. The act performing on this particular night was The Beatles, who played to a packed club, and managed to capture a fanbase in Britain's most important northern city, for the first time.

The Beatles had played Manchester a year earlier and been given a resounding thumbs-down, with manager Rick Dixon re-calling, in Dave Haslam's book *Manchester,* that 'there were thirty-seven people there, and none of them were very impressed.' Though the Beatles were a little way off their first single success with 'Love Me Do', they had already built up a formidable live reputation beyond The Cavern, having honed their skills in sometimes hellish, always hi-energy live stints in Hamburg. The Mancunian indifference that first evening is typical: Manchester is huge, self-contained, almost a state-within-a-state, and (in a commendable way) not too easily impressed by outside influences. It's an attitude borne out of self-reliance somehow encapsulated in that ever proud Mancunian Ian Brown's quote about his hometown: 'It's got everything except a beach.'

Manchester's contribution to music in the UK and the world has always been there, always a match for any other city, always challenging and often quirky. It is a twist of fate that Ian Brown was born two days *after* the 'Fab Four' finally took the city by storm. Had the two dates coincided, perhaps it would have been a better omen for the Stone Roses; maybe then they would have fulfilled their potential and actually become 'the greatest English band since the Beatles' – a label with which they have been dogged over the years. But the story of the Roses and Ian Brown is *the* antidote to fairy-tale rock 'n' roll stories. Along with the clichéd moments (and characters) there are dramatic feuds, heart-warming and heart-chilling events, low farce and high comedy. And for

Ian Brown himself, part of his fascination as a musical icon lies, as we shall see, in his position as rogue prince, rather than Prince Charming. So his birthday, 20th February 1963 is, as some in the North West might say, 'sound'.

To skew fate even further, Ian Brown wasn't (as some reference sources state) actually born in Manchester at all. His birthplace, Warrington, Cheshire, is a town situated between Manchester and Liverpool, just across the border from Lancashire. The Cheshire Plains are now dotted with the palatial homes of millionaire footballers, but Warrington, along with St Helens, Widnes and Runcorn, is decidedly a 'Rugby League' town.

Ian was given the middle name George after his father, a local joiner. His mother, a telephone receptionist, worked at Warrington's huge BT call centre. He was the eldest child, with a brother, David, and a sister, Sharon. Ian had a fairly typical northern working-class upbringing, right down to the non-conformist, anti-establishment attitude borne in him, perhaps more traceable to his mother who was 'an outspoken woman'. He has later said: 'I have no fear of people from my mum'. Little trace of his father's character is to be found however, who is described as 'sweet and shy'. Ian has retained his rebellious nature to this day, but it was in evidence as far back as primary school when he refused to become a milk monitor – 'I think I was supposed to feel proud… I refused. Damn right too. I'm still quite proud of that.' As he said in 1998 to *Q*: 'I have never liked people telling me what to do.'

Likewise he is quoted in *Mojo* as saying: 'I always had attitude. I don't know where that came from. My dad's a real quiet guy. (The attitude) was part of my personality – it wasn't something I was putting on just to get attention. I did feel these things you feel when you're young: indestructible, unstoppable.'

Another formative influence on Ian's character was the indomitable spirit shown by one of his grandfathers who used to grow and sell his own flowers before the Second World War. When the war came he lost his land and the use of both of his legs: 'as a young man he had everything,' Ian recalled, 'then for the rest of his life he can't walk further than ten yards'. His grandfather's return to gardening and unremittingly positive attitude made a huge impression on the young Ian.

He has described Warrington as 'grim, but fun', though the Brown family didn't stay there long, moving to the more pleasant Timperley, nearer to Manchester, and a slight move up the social scale. Timperley has, within it, the rather plush Altrincham, juxtaposed with the notorious Wythenshaw council estate. Paradoxically, the working-class Browns found themselves at the 'posher end of town', but Ian hung on to his 'rough edge', becoming well-known in the area as streetwise and sporting an 'attitude', elements that remain with him today.

The development of such characteristics seems inevitable when one considers who Ian's earliest hero was. At just five years old he had first caught sight, on television, of one of the most renowned sports figures of the era: the incomparable Muhammad Ali. At this time, 1968, Ali was not actually fighting, having been sentenced to five years in prison for draft evasion (against which he was appealing). Presumably the young Ian Brown had still seen footage of one of his earlier fights and been exposed to the awesome charisma, wit and intelligence of Ali, the antithesis of the punch-drunk boxer. Now a hugely famous icon the world over, at that time he was still a lesser-known hero, especially for a five-year-old boy growing up in Lancashire. Yet Ian's entire bedroom was festooned with posters of the former Cassius Clay, and this earliest of influences has proven to be an enduring one on Brown, both as a performer and a man – a rare instance of a non-music legend having a significant effect on a musical star.

As the Brown family settled into Timperley, other influences began to take hold, football being a fairly predictable one. Ian came down on the United side of the Manchester football divide, and in 1969 United were irresistible. Not only had they become the first English club to win the European Cup the year before, they also boasted a handful of the most talented players in the game. The perennially popular Bobby Charlton – already one of the best-known English players in the world – and the lethal goal-scorer Denis Law, were, as a duo, enough for most teams to boast about. However, the jewel in their crown at that time, and a more attractive figure to Brown, was the legendary George Best, the most glamorous pre-Beckham footballer the country had known. Later, on trips into Manchester with his mates, Ian would actually get to befriend Best, when they started hanging around his boutique. He was always kind, eventually turning up with sweets for them. When Best retired from football by all accounts Ian burst into tears and had to be consoled by his father. Brown can still be seen at United games today – though he has also been spotted, with his dad, cheering on Warrington at the much less glitzy Rugby League game.

In 1973, when Ian was ten, Muhammad Ali and the Manchester United team were joined in his line of heroes by another idol of the age. If 1973 wasn't an auspicious one for his team (they were relegated at the end of the season), it most certainly was in terms of the worldwide popularity of martial arts superstar, Bruce Lee. Lee had been making films for some time, but this was his breakthrough year and across the UK, cinemas were showing double bills of *Fists Of Fury* and *Enter The Dragon*. The latter is generally considered Lee's masterpiece, an exhilarating cocktail of high-speed martial arts that is still impressive today. Tragically, this was the last film that he made, as, soon after its release he succumbed to a death that is still shrouded in mystery. Bruce Lee's iconic status was, with grim inevitability, further reinforced by his untimely passing, even as the film was playing the circuit, but Lee and his skills in the martial arts had already taken a hold on Ian Brown.

He threw himself into learning the physically and mentally demanding discipline of karate, displaying a real sense of commitment (something that had been noted absent by his teachers) by cycling four miles to his lessons, even after a day at school, as well as at weekends. He continued karate classes for some years and was well on his way to black belt status – he'd even at one stage considered going to Japan to improve his skills still further – before he finally called it a day at the age of seventeen. For someone who has gone on record as stating he has only ever had one fight in his life, this is a noteworthy achievement, revealing a sense of ambition and desire for self-improvement that belied the rebellious nature he was cultivating simultaneously.

The forum for this was, of course, school. He had quickly built up a reputation for himself as a bit of a handful. The milk monitor incident was merely a prelude to a long run of trouble-making. He has said that from the age of four he had an obstinate streak that started getting him into trouble at school. He was well known as a classroom joker, an over-eager impressionist, always trying to grab the lead roles, as an impersonator of teachers and in general, a disruptive influence. He told *Q* in 1998, 'A lot of the teachers were wary of me 'cos I was always quick to answer back, not that I was particularly naughty, but I did have an attitude.'

So, though carrying a notorious reputation, Brown was far from being a delinquent. As he grew into his teens he developed two further enduring characteristics: a wanderlust and an ever deepening love of music. The Brown family home had always been one that echoed with music. When Ian was eight, an aunt had given him a large selection of seven-inch singles, which he played non-stop on his self-stacking Dansette record player, and with that, his interest in music intensified. Each record that thudded down onto the turntable was a pop classic: music from the Beatles, the Stones, the Supremes, Tom Jones and so on. This is where Brown's pop sensibilities undoubtedly germinated. The purveyor of three-minute classics said later 'for years, from seven until I was fourteen, I thought there were only singles, I didn't know there were any albums.'

He bought his first record in 1972, when he was twelve – 'Metal Guru' by T-Rex, the glam rock classic. But the musical style that had the formative influence on Brown was Northern Soul. Developing out of the mod clubs of the 1960s, the essentially revivalist Northern Soul craze, which is still with us today, has managed to survive the onslaught of a host of other music trends through the years. The purist and perhaps elitist approach of fans and organisers, setting great store by the original soul records on the rarest of labels, is counterbalanced by the great spectacle that is a Northern Soul club in full swing. By the mid-seventies it was at its height, the highs being fuelled by plentiful supplies of amphetamine – the Northern Soul dancer's drug of choice. It's easy to see now that this long-lasting craze was a significant precursor to the emergence of Acid House in the late eighties – the development of which Brown and the Roses played no small part in.

The Twisted Wheel in Manchester and the Wigan Casino were the premier Northern Soul venues at this heady time. Although still only in his early teens, Ian did manage to get into a less well-known club, the Droylsden Concorde Suite, for a soul all-nighter where he experienced the headlong rush of this anthemic sound.

Here was another destination for someone who loved to move around. Since he was eight, Ian had been wandering down to the city centre, checking out the scene – even venturing into the Oasis café where The Beatles had played. He began to go further afield with a small gang of friends from school – to Leeds, York, Blackpool. He told *Sounds* in 1988: 'I've always been on the move. I hung about with lads all over the city. I've been to every seaside resort in England and most cities. I've been to most of Europe just moving about.'

The gang would buy clothes and records, hang around, looking or not looking for trouble, depending on the circumstances, and then start the long journey back. All common and fairly harmless pursuits for mid-seventies teenagers with a bit – or indeed an excess – of unreleased tension. But Ian would also find some measure of release in his next musical discovery.

When Brown was fourteen, he heard punk rock for the first time. 'Punk changed everything,' he said later, 'the band I most got into was the Sex Pistols. My mate had "Anarchy In The UK". He got it in Woolies for 29p 'cos after that Bill Grundy Show they put the record in the bargain bin!' It was at this infamous appearance on the Tonight show, hosted by Bill Grundy, that the Sex Pistols – flanked by hangers on such as that femme-fatale of the scene, Siouxsie Sioux – created the flashpoint through which the nation was alerted to the 'menace of punk'. Of course, the show is remembered less for the emerging music phenomenon it was reporting on, than for the antagonistic Grundy, goading the only-too-willing Pistols to swear and generally cause outrage among tea-time audiences. The scale of the impact this broadcast had, and the notoriety it quickly gained, is reflected in the fact that the transmission was not even a nationwide one, but limited to certain regions and, ironically, was never aired by Granada Television, the only commercial network broadcasting in Brown's neck of the woods. The aggressive personas adopted by punk singers became another important and enduring influence on Brown, his onstage presence frequently resembling an amalgam of Johnny Rotten and his old hero, Muhammad Ali. Ian was still too young to see the Pistols play their landmark gig in Manchester, so the punk influence that actually made him seriously consider getting a band together was, fittingly, an outfit from round the corner in Wythenshawe – Slaughter and the Dogs.

Slaughter and the Dogs, or Slaughter as they came to be known to fans, are one of those bands that emerged from the punk era destined, if not doomed, to be 'remembered' in music history only once the Pistols, the Clash, the Damned et al have been mentioned first – and then often by people who have ended up far more famous than they ever were. So, just as Nick Cave exudes a teenager's enthusiasm for those darlings of post-punk, the Pop Group, Ian Brown has heaped praise on Slaughter who are, irrevocably, 'Championship' material rather than 'Premiership' – mere mortals instead of immortals.

This is not to say though that Slaughter and the Dogs were a bad band. In strictly punk terms their conspicuous lack of musical prowess made them exemplars while their all-round energy and anthemic flourishes made them an alluring live act. David Bowie's erstwhile cohort Mick Ronson produced their first glammed-up album and they had two landmark singles, "Where Have All The Boot Boys Gone?" and "Cranked Up Really High", released around the time that Ian discovered them. The latter was heavily redolent of a night in a club, full of speed and/or booze, a kind of punk Northern Soul number – this was Ian Brown's favourite, and, during the press for the release of his first solo album, he was still inspired enough to intone the name of Slaughter and the Dogs.

'Yeah, I got into them through that single "Cranked Up Really High". My next door neighbour was a friend of Rossi, the guitarist. I saw them at Wythenshawe Forum and the Belle Vue a few times.'

Ian was now getting to gigs on a regular basis. In fact, the first band he had seen – with a friend from school and the friend's twelve-year-old sister - was the legendary Joy Division. This gig is famous less for the band's performance as for Brown's later revelation that singer Ian Curtis had shocked him, his friend and – most pertinently - the twelve-year-old girl, when she, having asked Curtis for one of his badges, was told she could have it "… for a blow job." Little is known about Ian's reaction to this particular performance, but it is clear that as his energies started to turn more and more towards music, the 'Manchester gloom' perpetrated by this unique outfit, heroes to the fabled 'raincoat brigade', was not for Ian Brown. 'I never felt hip,' he said later, 'That was always a big thing in Manchester… all those Factory bands. It was all so insular and I never felt close to any of that.'

He began to explore music in depth, not only going to gigs, but also making regular trips to the Virgin store on Lever Street in the city centre and buying up a host of the once-occasional punk singles that had quickly become a stampede. Though this was the hangout for all the Manchester punks, swapping gossip and selling fanzines that are now collectors' items, he seems to have demurred at becoming a punk himself, even when he was seeing some stellar punk outfits: 'I saw the Buzzcocks a few times – at the Mayflower in Belle Vue and at a signing at Virgin Records. I saw the Clash in '77.'

Brown even resisted the temptation to become a no-holds-barred punk throughout a stint of roadie-ing for a punk band. He told *Record Collector*: 'I used to go watch the Angelic Upstarts! Mensi – top kid! I roadied for them a few times. I've seen them fifteen, twenty times. Top band.' The Upstarts were part of a clutch of groups from the era when punk was actually evolving into the next musical phase, and record companies, with almost missionary zeal, seized on above average and savage outfits such as the Upstarts, even though their best singles – in their case, 'A Clockwork Orange' – could only ever hope to scrape into the Top Forty.

Right in the midst of all these experiences, it would have been hard for Ian to discern that punk was actually on its last legs. He was still having a great time and Manchester was at the forefront of this revolution – Jon Savage has written that 'in early 1977, Manchester started to develop as Britain's second punk city after London and, as the capital quickly became punk-saturated'. By the end of 1977, however, Joy Division had released their *An Ideal For Living* EP and, with hindsight, it's clear to see that the future was not punk, but post-punk. The more subtle and angular sounds of, first Joy Division, then the Fall and Magazine, began the ascendancy of the 'Factory Bands' in an alternative music scene that Ian was now part of.

Music was now taking up a lot of Ian Brown's time and energy, and, sooner or later, he would need to turn ideas into action. To do that, however, he would have to find a musical partner. That collaborator turned up in the form of an old friend from school, who shared his passion for punk rock – John Squire.

II

While there are few fairy-tale elements to the story of Ian Brown and the Stone Roses, one pre-requisite of a classic rock n' roll tale - and peculiar to the early Roses circumstances - is the metamorphosis of a childhood friendship into a formidable song-writing partnership, resulting in the formation of a hugely successful band.

Ian Brown and John Squire's collaboration echoes those between John Lennon and Paul McCartney, and Mick Jagger and Keith Richards. Just as the acerbic Lennon rather overshadowed the arch-romantic McCartney, the introverted Squire would often be pulled along by the outgoing Brown; Jagger was a compelling front-man, as Brown would go on to be, while Richards and Squire, both swiftly advanced from mastering the guitar to writing tunes on another level entirely – and becoming bona fide guitar heroes. Another similarity between the Lennon/McCartney and Squire/Brown axis, is the more ominous one of both partnerships and their bands ending in spectacular fallings-out. In their early years as friends it would have seemed impossible for either of these partnerships to have disintegrated. These were both true friendships based on the age-old adage that opposites attract.

The first-ever meeting between Brown and Squire was virtually a replica of the recorded early childhood meeting between Jagger and Richards – taking place in a sandpit. John has recalled (Ian himself can't remember, but doesn't dispute it) that Ian was playing naked in the sand. As proof of Ian's extrovert side this story couldn't be bettered and the contrasting nature of John is confirmed by Ian's clearest recollection: 'I do recall his shy stare, which was quite intriguing even then. There was something about him.' As the owner of a decidedly piercing stare himself, this is a kind of backhanded compliment.

Unlike Jagger and Richards however, Brown and Squire did not attend the same primary school, though they were near neighbours, John living on Sylvan Avenue in Timperley, where even, the Bee Gees had once lived. They would eventually be in the same class together at secondary school, but John's early school life couldn't have been more different from Ian's. John's quiet nature sometimes concerned his teachers, but they soon found that he possessed a deeply creative side, manifested in art classes, where he began to excel, often being excused from P.E. so he could develop his artistic talents.

Outside school, both boys grew up in close proximity, they never really connected early on: Ian pasted up his posters of Ali, tore away to his karate lessons and began to wander, while John spent a lot of time at home, putting many hours of work into his drawing. He has said since, somewhat defensively: 'I was always a loner. I prefer it.'

Once they were secondary school age and ended up in the same class at Altrincham Grammar, their common interest in music created new contact. Where Ian had a scattershot 'singles' education at first, along with the Northern Soul influence, John tended to immerse himself in older bands (an addiction that would have far-reaching consequences) listening to albums, and developing an in-depth knowledge of the Beatles and the Beach Boys, for example. Like his friend, he also became interested in punk and it was this shared passion that brought about regular meetings, meeting after school round at each other's houses.

'We became friendly at thirteen or fourteen,' said Ian, 'I took "God Save The Queen", the first Clash LP and "One Chord Wonders" by the Adverts round to his house. I played him these punk records, and then a week later he'd bought the Clash and "God Save". He went mad about the Clash.' John went on to play the Clash album every single day around that time and when Ian walked into John's bedroom one day he was astonished to find that, where his own walls were covered with images of Ali, John had actually painted a mural celebrating Joe Strummer.

While their shared interest in music was at a similar level, it was John who took the first tentative steps towards actually making his own music. 'He got his guitar when he was fifteen,' recalls Ian, 'the first thing he learned to play was "Three Blind Mice". Then he'd play his guitar for me when I went round.' John now began to cultivate his twin passions of painting and guitar with equal gusto.

Two of John's earliest guitar heroes were, naturally, the two Joneses, Steve and Mick, from the premier punk bands of the day, as well as the New York Dolls' Johnny Thunders. He quickly outgrew 'thrash' guitar, however, and attempted to master more intricate styles. His father helpfully rewired his record player so he could slow down records by Hendrix, Clapton and Jeff Beck enough to learn their guitar lines. His immersion was total. He admitted to *Total Guitar*: 'I probably spent too long practising on my own'. The fact that the first time he met another 'proper guitarist' was just before the first Stone Roses album says it all.

By 1979, both Ian and John were armed with a fairly respectable haul of 'O' levels. Of leaving school Ian said later: 'The first thing I did was scrub pots. Been left school two days and I'm in this big oven in a hotel with the chef kicking me. I stood it about three weeks.'

He and John thus swapped Altrincham Grammar for South Trafford College of Further Education, a popular option of the time. Further education was 'optional' in the loosest sense of the word, and there was a markedly less-disciplined environment than school. At South Trafford, there was nowhere near the same amount of invigilating or enforcing of students' pursuit of their education. Instead, it provided an opportunity for Squire and Brown to bunk off their lessons, go to the cafés and discuss their greatest ambition: to form a band.

There had been loose gatherings with mates from the school and college, centred round John's guitar playing but, as is often the way in band histories, the name emerged a little while before the songs actually did. So during '79 the Patrol were formed, the fledgling line-up of the band comprising Squire on guitar, Brown on bass and Simon Wolstencroft on drums.

Wolstencroft was in the same year as Squire and Brown at South Trafford, and possessed a considerable musical pedigree in that he had already been in a band, not to mention having actually ventured inside a real rehearsal room. The first session by the Patrol took place in Wolstencroft's house and resulted in some rough Clash-like 'tunes'. Though Ian would respond gamely on bass in these first rehearsals, it wasn't long before he lost enthusiasm for the instrument and, while Squire's skills developed, Ian never really got beyond the basics. A sense of disenchantment in Ian could be construed from his spasms of wanderlust, often travelling on his own and as far a field as Blackpool, but, nevertheless, the Patrol as a group began to think about getting a singer.

Brown and Wolstencroft were in the refectory at the college one day when a likely candidate presented himself in an unusual way. The hubbub of the room was suddenly dispelled by row between a pair of boys that quickly escalated into a full-blown fight. One of the perpetrators was a skinhead Ian had noticed in and around the college before.

Andy Couzens had wreaked terrible revenge on a fellow student (left crying by the end of the brawl) who had been having a go at Andy's younger brother the night before. Having witnessed Couzens' opponent lying across one of the refectory tables, a suitably impressed Ian Brown strolled over to Couzens and asked him if he wanted to be in a band. Couzens immediately said yes, and when Ian met that answer with another question ('Can you sing?') Couzens clearly didn't ask for time to think it over as his first rehearsal with the band took place that same evening – despite it still remaining unclear as to whether he could actually sing or not.

It transpired that Couzens couldn't, but, rather in the spirit of Ian's beloved Slaughter and the Dogs, whatever Couzens lacked in musical ability, he did his best to make up for with enthusiasm. Though he was intensely nervous (he had his back turned to his new colleagues throughout), he finally let out a stream of impassioned, hysterical shouts; while the majority of his vocals may not have been tuneful, the rest of the band were impressed enough to invite him to join them.

It's as well to remember here that Brown and Squire, the eventual purveyors of perfect three-minute-pop, were still totally enthralled by punk at this stage. The songs that started to emerge during the ensuing sessions would betray the influence of the kind

25

of political punk espoused by the Clash, with such titles as "Jail Of The Assassins" and "25 Rifles". These early offerings were essentially parodies of Clash songs like "Bankrobber" and "Spanish Guns". As Squire broke out of the bedroom at last, he also chose to travel the country, along with many other fans, following the Clash's '16 Tons' tour, and catching his idols in an era when many considered them to be at the height of their live playing power. Squire was in the deepest phase of his Clash fascination, and in Wolstencroft he found a willing cohort too.

The Patrol had their own 'fan' in the form of a mutual friend who began hanging out with the band and even attending rehearsals – someone who would become a key witness and participant in the early Stone Roses story. Pete Garner had bumped into Ian and John walking through the fields near where they lived. Though he didn't go to the same college (Garner went to Burnage High School, also attended by future Roses member Aziz Ibrahim), he became friendly with the Patrol, sharing their love of punk and quickly becoming 'one of the gang'.

It was Garner and Brown who discovered one day that their idols, the Clash, were rehearsing somewhere in Manchester. Following a hunch, they made their way to the Pluto Recording Studios and hung around outside. Sure enough, their heroes turned up to work on the afore-mentioned "Bankrobber". The star-struck pair managed to do some fast-talking and were somehow spirited into the studios as part of the Clash entourage.

The Clash were always well-known for their generosity to fans, once, for instance, famously stationing themselves outside a venue to explain in person why that night's gig had been cancelled. Ian and Pete were transfixed as most of the band took time to have some words with these new-found acolytes. Cruelly, John Squire of all people, was committed elsewhere that day and missed the momentous encounter. He has never commented, but perhaps missing the session was in some ways fortunate, since the one member of the Clash who wasn't wholly welcoming, adopting a more conventional rock star demeanour, was none other than his idol, Joe Strummer. Ian's comment was: '... it was a bit of a let down. I thought he was a bit of a dick, to be honest.'

Even so, one assumes that for the band this Clash experience was an inspiration. Certainly, more songs started to pour out of the Patrol's rehearsals – to the extent that they were close to performing for the first time. The fact that Garner was attending these rehearsals while not playing anything didn't quite mean that he had nothing better to do. Again emulating the Clash, the Patrol subscribed to the idea that a band must have a gang mentality and, in between creating songs, everyone, Garner included, would be discussing music obsessively, while attempting to formulate the band's musical plan for future audiences.

In March 1980, the Patrol played to their first audience, managing to get themselves onto a bill at the Sale Annexe Youth Club, admission charge, 30p. They were supported by a band called Suburban Chaos and Andy Couzens has recalled to author, John Robb, that they did rather well: 'We went down good, we were shocked! We were rehearsing so much it was as good as that stuff was going to get.'

Naturally, more gigs followed, but the band would manage only once to break out of the tiniest of venues with this music, which, however enthusiastically played was still, at the end of the day, a Clash derivative. And this element they had in common with many of the bands around at the time – like Suburban Chaos, or the exquisitely named Corrosive Youth.

The one time they got a gig at a larger venue – the Mayflower in Gorton – came about because they just happened to be an available replacement for none other than Adam and the Ants, who had broken down on the motorway. Thrust on to the stage by a panicked promoter in front of a disgruntled local punk audience, who had already antagonised Ant's roadies, the Patrol acquitted themselves well, playing a decent set that ended peaceably. But even at this more prestigious gig, there were not many more than fifty people in attendance.

Not surprisingly, there was only one Patrol demo to go with the one 'larger' gig. Recorded on a 4 track in a Rusholme studio, it was limited to one hundred copies, and amounted to three songs: "Jail Of The Assassins", "25 Rifles" and "Too Many Tons". This riff-heavy compilation, the first recording of Ian and John together, shows up John's continuing development of the guitar in contrast to Ian's distinct lack of any real connection with the bass, though he hammers away enthusiastically throughout.

With the demo accomplished, the Patrol returned to the cycle of smaller gigs – though this was to be the final lap for them. Over the months, they had developed the semblance of a stage act, heavily influenced by the time-honoured confrontationalism of punk. Andy Couzens has commented interestingly on Ian's contribution – 'Ian always had to have a microphone so that he could shout at people' – suggesting that even at this stage, the role of front man was more to his liking.

There were, no doubt, feelings of déjà vu when they found themselves on a bill at Dunham Massey village hall with none other than Suburban Chaos and Corrosive Youth. But the last gig by the Patrol was, fittingly, back at South Trafford College in November 1980, admission 50p, where they were joined in the line up by Scorched Earth and Strange Behaviour.

The Patrol had already talked about refining their music and moving away from the Clash-based sound, but a more significant shift came about as the result of a spontaneous incident at the end of this final set, which pointed the way to their future. Ian grabbed hold of a microphone and began shouting out lyrics from The Sweet's glam stomper "The Blockbuster". Pete Garner picked up the bass, and since "Blockbuster" has one of the simplest bass-lines around, was able to carry the song along. Thus, Ian had his first real taste of being front man on stage. It was this improvisatory moment that foreshadowed the first line-up of the Stone Roses, and without any formal sign-off – or bitterness – it proved to be the end of the Patrol.

III

Ian Brown's bass-playing days were definitely at an end too. He sold his instrument for a £100, bought a scooter and started looking round for a scooter club to join. There had been hints of his growing boredom with the band and clearly Ian's penchant for hitting the open road wasn't about to be fulfilled by cadging small to medium gigs in and around Manchester. He was still very young, barely an adult, and, as was typical by now, he couldn't simply take a *passing* interest in any chosen lifestyle.

Ian's scooter craze was of course linked to his earlier interest in Northern Soul – the soundtrack to the life of the scooter boys. He bought a 1966 Lambretta J 125 from Braithwaite's, a popular scooter stockist in Stockport. Now a legendary model of course, the golden era for the Lambretta was actually in 1968 to 1973, when the mods, skinheads, greasers *et al* were abroad and the nearest fights to Ian took place in Blackpool and Stockport.

A scooter revival began however, in the late seventies and there remained some remnants of the craze when Ian bought his machine. The soundtrack of the scooter brigade had now been extended to include the ubiquitous Angelic Upstarts, the Cockney Rejects and bands like them. These were the bands championed by Garry Bushell of *Sounds*, who awarded them some coverage while they were being totally ignored by *Melody Maker* and *NME*.

The revival was demonstrably working-class and Ian was perhaps making a class statement, following his instincts by binning the bass and straddling a scooter. Ian has made his feelings about the hypercritical music press (i.e. *NME* and *Melody Maker* – the London-based papers), abundantly clear. To his mind they were encouraging hifalutin pretension in rock bands while snobbishly turning their backs on the mod revival bands: 'I didn't like it when all these culture bands started taking themselves really seriously. As if they were creating these monumental works of art... The music press was at fault because it encouraged them too much... made them feel like stars before they were ready, often with disastrous results. I wasn't particularly interested in becoming part of it."

One could speculate freely about which bands Ian was referring to here, but there was clearly a rejection of the current music scene, rather than of music itself, his disenchantment perhaps being fuelled by the knowledge that it was the end of the road for the Patrol, with nothing, as yet, to replace it.

So, in the absence of any new personal musical venture, Ian threw himself into the scooter life. He reaffirmed his Northern Soul loyalties by joining a North Manchester scooter club, rather than one south of the city, as the favoured music was of these areas more rock-based. Neither did he look towards East Manchester, which had a heavy-metal vibe. During this phase of Ian's life he owned five scooters, joining a number of different clubs and putting in all the hours of maintenance, decorating and general cosseting of the vehicles expected of any self-respecting scooter boy. One of his bikes also had 'Cranked Up Really High' emblazoned on it, invoking the name of Slaughter and the Dogs once more. He went on scooter rallies and, with his own wheels, his journeying took on new dimensions, taking him as far afield as Brighton, the Isle of Wight and even the highlands of Scotland.

This new interest provided some of the fundamental opportunities any 17 year old would wish for – to play music, have a scene to belong to and meet girls. 'When I was 17 I used to put a Northern Soul club on with my mate in Salford at the Black Lion in Blackfriars Street,' Ian said later. 'We used to hire a room for £15 and all our mates would come down. We used to build scooters to go to the all-nighters – just to get girls really.'

Throughout this craze, Ian never forgot his friend from the Patrol, and from the outset, tried to get John into scooters, in the same way he had previously got him into punk. Where John had been an instant convert to Punk, with scooters it took two years to get him fully on board. Ian dragged him to scooter meetings galore but it was only after finally seeing that ultimate paean to the Mod movement, in the film *Quadrophenia* that John at last succumbed, instantly proving his commitment by assembling his own Lambretta – rebuilding a GP200 from the frame.

Both Brown and Squire have looked back at this era with fondness, the latter stating: 'A Lambretta is a very desirable object. I got one. Did it up, painted it. I wanted to show it off to other people who had scooters.' Typically, John had a Clash quote painted on his bike: 'Too Chicken To Even Try It' from "White Riot". Ian has also recalled some of the occasional violence, including spats with fellow future rock stars: 'We used to go to the Beehive in Eccles and the scooter boys used to fight with the lads from that area – where the (Happy) Mondays were from, Swinton.'

Patrol ex-member Andy Couzens also joined them on the odd occasion, including a bone-jarring journey to Weston-super-Mare which took them over two days to complete and nearly put them off scooters forever. The violence, though, was no deterrent as he had rather reverted to South Trafford College type, becoming embroiled in that other teenage craze: football hooliganism.

Pete Garner, meanwhile, had opted to go into full-time employment and had, rather fortuitously, got himself a job in a store called Paperchase. A long way from the future greetings card chain, this was a shop that sold magazines, fanzines and paraphernalia as well as records. It was an old-style record shop that fitted Garner's lifestyle perfectly, though far from being a 'megastore' such as the local Virgin, which might have promised some kind of career.

Couzens, Squire and Brown were drifting in the way young people of this age frequently do. Couzens survived doing odd building jobs. Squire's entry into the scooter lifestyle had meant he had neglected his guitar playing to an extent, but as some of the initial enthusiasm for the Mod lifestyle started to wane, he slowly but surely reverted to putting in solitary hours of guitar practice, building up his skills while waiting for the right opening to utilise his creative talents.

Perversely, it was the restless, nomadic Brown who took the really humdrum job. Incredibly, it's said that Ian even went as far as nagging his ex band-mate to supply him with a lead to an interview for a job being offered by Couzens' uncle. It would seem that Ian genuinely wanted this job – as a salesman in a caravan business! Ian was successful in the interview and began a new era ushering mostly middle-aged couples around a yard in Poynton, selling all the essential equipment for life in a mobile home, as well as the caravans themselves.

Horrified fans of the consummate star of the present-day can be reassured by the fact that this job lasted only a few months with Ian walking out in the end. It seems far-fetched to believe that Ian Brown *really* had any genuine interest in a career in caravan sales and the truth surely must be he was at that time utterly at a loss as to what to do with himself when he wasn't riding his scooters. His abrupt departure and subsequent behaviour confirm this.

The era that Ian and the rest were living in now – the dawn of the eighties – was one of the bleakest in post-war British history. Margaret Thatcher had been elected Prime Minister in 1979 and, though she had promised to bring about some kind of unity to a country beset by unemployment and industrial unrest, her government's programme amounted to an attack on unions and a serious undermining of the social fabric – something underlined by strikes that would become more bitter as the decade progressed, as well as a wave of riots and disturbances which took place across the country.

The Manchester of these Thatcherite days was a bleak landscape indeed, in more ways than one. Whereas the sixties Manchester, into which Ian Brown was born, had a strong manufacturing base, meaning that jobs were fairly easy to come by, and new ones being generated as industries grew, by the eighties, Manchester's manufacturing industries were starting to erode. Slowly the city area was transformed into a domain of call centres, like the one that Brown's Mum worked in. Clearly, that kind of prospect didn't fit with Ian's plans – if he had any at the time.

After the caravan stint in Poynton, Ian seems to have disappeared from the lives of the ex-members of the Patrol for nigh on a year. A 'lost weekend' may be overstating it, as he continued to be spotted by mutual friends at gigs, such as those of the Meteors, of whom he was a big fan, and rockabilly punk nights. Squire, meanwhile, was back playing the guitar on his own, and favoured Bowie/Roxy nights at the Pips nightclub.

Andy Couzens has declared that Ian Brown entered a murky world around this time. Readers well versed in band histories of this era will have noted the Meteors were the leading lights of what came to be known as the Oi! faction of bands, championed by *Sounds*' Garry Bushell. Many of these bands had, if not affiliations, then sympathies with right-wing groups. Couzens told Manchester rock journalist Mick Middles that Ian Brown 'dabbled with the NF and all that'.

Certainly, if he was going to as many Meteors gigs as is reported, he would have been exposed to plenty of right-wing propaganda, but Couzens fell short of saying that Ian dabbled in any of the extreme violence – one of the most disturbing offshoots of the movement. Right-wing propaganda was pretty common among scooter clubs too, so, like many of the scooter boys of the time, he may have flirted with the ideas. But they were no doubt dispelled when the next musical distraction came along.

Of all the Patrol members, John Squire was to fall on his feet when it came to getting a job – and it was to become a later claim to fame too. Succeeding no less a personage than Bernard Sumner of Joy Division and New Order, John got a job at the animation studios, Cosgrove Hall. Founded in 1976 in Chorlton-Cum-Hardy by Brian Cosgrove and Mark Hall, Cosgrove Hall is a singular Manchester success story. Eschewing the traditional route of success in their industry by moving to London, they affirmed their roots further by naming their first series *Chorlton and The Wheelies*. This show has since gone on to become a cult classic but has been eclipsed by the success of *Dangermouse*, one of the most popular children's shows ever, seen in over 112 countries, and even managing to get screenings on American television – a remarkable achievement.

John was lucky to fall into a highly creative and refreshingly bohemian workplace where he flourished. Scraping away at the heads of models and sketching movements, he worked on *Danger-mouse* itself, as well as the future BAFTA award-winning *Wind In*

The Willows. There was even a rumour that it was John's design that was used for the Bertie Bassett liquorice commission.

So John now had a rewarding job and plenty of disposable income too. This led him inexorably to music and to the Paperchase store where his former fellow band member, Pete Garner, was standing behind the counter. Hooking up for drinks to discuss an unrealised animation project, they soon switched to talking about putting a new band together, a casual rehearsal revealing to Garner Squire's astonishing development on the guitar.

John had seen something of Andy Couzens around here and there, and knew he had, rather typically, been asked to leave college for launching an attack on a teacher before telling the principal 'to go fuck himself'. Now he had a bit of extra time on his hands (and was playing guitar), it was agreed to approach him and see whether he would like to hook up with John and Pete and have a go at another band. They drafted in a drummer who was quickly replaced by another, and another after that, until the whole thing fizzled out before they had even alighted on a name.

It was an abortive experiment, but, once again, John's burgeoning talent as a guitarist and a songwriter shone through, and there wasn't to be much of a delay before they got something else off the ground. So they re-convened, this time *with* a name and quickly pressed into service a future member of the Stone Roses, whom the elusive Ian had met some years before.

Back when he was sixteen, Ian had been drafted into an ad-hoc gang in his area, a 'posse' which were dispatched to North Manchester: 'We'd heard about this kid with a swastika on his head, some bonehead... who was bullying kids. So we got up a crew to sort him out.' The 'venue' for this brawl was a council house and once there Ian recalled: 'I remember seeing Mani sat down. I'm thinking, he ain't no fighter. So, one or two of these kids dealt with the bonehead, put him to rest – and that's how we met.'

Gary 'Mani' Mountfield was born in the same year as Ian and John in Crumpsall, growing up in the tough area of Moston, on Manchester's north side. Mani was, at first, more football than music-obsessed and, had he possessed the talent, would certainly have chosen football over music. A lifelong and diehard Manchester United fan, his parents were, for a time, even friends with George Best, whom Mani remembered would occasionally turn up for a late night drink with his Mum and Dad. Where Ian's early life cultural pursuit had been karate and John's drawing, for Mani life was really all about Manchester United. He would attend every game he could, as he still does today, and was even reputedly caught on TV cameras, much to his parents' anger, gobbing from his place on the terraces.

Once he realised that he didn't have enough talent to make it as a professional footballer, however, he made it his aim to be in a band. Football or music, as the Gallagher brothers have since attested, were the only conceivable career options for working-class Manchester kids. And, as young Ian and John were joining the punk revolution in the leafy suburb of Timperley, Mani was doing likewise in the north side, choosing the bass as his instrument. The bass guitar was a popular choice for aspiring punks with only rudimentary musical skills, the most obvious examples being Sid Vicious and Paul Simonon. But Mani, unlike Ian, embraced the instrument and also in contrast to Vicious or Simonon, proved to have an outstanding talent as a punk bass player. Primarily, though he also developed an interest in Northern Soul: his mastering of both styles proved to be a powerful influence on his future bass playing.

He was soon taking up duties in a host of punk outfits, including a youth club band called Urban Paranoia who, with a name like that, would have been at home on a bill with the Patrol. Following his first encounter with Ian, Mani became well-known to the ex-Patrol bunch. While he started off as a punk, Mani has also become known as a trailblazer of the 'Perry Boy' look which, outside of Manchester and the North was known as 'casual'. A much more agreeable forerunner of the modern-day 'Chav' look, Mani's Perry Boy style was one that he has claimed to have brought to the rest of the Roses, but, in truth, when one looks at archive photos, he is the only member who really appears comfortable in the garb.

Mani was even present, in 1983, during John's first acid trip: 'We walked into town tripping our tits off,' he later told *Mojo*, 'we bought these big Chocolate Forest ice lollies and we were walking around in a right state, seeing rabbits and all kinds of shit.'

For John, Andy and Pete, then, Mani was well worth inviting along for their next musical experiment, to be called the Waterfront, after Squire's ill-advised suggestion, the 'Fireside Chaps', was mercifully rejected. Also included were a drummer, Chris Goodwin from Oldham, suggested by Mani, and a singer from Moston, like Mani, known as Kaiser, real name Dave Kartey.

Formed in 1982, probably the high watermark of the post-punk era, the Waterfront retained some of the attack-minded facets of a punk band on stage, alongside the fairly conventional rock/pop format of the songs that the band's name suggested. Most notable of the punk-style acknowledgements was Kaiser's habit of head-butting the microphone, Manchester music author Mick Middles, has suggested that the shadow of late-seventies football violence also hung over one song in particular, 'Normandy (On A Beach In)', a musical memoir of Kaiser's thuggery during a football tournament in France. Kaiser however, recalls it as something of a tribute to the soldiers who lost their lives in the Second World War. This song was included on a demo produced by the band after a few months, which duly came to the attention of Ian Brown, back from one of his scooter runs. It encouraged him to make contact again with all of the ex-Patrol guys.

'The Waterfront were great,' Ian later told *Record Collector*. They were like Orange Juice. He (John) played me a tape and it sounded really good. I was impressed I knew somebody who could play with that quality.'

Apart from the similarity to Orange Juice, much-revered at that time, the outstanding feature of the demo was the quality of John's playing: he was clearly attaining his own style; the recording was alive with actual guitar flourishes. Ian was encouraged to move a step closer, attending the odd rehearsal, and it was John who asked him to try out on vocals, with a view to his sharing duties with Kaiser.

Another amazing brush with a musical legend emboldened Ian now. The event took place at a party in the flat that he had moved to in Hulme. Hulme was well-known at that time as a 'boho drop-out zone' and less well-known, at that time, as the birthplace of Morrissey, who was then on the cusp of a fateful meeting with Johnny Marr. The party, for Ian's girlfriend's 21st, was graced by the presence of none other than Geno Washington, one of the giants of Northern Soul, whose searing talents had recently been celebrated in the Dexy's Number One, "Geno". Washington was fresh from a gig at Manchester University, searching for some spliff, and looking for directions to the Reno club in Moss Side. Following some conversation, Washington said to Ian: 'You're a star. Be an actor. Be a singer.' This was just a few days after John had asked Ian to be in the band – fate was seemingly taking him by the hand.

'I knew that Geno was being honest,' Ian told *Vox* magazine later, '… and I thought I'll go with that. I've got to. I just have to… .'

Ian came into the outfit, singing at rehearsals with Kaiser. As with the Patrol, camaraderie developed between all the members – most importantly, strengthening a three-way understanding between Ian, John and Mani. There were 'extra-curricular' activities too, such as late-night film screenings at someone's house, embellished by Mani's inimitable impressions, his party piece (of all people for a working class Manc) being Woody Allen.

But, then, abruptly, Ian became disenchanted once more and left. This time, to become a civil servant (in the DHSS office on Dene Road in Sale), and, as he had previously done with the caravan yard, he applied himself vigorously to the job. It would seem that even with fate taking a hand as it had done in the miraculous encounter with Geno Washington, Ian had had either a crisis of confidence or an intimation that the Waterfront were not going to make it. Since he was now living with his girlfriend, Mitch, and planning to have children with her, the latter seems more likely, a sure indication that he was not willing to risk everything on a venture that was more than likely to fail. His departure signalled the end of the Waterfront. Just as a new band from Manchester emerged.

IV

Historians of Britain's independent music scene will already be aware that the period between 1983 and 1984 is generally remembered, in the music press and literature, with a kind of misty-eyed zeal. The cause of this was none other than Ian Brown's near neighbour Morrissey and his band the Smiths. In fact, practically the whole lifetime of the Smiths, stretching from 1983 to 1986, is recalled in this manner, and it is relevant to the Stone Roses story to investigate their impact, which had a far-reaching influence on music in general and on the Roses in particular.

A devastating four-piece, the Smiths' secret weapon lay in the magical blend of Johnny Marr's unique, 'pastoral' guitar sound echoing the Byrds, with the dry, sometimes savage, and frequently obscure humour of Morrissey. In his utterly unique and justly celebrated lyrics, Morrissey was the first, and possibly the last, artist to bring Oscar Wilde into the frame of reference for rock stars. The skills of bassist Andy Rourke (whom Ian knew quite well) and drummer Mike Joyce, complemented the singer and lead guitarist beautifully and, though they were slightly hampered by Morrissey's occasionally idiosyncratic delivery, the Smiths produced a memorable musical style all their own. This has rightly been hailed as a quintessentially English style with, perhaps, only the Kinks before them having achieved anything similar in British pop music, dominated as it has been, throughout its history, by American influences.

Their impact on the independent scene was remarkable enough. In Manchester, Joy Division and later New Order were undoubtedly seminal outfits, but seemed destined to remain non-mainstream acts. Much the same could be said of Liverpool's Echo & The Bunnymen, whose Doors and Velvet Underground influences, won them some national acclaim. But even the Bunnymen were swiftly dispatched by the Smiths, who were, in effect, at the vanguard of the independent scene within a few weeks of their first single "Hand In Glove". Now, more than at any time previously, it could be said that there was an independent 'movement' where 'indie' labels – most notably, Rough Trade – were riding the crest of a wave and, for many, fulfilling the legacy of the punk movement before them.

Incredibly, the Smiths, with none of the shock value of the Sex Pistols, began to make major inroads into the charts, with a run of consistently brilliant singles. And with them they brought a whole new dimension to the music on offer, aided by the maximum marketing that Rough Trade could afford – peanuts, it should be noted, compared to that which a major label would have spent. This, remember, was an era where groups like (the admittedly fairly inoffensive) ABC and (downright offensive) Dollar were finding favour among the music press, (even in the NME), despite the fact that these, and bands of their ilk, to paraphrase Morrissey 'said nothing to them about their lives.' 'Them' being the thousands of disaffected youths who bought the Smiths records in their droves and who, in truth, *had* found a band that could articulate for them what the aforementioned outfits could not.

Though they are still described as a Manchester band as frequently as they are described a 'quintessentially English' band, it's probably safe to say that they didn't set *that* much store by the Manchester tag. An early 'subliminal' sign of that, perhaps, was the 12" version of the breakthrough 'This Charming Man' single which included a 'Manchester' version and a 'London' one – the latter being considerably more lush, and receiving the most airplay. They were adored by the London-based music press from the off, and, while they were photographed in Salford for *The Queen Is Dead* cover shots, they were in no way part of the 'Manchester Scene' in such a way as New Order at the Factory were or, indeed, of the 'Madchester' scene from which the Roses and the Happy Mondays sprang from. Though no Smiths member dissed Manchester explicitly, Morrissey's lyrics, it must be said, often told tales of people leaving Manchester (songs like "London" and "Is It Really So Strange?"); then there's the lyric to "Suffer Little Children": 'Oh Manchester, so much to answer for'. There was an insularity heavily implicit in Morrissey's attitude and once he pointedly described the band as 'an absolutely closed society'.

When, in the band's lifetime, Morrissey left Manchester for London, and thence to the States (never, to date, to return) it probably becomes fair to say that he didn't much worry about the Smiths being a 'Manchester Band'.

While all this may have not been fully appreciated by Ian Brown and the other fledgling Roses, the Smiths were in fact an important issue for them, even then. As the loose ensemble of musicians who had been the Waterfront met up once more – initially without Ian – one unifying force amongst them was an utter *contempt* for the Smiths. Pete Garner, speaking to Mick Middles couldn't have put it more bluntly: 'I can't remember hating a band more than the Smiths... people kept saying how they represented Manchester. They didn't represent Manchester at all. They didn't represent me, or any of my mates. I felt this very strongly at the time. We needed a band who represented us.'

Brown, when asked later by *Record Collector* what he thought of them, was a little less damning, saying: 'I liked the fact the Smiths came from our home town, and I knew Andy Rourke when I was a kid, so I was happy for them. I liked "What Difference Does It Make" but after that, not really.'

While Squire also recognised a positive side to the Smiths (namely Marr's exquisite guitar lines) a general anti-Smiths feeling was common to the embryonic Roses, stemming from their conviction that, not only were the Smiths unrepresentative of Manchester's youth and for that matter, young people everywhere, but also that they were effete and contrived. Part of the undoubted power and appeal of the Stone Roses-to-come, both in their hometown and beyond, was their directness and lack of affectation, epitomised in their identification with 'Madchester'.

The level of success enjoyed by the Smiths with their 'independent' background had a huge impact on the music press and the music business in general. The Smiths had caused much speculation that, if an 'indie' band could make their mark with hit singles and get on to the all-important playlists, hit albums from independents were, clearly, more possible than ever. The music press championed the Smiths from beginning to end, and, even when they finally disintegrated, were prone to hailing upcoming bands 'the new Smiths'. This honoured title or jinx, depending on how you view things, was extended to bands supporting the Smiths, ones that Morrissey personally liked (James), bands that sounded remarkably like them (Gene) and bands that had a sensitive singer and a particularly gifted guitarist (The House of Love). Such hyperbole did most of these bands no favours at all, and what's clear now is that it took the emergence of the Stone Roses to find a band worthy of this accolade and the success of the Stone Roses' first album was, at least in part, due to the Smiths having paved the way before them.

Having said this, the success of the Smiths did not immediately translate into an exciting era for Ian Brown, John Squire, Pete Garner and Andy Couzens and, according to Ian, 'Manchester was so dull at that point.' It was, then, a timely move by Andy Couzens (the only one of the quartet without a nine-to-five routine over this period) one that proved the catalyst towards some semblance of a reunion, when he dropped round to Ian's Hulme flat one day. Ian was at the dole office, John still at Cosgrove Hall, and Andy holding down his job at Paperchase. John and Pete were getting at least some measure of job satisfaction, and, as with so many young former band members, had shelved any immediate thoughts of rock stardom, trading them in for regular work and job security. Couzens, therefore, deserves some credit for taking it upon himself to try and persuade Brown to have yet another go at the band, particularly as Ian would have been, at this time, easily the most reluctant to get involved. He has said of the mooted band re-launch suggestion: 'I had given up on it (rock 'n' roll) in one sense.'

Also, while Couzens he had been drifting, in and out of jobs, fights etc in his accustomed manner, he had also been keeping a close eye on what was going on in music, attending gigs on a more regular basis than ever. Convinced that there was a place for a new line-up, and sticking to the Patrol core of people (Mani had drifted off to play with other bands), he was disposed to be persuasive

– and if he managed to persuade Brown, the others were almost certain to follow.

Ian: 'It didn't take long for me and Andy to start getting excited again. A lot depended on how John would react. He was the only one who knew what he was doing, in musical terms. But he was so obviously searching for a band, or for something, that he instantly agreed to have a go. We just started practising.'

So the line-up was decided as follows: Ian now confirmed on vocals, John and Andy on guitars, Pete on bass. As for a drummer, they decided to turn again to Si Wolstencroft. After the Patrol, Wolstencroft, had been recommended to the pre-Smiths Johnny Marr and Andy Rourke. Marr was still a way off from creating his 'pastoral' Byrds sound, having one of his periodic funk fixations (only hinted at on Smiths tracks such as "Barbarism Begins At Home" and "The Draize Train", but strongly evident in some of his work with Electronic). Rather fittingly, for a funk band, they became known as Freaky Party, but it was a frustrating year for all concerned as they failed to find a singer and, despite endless rehearsals honing their sound, they never actually even played live. They kept in touch and Wolstencroft, *the* nearly man of indie percussion, had briefly been in favour as a drummer once the Smiths were formed, and played on demos for "The Hand That Rocks The Cradle" and "Suffer Little Children". According to Ian, he left 'because he thought Morrissey was a weirdo!'

Once Wolstencroft was in this line-up, the name, Stone Roses, was decided on immediately. Unaware, it seems, of a 1956 spy novel by Sarah Gainham, set in Prague called *The Stone Roses*, and, contrary to stories widely circulated that the band were initially called English Rose, the name was in fact adopted via a suggestion by John, atoning himself perhaps for his previous 'Fireside Chaps' offering.

Ian: 'It was a name that John came up with ... meaning 'opposites'. Stone Roses... like Led Zeppelin in a way. Heavy and light. It sounded a good name, well balanced. I always liked it.'

43

Ian conducted a straw poll at the DHSS office and got the thumbs up from non-musical colleagues so that fully convinced him.

The first Stone Roses rehearsals were fairly arduous yet enjoyable affairs, with the band often playing for five hours at a time. The early indications were good, with Squire predictably coming to the fore, although reservations were aired about Ian's voice as being 'too weak'. Pressed by the others to have singing lessons, Ian gave it a go, making regular visits to Mrs Rhodes, a vocal tutor with an accompanying 80 year old pianist. Like many of her ilk, Mrs Rhodes was a stern taskmaster, in no way intimidated by this young streetwise pupil, wringing him through renditions of "Strawberry Fields Forever" and "After The Gold Rush" – 'she'd get me there at six o'clock, open the window, with everyone coming home from work. She'd have me wailing… out the window. The crowds looking up and she's saying: 'if you can't do it, go home.' So I thought, fuck it, I'll stick it out'. Ian went every weekday night for three weeks but on his return the band found that, while he had learned important lessons on how to exercise and develop his voice, there remained some lightness to his vocals. They pressed on, though this problem would resurface later.

After six months the Roses were presented with a more immediate problem when Wolstencroft announced that he was leaving. He had openly, and with the rest of the band's consent, been doing occasional auditions for other groups, and an offer that he felt he couldn't refuse had come up. It came from ex-Special Terry Hall's Colourfield, also featuring Craig Gannon who, you guessed it, would play with the Smiths later.

While they wished Wolstencroft well, this was a disaster for the early Stone Roses and they were forced to continue working on their songs drummer-less. Mani's friend Chris Goodwin was approached, but felt he could only manage one rehearsal with them and another audition proved to be something of a farce. Howard Daniels, who'd had a year's experience with a recorded band, the Skeletal Family was deemed to be worth giving a shot. Unfortunately, the Skeletal Family were a goth band, part of a burgeoning scene that had never held much allure for the members of the Roses, and more importantly, carried a style of drumming that wouldn't have suited the Roses songs in a million years. Daniels, bedecked in trademark black and fully armed with a daunting drum kit, pounded out the kind of tribal beats that, while *de rigueur* in Goth circles, reduced the Roses to a stunned silence. 'He was a complete dickhead,' said Andy Couzens.

The songs that the still drummer-less Roses were working on, however, were taking shape. Though still carrying distant echoes of their punk heroes, the sound also began to encompass more recent influences – Orange Juice (still), Empire (the 'halfway hotel' band for Billy Idol before solo stardom) and Tony James (prior to Sigue Sigue Sputnik). The continuing punk influence is reflected in some of their more ropey titles: "Misery Dictionary", "Mission Impossible" and "Tragic Roundabout". "Nowhere Fast", another title with punk overtones, was, irony of ironies, the namesake of a song by the Smiths on their only number one album, *Meat Is Murder*, released the following year.

Despite the fact that the songs were coming thick and fast, the problem of getting someone on the drumming stool was becoming increasingly urgent, and, in May 1984, the Roses placed yet another ad in A1 Music, the guitar emporium in Wakefield Street. Had they known that the music style of choice from the first drummer to book himself in for an audition, was, … shock, horror… Heavy Metal (even worse than Goth!) they might have asked him not to bother turning up. Luckily for the Roses, however, the drummer on the other end of the phone, a kid who called himself 'Reni', did not at that point, mention his musical preference.

Reni (real name, Alan Wren) was born in the Ardwick/Gorton area, a collection of rough estates that cluster around Manchester city centre – he was, if anything, the most streetwise of the Stone Roses. Born in 1964, he was also the youngest by nearly two years – quite a gap for people in their early twenties. But Reni more than made up for his tender age with his outstanding musicianship, which was to astonish all of the Roses, including John

45

– the hardest taskmaster and the most advanced musically. In the tradition of many virtuosos, Reni was introduced to his instrument at a very early age, playing along with various acts throughout his childhood and into his teens, on drum kits set up by his parents in the pub they ran.

Known all over his area as 'the kid with the drums', he naturally gravitated to playing in the bands of various mates. A few months before he answered the Roses ad, a fellow drumming friend of his, Simon Wright, had famously got into AC/DC after an audition. To a diehard Heavy Metal fan such as Reni this must have been galling, as well as an incitement to further his own drumming career. By the time he met the Roses he was already in two bands, playing whenever he had the chance and justifiably confident of his abilities, not to mention his chances of getting into the Roses.

In view of their musical differences, it seemed highly unlikely at this point, that any sort of musical partnership would result between Reni and the rest of the band. Also the advert had been quite explicit about their major influences: Generation X, The Clash, Empire – hardly an encouraging catalogue to a heavy metal fan. And Reni was not hugely impressed by what he heard from them– 'I thought they were a horrible racket,' he said. What had impressed him, though, was their self-belief and determination to succeed and so the audition turned out to be something of a revelation, in more ways than one.

Reni appeared in a long coat, furry moonboots and unfeasibly tight jeans – not an auspicious start. But, without further ado, he got on to the drum stool and tore into the songs, the tricky arrangement of "Nowhere Fast" being absorbed and assimilated in a matter of minutes. By the end of that track alone, the band were literally agog, marvelling at Reni's power and improvisational skills. At the end of the rehearsal, they were desperate for Reni to join, and fortunately for them he immediately said yes: '(They) were such an oddball collection of long hairs, scruffs and smoothies that I just had to join.'

The position of drummer in a rock band has long been a source for humour, the butt of jokes good and bad, and it's difficult not to accept – even if you are a drummer – that the role lacks the charisma of other positions in a band's line up. But Reni was the first British or American drummer for a long, long time to possess that aura held by all great musicians. And his musicianship should never be discounted. Arguably, of all the eventual Stone Roses musicians, despite Mani's superlative skills on bass and Squire's deserved 'guitar hero' status, it is only Reni who can be classed as a *genius* on his instrument. Ian has attested to this and provided another lofty citation too: '(Reni) could play anything… He had a musical talent that none of us had. We all had to graft and work, but he was born with it. Pete Townshend saw our first gig and said he was the best drummer he'd seen since Keith Moon.' And that first Stone Roses gig, now that Reni was on board, was not far away.

V

Ian Brown is to be credited with landing the Stone Roses with their first highly prestigious London gig, late in 1984, which featured one of the band's now habitual brushes with living legends of the music business. As soon as Reni joined, the band was fully fired up and songs began to pour out of them. Over the summer, they rehearsed at Spirit Studios in Chorlton, near Cosgrove Hall, and it was here that the first version of "I Wanna Be Adored" was played. At the studios they also made an important contact in Steve Adge, who helped run Spirit, and was an influential figure within Manchester's music business to boot. Very soon they were using the recording booth to make a demo, which was copied on to a hundred cassettes, and featuring the first of John Squire's cover designs – the band's hand-drawn logo stuck on to a paisley shirt.

Then Ian saw an ad in *Sounds*, asking for bands to take part in an anti-heroin benefit. With his usual mixture of supreme confidence and bravado, he sent the demo along to the Moonlight in Hampstead, hinting at a massive following, when in truth, they had yet to emerge from the recording studio. He also appealed to the organisers' sense of civic duty – 'I'm surrounded by skagheads', he wrote, 'I wanna smash 'em. Can you give us a show?'

Having received the nod from the Moonlight, and with the gig scheduled to take place in eight weeks time, the band threw themselves into rehearsals, honing the songs from the demo. "Misery Dictionary" was re-named "So Young", the band now convinced that the former title sounded too reminiscent of the dreaded Smiths. The songs as a whole struck out in a new direction, with less of the punk influence, and stretching towards what would become the quintessential 'Stone Roses sound.' And, even before they played the Moonlight, people around Manchester and beyond were becoming aware of, as well as being won over by, this totally fresh approach in their music.

A month before the gig, a trip to London was arranged to meet Caroline Reed, who had received the demo from Ian. She had played the tape to her colleague, Andrew Tunnicliffe and, in no time, it seems the entire Moonlight management company had been bowled over by what they heard. Andrew and Caroline were, in fact, seriously thinking about managing the Stone Roses, and the band duly piled into Couzens' van, travelling down to meet the Moonlight pair in Hammersmith. While the Roses displayed a steely determination, and even an air of arrogance ('Loads of people said we seemed aggressive at the time' Couzens admitted), Andrew and Caroline, were far from put off. However, nothing was finalised, in terms of a deal, during this initial meeting.

With a management deal already on the cards for the Stone Roses, before they'd even played a gig, the Moonlight benefit could now be viewed with less apprehension. They were sharing the bill with bands High Noon and the 'Goth' outfit, Mercenary Skank, as well as a secret 'special guest star'.

The Roses were in on this 'secret' and, by the time they arrived in London for sound-checking, they were not only buzzing from the amphetamine consumed by all (except Reni) but also at the idea of meeting Mod legend, Pete Townshend, whose *Quadrophenia* had helped inspire hundreds of kids, Ian and John included, to get on their scooters.

For the soundcheck, they chose to do a cover of the psychedelic classic, "Open Your Eyes". A measure of the advances the band had been making was evident by the overwhelming response (during a *soundcheck*) from the crowd gathered there. By the time they went on stage, second in the line up, to High Noon, the band was full of energy, brimming with confidence and, unsurprisingly, got a rapturous reception to their set.

And, to cap it all, coming off the stage, they were confronted by Pete Townshend himself. Recently returned from the US, playing to 50,000 people with the Who at Shea Stadium, he was on the lookout for a couple of guitarists (who would actually come from Mercenary Skank) and a drummer – he had, as has been stated, been completely blown away by Reni. Ian said later: '… Townshend was like, you look really good up there and your drummer's great. Then he said, as an end-of-the-night thing, I wanna play a couple of tunes. Do you want to do it? Reni's like, yeah! We'd do soundchecks and Reni had people with their mouths open.'

And, on stage, with Townshend, Reni did it again, staggering the audience with a blistering accompaniment to "Substitute" and "Pictures Of Lily" – tracks he claimed *not* to know. The rest of the Roses were rightly concerned that Reni would be poached by Townshend, but as Reni later told *Mojo* 'I was in the only rock band on the planet. Townshend only had the Who. No contest.'

A journalist from *Sounds,* present at the gig, promised them he'd not only be reviewing their performance, but also intended to organise an interview with them in the next few weeks. However, the *Sounds* introductory piece on the Roses actually finally appeared in January 1985, a later live review, and was in fact written by someone who hated the band. Not that this would hold them back. Following the Moonlight Benefit the Stone Roses were out there and flying.

Fresh, then, from what had clearly been a triumph for the band, the Roses' thoughts naturally turned to the management deal that might be in the offing. Caroline Reed had already booked them for a couple of gigs, but they were as yet unaware that someone else, having received a hefty tip off about the band, was waiting in the wings.

The person in question was Howard Jones, a figure with considerable *nous* in the Manchester music scene. Jones, originally from Stoke-On-Trent, sought more invigorating cultural climes once he became an art student and at the age of twenty, he moved to Bristol. While Bristol had some interesting music going on, this was the early eighties, long before artists such as Portishead and Massive Attack appeared on the indie scene, so Jones was forced to look towards alternative music genres. Following a successful run as promoter of a slew of progressive rock acts he was, rather mysteriously, 'run out of town.' Having previously made friends in Manchester, he returned north just as the punk craze seized the city of Ian Brown *et al.* Clearly able to switch cleanly from prog to punk, Jones witnessed some frenzied and infamous gigs at the legendary Electric Circus. Seeing it close-down after failing to secure a food licence, Jones, ever the opportunist, went about setting up an alternative club, Rafters, which quickly earned a reputation.

Jones built a network of music contacts in Manchester, as he had previously done in Bristol, and after impressing New Order manager Rob Gretton with his promoting skills, he got an offer to become general manager of the most renowned Manchester club of all, the Hacienda, the 'public face' of Factory Records. Jones experienced the thrill of seeing some of the most memorable gigs of the era there, but his closeness to the music – an all-important aspect to him – was eventually threatened by the increasingly Byzantine business affairs of the club, and Jones deeply resented this. So, as the Stone Roses were preparing for their first London gig and being wooed by Reed and Tunnicliffe, Jones left the Hacienda and was asking his contacts for any band recommendations – with a view to management.

One of these contacts was Steve Adge at Spirit Studios, who one day gave Jones a call while the Roses were downstairs in the rehearsal rooms: 'They need a manager,' Steve said, 'and I think they might really like you.' Adge spread the same message to the Roses and it was arranged for Jones to attend one of the rehearsals at Spirit, so they could see what they thought of each other.

Typically, the band made a point of ignoring Jones throughout and refused to turn the sound down. After twenty-five minutes of the band at full blast, Jones' reaction, was a mixed one. Describing them to John Robb as 'absolutely fucking diabolical' he balanced this with a more positive perception of their 'arrogance' - by viewing it as self-belief. Aside from the obligatory eulogies of Reni – 'the most brilliant drummer I had ever seen or have ever seen since' – Jones was struck also by Ian Brown and his lyrics: 'I eventually got to know Ian and got to realise how deep a thinker he really is... I thought: this guy is a great songwriter.'

He cast a critical eye on the band's presentation too, including John's bandanna and Pete's haircut, but he was encouraged to work some favours – with the band's assent – and book studio time for them. The recordings produced at this point included early versions of "Going Down" and "Shoot You Down".

Jones was confident enough in these recordings to approach another luminary of the Manchester music scene, Martin Hannett, the legendary producer of the Joy Division albums. It was lucky that Jones had left the Hacienda by this time, because Hannett had spectacularly fallen out with Factory over a Fairlight computer and a new studio, the money for which was being spent on the club. Not that Hannett held any grudges against Jones. While it was an attractive idea for the Roses to be working with a named producer such as Hannett, process was stymied by Jones and Hannett's increasing chumminess, which resulted in their hatching a misguided plan to set up a rival label to Factory, whom Hannett couldn't forgive.

Once the Roses were aware of this idea, they had serious misgivings. The risk factor was only increased by the notion of a new, independent record company putting out the first Stone Roses record, despite the kudos of having the Hannett name attached – and Hannett, though brilliant, was known to be wildly erratic even in his lighter moments. The Roses may by this time have been on the look out for a bigger deal, but they initially went along with Jones' plans: until that was, he erred very badly.

The next wheeze from Jones came totally out of the blue, contradicted his earlier effusive comments, and it was a suggestion which quite literally left the band speechless: sack Reni. It would appear that Jones found Reni's drumming a disruptive influence as well as, it would seem, the man himself. Reni was, after all, easily the most rumbustious of the Stone Roses, and perhaps Jones thought he would be too tough to handle. It's difficult to see how Jones could even have entertained the notion that such a bizarre suggestion would seriously be considered by the other band members. But he was a clever and persuasive man and, unbelievably, in a Reni-less meeting, he not only succeeded in getting the Roses to agree with him, but also to go and break the news to the drummer in person. However, in a grand display of 'sense finally triumphing over lunacy', as they left on the mission, the band members drove off in the opposite direction from Jones, only to return some time later – with Reni on board!

Reni was the Roses trump card of course and no one could persuade the rest of the band to get rid of him. Even when recalling the episode later, Ian was incredulous: 'That was just an example of the madness of the time. Sack Reni? Reni was the main reason why the Stone Roses were so special. To sack Reni would have been the dumbest thing ever.'

Despite this ludicrous run of events, the Roses were still prepared to go into a studio with Martin Hannett to make a recording for what would be their first single. They were booked into Strawberry Studios, where Hannett was owed copious amounts of studio time, and immediately began work. "So Young" was selected as the eventual A-side; it was a strong song with an equally strong lyric, with the band's original composition now added to by Brown, reflecting the everyday waste and pernicious languor observed in the streets around Hulme, where he lived. He described it thus: "It was as if these kids... really bright kids too, were falling right into the Hulme stereotype and it was just so pointless. It certainly wasn't romantic, it was grubby and cheap." Ian, in sharp contrast to the Morrissey – 'sit in your bedroom and mope' – camp, seemed to be suggesting a more active, positive approach to life, epitomised both in Brown's strong work ethic as well as his former dedication to the discipline of karate.

Morrissey's lyrics are full of allusions to passivity and negativity. Lyrics like 'if you must go to work tomorrow, then I really wouldn't bother' spoke of years of wilful but ultimately directionless unemployment. Ian's lyrics, such as 'Where there's life there's gotta be hope, where there's a will there's a way' actually sent out a stronger, more upbeat message, countering Morrissey's trademark insularity. 'It was an angry song,' he said of "So Young" later, 'but a positive song'; Hannett's original production had an 'unnerving power' Ian told *Record Collector* later, despite Hannett being in the midst of drug problems during this period, through which he lurched alarmingly from steering the ship brilliantly, to literally falling asleep at the desk, so that an engineer had to step in (or over him) to take over.

Meanwhile, Jones was trying to come up with a Factory-style strategy for the single's release, irritating the Roses further, but all his plans for alternative versions (including a Nashville session) came to nothing. The single eventually came out without too much gimmicky artwork so for now Jones had to redeem himself by utilising another one of his contacts.

Tony 'The Greek' Michaelides, of Manchester Piccadilly Radio, had established a show called the *Last Radio Programme* making him something of a Northern counterpart to John Peel. He was instrumental in getting first radio airplay for many bands in Manchester and the surrounding area, and for Howard Jones he was the first port of call once the single was ready. On receiving Jones' 'bowled-over-with-enthusiasm' call, he was initially sceptical, (he had, of course, heard it all before) but being well-disposed towards the Roses manager, and having taken delivery of the recording in person from Jones and Pete Garner, he gave it a listen and his reaction was, overall, positive – 'there was something about this tape that completely floored me.'

Michaelides certainly wasn't averse to giving it a spin on his show and the response to its airing was a good one. Although well aware that many of the calls of support could have been from the Roses themselves and their mates (again, he'd 'seen it all before') – he still felt there was something special about this band and thus tried to engender ways of getting them more airplay. An obvious method was, as is often the way, staring him in the face.

One of the *Last Radio Programme*'s selling points was a series of 'unplugged' sessions, actually inaugurated by the Buzzcocks' Pete Shelley, who had turned up in the studio with his 12-string guitar one evening and knocked out unfamiliar but well-received versions of some of his best known tunes. When bandmate Steve Diggle turned up the following week and did a similar thing a precedent was set for a popular series.

The Roses performing this kind of session at the time would have been tricky, not least because Brown's voice was nowhere near powerful enough. So Michaelides thought of the next most logical step – a full band session with amps and all – and, in this way, the Roses *en masse* were booked in to play. The Roses blazed through the session with their by now customary ragged aplomb, horrifying the afternoon soul DJ, whose records were backed with Reni's thudding drumming, as they soundchecked. They made mistakes on air, but carried on regardless and reputedly threw chairs about the studio. The session was a highly successful one in the eyes of the host, who felt it was 'the most significant thing I ever did', and the session tape has gone on to be one of the most sought-after Roses bootlegs, not least because it contains the first recorded version of "I Wanna Be Adored".

This led to a surge of interest in the band and when Michaelides was asked to put together a line-up for a showcase of Manchester bands, at Dingwalls in Camden, he wasn't about to leave the Roses out of it. As the band prepared for another London gig they all hoped it would prove to be a further significant step forwards.

Jones may have raised their expectations somewhat as he busied himself, giving every A&R man he knew in London the kind of call that he'd previously given Michaelides. And it was Michaelides himself who, now hoping that the 'Manchester Bands' Showcase' would revolve around one band only, put Jones in touch with his friend, Simon Potts, A&R man at Elektra. None of the other bands joining the Roses that night were, to be fair, destined to go on to greater things, and in fact two of them had gained their places simply by virtue of being indiscriminately fished out of the tape bin at Michalides' office. It certainly didn't sound as if any stiff competition was about to present itself. Clearly it was *meant* to be the Roses' night.

In the event, still only the second Stone Roses gig, the band and Jones were horrified when it became apparent that, of all the A&R men invited, only Potts turned up – and part of the reason he was there was because his friend, Michaelides was staying at his house that night. Here Jones had been truly naïve: whether the Roses knew it or not, he at least should have known that even five London A&R men at a showcase for *Manchester* bands would have been nigh on a miracle. It was another black mark against Jones.

If Jones didn't get much out of the gig, the band were determined to use it to their advantage, revealing a dynamic presence on stage, especially Ian, who was clearly growing into his role of frontman, relatively new to it as he was. Said Michaeides: 'Ian was fantastic. He didn't seem to care that the audience was flimsy… he just wanted to show off… walking right up to people and just showing off.' Ian said later: 'I'd jump off the stage in the early days. I was always walking round the crowd singing. When we started getting known we didn't enjoy the shows as much because I had to stay on the stage, but in the early days I sang to the girls to get the lads wound up. And it worked – people remembered us'

Michaelides was also gratified by the strong impression that they made on Potts; it would have been too much to hope for him to sign them up there and then – but if the one A&R man who turned up liked them instantly, that was something at least the band could draw from.

Along with the airplay for the single, the session and the gig and Dingwall's, there had been a smattering of press for the Roses: the magazine *City Life* for instance, wittily describing their music as 'deviant Mersey beat'. There was also an eager audience building up for them.

In Manchester, during the early months of 1985, as the Stone Roses were well aware, the music scene had become, in this state-within-a-state, a kind of capsule where a 'word-of-mouth' movement existed totally independent of the music press – an independent offshoot of the independent movement, if you like. In this atmosphere, you would have the phenomenon of a band like the Chameleons, virtually ignored everywhere except Manchester, being booked to play the Free Trade Hall where artists such as Bob Dylan had performed.

Another feature of this scene was the 'warehouse parties', impromptu gigs in railway arches and the like, which had become increasingly popular. As we have seen, the Roses were well-connected in Manchester's music scene and would have known about this underground network of information and events from the beginning. In turn, once the Roses decided to promote themselves via this grapevine, it didn't take long for word to spread about them, meaning that they could bring in a decent local audience in no time. Ian later recalled one in *Sounds* magazine: 'They were packed out. At the first one there was about a thousand people – it was where we got our crowd from'.

Only Howard Jones was bemused when they started to draw sizeable audiences to these gigs, certainly not the band. As Jones said later, '(The Roses) just thought… people will come.' And come they did, in their hundreds. Jones learned from this and acted quickly, arranging the Roses' first gig in the North, in Preston – without any publicity at all, and simply relying on word of mouth to get people there. Preston was just big enough to contain a gig with the potentially large audience that Jones was hoping for, while just near enough to Manchester to haul in the Manchester crowd. The venue was Preston Clouds: in common with many clubs of this era, it transformed itself into an 'indie' club on Fridays, in contrast to the traditional disco it ran through the rest of the week.

This time, Jones had been able to get some important people along, a whole bunch of journalists – local correspondents for the *NME, Melody Maker* etc. – who were, by now, catching on to the Roses. There was a real sense of anticipation before the show began, as 'a good few hundred fans' started trickling into Preston, mainly from Manchester. But this atmosphere was soured at the soundcheck when they discovered that the club weren't about to break the bank in putting on this gig, and provided only the substandard house sound system.

This was not the best motivation for the gig, as the Roses didn't want their sound compromised in front of all the journalists gathered, as well as letting down their fans. Jones had to do some of the hardest work of his life to buoy them up and, though he finally persuaded them to go out on stage, he could do little about what ensued. Within five minutes the PA was playing up, the mood in the crowd (a volatile mix of pissed-up Manchester and

Preston youth) turned ugly and before long, fights were breaking out. The mood was probably not lightened by John, who waiting for another problem to be sorted out, kick-started the band into a sardonic cover of Sigue Sigue Sputnik's 'Love Missile'. More fights ensued, causing Ian to yell into his microphone 'Stop fighting you fucking morons'. This just aggravated the situation, and, with some of the gathered press being plucked out of the crowd, a full-scale riot commenced, culminating in Reni kicking over his drum kit and Pete smashing up his bass.

It would hardly be fair to say that the whole band fled the stage: Ian and Andy were tough characters who had seen their fair share of fights and observed the melee from the stage for a few minutes. But the gig, which had lacked a beginning and middle, saw no end either, as ninety per cent of the audience were simply oblivious to the band's departure. Ian would perhaps, in retrospect, have been better staying where he was as, in an understandably tense dressing room only a few feet from a riot, an *NME* journalist insisted on holding a frustrating hurried interview with him which wasn't even published in the end. Jones also had to contend with the drunken, disruptive appearance of Mani, who had wangled his way backstage, only to be pretty swiftly ejected. One would think Jones must have had his head in his hands on several occasions, wondering what had gone wrong on what had promised to be such a fortuitous occasion. He was starting to make too many mistakes.

VI

Post-Preston, the band would probably have done anything for a quiet life. The fact that they swapped a riot in an industrial UK town for a full-scale tour in the more restrained environment of Sweden was thanks not to Howard Jones but to Ian. That is to say he fished a number out of his pocket in the spring of '85, thrust it at Jones, and said: 'Ring him up and sort out a Swedish tour.'

When he wasn't with the Roses, Ian had been taking his fondness for travel to the next level by embarking on occasional hitch-hiking tours around Europe. While abroad however, he always had at the forefront of his mind that he was lead singer in a band, and he would make a point of promoting the band to anyone who would listen – and, more importantly, anyone who might be able to further their cause. Andreas Linkaard, whom Ian met on a train in Germany, turned out to be one of these people. Linkaard had a friend who was a promoter, as Ian was to fondly recall later.

'I met this kid whose friend was a promoter so I told him we were a big group from Manchester. He set up about eight or nine shows. We were living in his flat in Stockholm for about a month. It was great.'

But even for one who enjoyed travelling as much as Ian, from all accounts there were as many nightmarish aspects to the planned tour as there were highpoints. Jones had pulled his finger out and done some pretty hasty organising, and so they left two weeks after the Preston Clouds gig, although as it turned out, only two gigs were actually confirmed. Nevertheless, Jones had arranged return tickets on the car ferry and sorted out their 'accommodation' – all he asked of the band was that they turn up on time, so as not to miss the ferry, and that they each rustle up £50 towards the costs.

After a ten-hour trip in Couzens' van they arrived just in time to catch the ferry, but the day of the crossing coincided with Reni's 21st birthday – and this inevitably resulted in a huge dent to their part of the kitty, as well as their spending money as they got as drunk as possible. On arrival, they clambered on to the quayside only to have their hangovers intensified by the brutal Swedish weather – having left a mild spring in Manchester, they now encountered strong winds and heavy rain. Bitterly cold and with raging headaches, to have checked into their accommodation would, at that point, have been blissful for them. But this was a pre-Ryanair era when a jaunt to Sweden wasn't simply a matter of a couple of hours flying time. They were still *fifteen* hours from their destination and meeting point with Andreas – Stockholm Railway Station. But not only were they freezing and with aching heads, they were also without petrol. Finding only twenty pounds left in the kitty, they were forced to beg strangers for help. They were lucky enough to stop a local who handed over 150 Swedish Kronor, though whether it was through kind-heartedness or fear of reprisals from this, by now, fearsome-looking mob is uncertain.

Miraculously, they managed eventually to meet up with Andreas, the journey having been stretched from fifteen hours to twenty-four. The band were none too pleased to find that Jones had already reserved the only proper bed within their so-called 'accommodation' for himself in Andreas' friend's draughty, part furnished flat, and took revenge by 'nobbling' his place of repose so that he crashed to the floor each evening, leaving him, after two weeks of such treatment, battered and bruised beyond endurance.

Their first gig, expertly arranged by Andreas for two days after their arrival on April 10th, took place in Linkoping, a largish town not far from Stockholm. Andreas had done a tremendous job of previewing the Roses in the local press and generally building up a welcome for them. Ian, however, had decided to make 'You're all Swedish twats' his first learned phrase and he was lucky that the inquisitive and remarkably equable Swedes gathered took it in good part. With the 'pleasantries' out of the way, the band performed well and even came out for an encore consisting of reprises of a couple of the songs just performed. The Swedish press were generous, though perhaps less so to Ian who they said 'runs around like he has rabies'. The following night they were at Norkopping and, again, they did well enough to warrant two encores.

But the band was in pretty dire straits, being perilously short of finances. The high cost of living in Sweden stunned them: it forced them to cajole a supermarket manager into purloining food for them, and they while incessantly put pressure on Howard Jones to get them more gigs. The band-manager relationship was becoming so strained that, at one point, Jones was kicked out of the van and left to walk back from a venue, in freezing temperatures. Nevertheless Jones used his Hacienda calling card ruthlessly and in three weeks they played at a host of places, including a spot supporting the Go-Betweens, this time causing another riot, though not half as bad as the one in Preston had been. Jones also got them into the Royal Palace, one of the top nightclubs in Sweden, as well as to the premiere of Terry Gilliam's *Brazil* at the Hard Rock Café. Such high-profile 'blags' were, however, counter-balanced by a host of humdrum parties gate-crashed by the Roses, who invariably headed straight for the kitchen to hunt for food. The Swedish experience proved, in hindsight, a beneficial one for the band as musicians – an intensive spate of playing that tightened their music up considerably, whilst providing the 'best' kind of introduction to the realities of life on the road.

On returning home, Howard Jones landed them an exciting Manchester gig. The International is a landmark venue in the history of Manchester's music scene. Often seen as a rival to the Hacienda, the International actually started out in the sixties as a disco, eventually becoming an important mid to large sized club, where acts ranging from Echo & The Bunnymen to REM and even Simply Red had played.

The Stone Roses walked on stage to a Tom Jones backing tape and Ian immediately set the tone by demanding attention from those still skulking at bar ('Hey, why don't you over there come over here') before going on to give a most uncompromising front-man performance. He berated the audience throughout for various transgressions ('stop talking fucker' or 'this is your last chance to shut the fuck up') and throwing down his mic in disgust on more than one occasion. Here was the old arrogance returning and translated into part of his onstage act. Apart from the odd person talking, the audience, including one Noel Gallagher, were rapt and fully won over by this now-polished band with the supremely self-confident singer. Also watching closely that night was international club manager, Gareth Evans, to whom Howard Jones had fleetingly introduced Ian and John, as they arrived at the club. They would be meeting him again properly, soon enough.

The Roses swiftly followed up this highly successful gig with another, which, while not so important in size of venue, was prestigious nevertheless, augmented by a high-level, professional performance from the band. Steve Adge from Spirit Studios had come up with the idea of putting on a warehouse party with the Roses, but, inspired by a trip to London – where such events were now commonly being held – was keen to make this party an 'all-nighter'. The Roses, who were duly billed to come on stage at the unholy hour of 1.30am, found the slot appealing as it was reputedly one which was, in venues 'down south' such as the Brixton Academy, reserved for headlining bands.

The 'northern version' was to be held at a railway arch that Adge rented from British Rail near Manchester Piccadilly, on Fairfield Street, without precisely explaining what he intended to use it for. This became another word-of-mouth extravaganza directly appealing to the core of musicians and music fans that knew of Spirit – tiny posters around the city centre being the only form of publicity. There were tickets, but they contained no indication of where the gig was – the buyer had to ring Spirit to find out how to get to the venue.

On the night of the gig it was these highly unconventional tactics that must have given the Roses, especially Ian, an attack of nerves – even though they were fully behind the spirit of the event. 'It was worrying,' he confessed, 'because we didn't really know if anyone was going to turn up or not.' Having sound-checked in the early evening, they waited apprehensively at Ian's flat in Hulme, for the time to, literally, 'face the music'. They needn't have concerned themselves however, as the crowd did come out that July night, finding Adge's 'venue' and taking immediate advantage of his innovative raffle-ticket system for purchasing alcohol. By the time the Roses got there, they found over three hundred high-spirited punters milling around.

Despite sound problems at the beginning, the band built up to a powerful, now legendary performance. Ian adopted a much less confrontational approach, where he was constantly in and out of the crowd, dancing before them and with them, in itself saying something about the event which was after all an embryonic form of the 'loved-up rave'. The Roses were in on this new dimension from the outset. Though their music still retained a few punk edges, the aggression invariably gave way to a more celebratory vein, fitting, the improvised, euphoric atmosphere. It was a triumph, a brilliant choice of gig that gained them a solid reputation in Manchester – where a night at the Hacienda might have meant so much less.

Now the Roses were fully primed to go into Strawberry Studios in August, where Martin Hannett was waiting for them, to start recording sessions for their album. Ian's final analysis of Hannett was: 'We caught him at the wrong time. He was a junkie, basically, a lovely, real nice man but out to lunch 23 hours a day.' And this was to be a frustrating session in other ways also, as the band felt the force of the musical shortcomings they still had.

On stage, they had become an exciting band to be sure, with Ian's performances and Reni's drumming being the highlights. But in terms of recordable output, they were still somewhat lacking: they really only had a handful of complete songs which you can perhaps get away with when playing live if the performance is electrifying enough, but certainly not when only the tape is running. As well as "So Young", this session would include "I Wanna Be Adored" and an early version of "This Is The One" but, frustratingly, they were clearly still a little way off producing enough material to record an album.

Up to this point, Ian and John hadn't specifically been working together to produce songs, the compositions arising out of a kind of a free-for-all, but work on "This Is The One" resulted in a step forward and on a possible new direction that would improve this jumbled set up for writing – even though it did come about as a result of Hannett locking the band in a room and telling them they weren't getting out until they'd written another tune. Ian and John decided to collaborate more closely on the writing, while the band as a whole began to broaden their listening, reaching beyond punk to the Beatles, the Byrds, Hendrix and more, artists whose influences would become all too apparent in the Stone Roses six-ties-flavoured sound. And though they were realistic enough to accept that they couldn't release an album on their repertoire as it stood, there was no reason why they couldn't use one of their finished songs, "So Young" as a single.

"So Young" was duly released in September of 1985 on Han-nett and Jones' Thin Line records, on the same day as the Happy Mondays' first single "Delightful" was put out by Factory Records. The single had a tough time of it, nationally, but it immediately went to the top of the local record shops' charts.

The first review of the single was in a local music paper, *Muze*, who called it 'big, loud and beautiful', while *City Life*'s comment – 'very un-Manchester' was hard to pin down as either praise or criticism. A 'national', *Zigzag*, stated it was 'good pro-duction that brings the best from a tested song' which was good news for Hannett presumably. On the whole, the Roses weren't too unhappy about the reception the single got and were certainly gratified by its success in local circles. For one thing, it increased their profile, and, having given them their best review to date, *Muze*'s Paula Greenwood, a big fan of the band, was also inter-ested enough to feature an interview with them. In this interview, Ian, as usual, came to the fore with some quotable lines, display-ing his and the band's self-confidence, as well as giving a sense of their destiny: 'we'll either be massive or fizzle out, there is no in-between for this band.'

It may or may not have been this sense of destiny, which led to Ian and Reni embarking on the cheapest and most direct of pub-licity campaigns shortly after this interview. In the dead of night, they raced around Manchester armed with a spray-can, daubing the band's name on the city's landmarks. While it was, no doubt, a bit of a lark at the time, they were astonished by the criticism that rained down on the band and their followers as a result. This came not only through the press – *The Manchester Evening News*, *Muze*, *City Life* – but also from a host of local radio shows. To them it was all part of the gang mentality and based on the premise that 'Me and Reni decided we'd been ignored long enough'.

There were now some indications of interest from A&R types, alerted, if not by Ian and Reni's antics, then by the single and a series of gigs, including one, ironically, at the Hacienda. This gig actually took place just prior to the release of "So Young", as a result of Hannett temporarily overcoming his grudge against the place. He was on hand both to mix the sound and tape the show. On one of his 'good nights', Hannett was able to create some supersonic sounds via John's guitar, which John himself was unaware were there. Typically, Ian walked into the crowd at this one – a rare occurrence at the Hacienda and one that did not go down particularly well. But the Roses had already decided that their sixties vibe was far too retro for the ultra-modern Hacienda, and their faces didn't really fit anyway, so it would probably be unwise to play there again.

The band was now back in the rehearsal studios and working on tightening their song- writing skills. These sessions did bear genuine fruit with the emergence of the song "Sally Cinnamon", hung as it on the strongest of melodies, proving another step forward, and resulting in the first bona fide Stone Roses pop song. It was also a tune built on the sixties influences, discarding any remaining echoes of punk, while retaining a contemporary edge.

The Roses saw the year out with some gigs and another warehouse party. In November, Mat Snow of the *NME* finally reviewed "So Young", but talked more about Martin Hannett than the actual song. In any case, realising that they weren't going to release an album yet, the Roses, and Ian in particular, wanted to 'move as far away from "So Young" as possible.' What this meant in real terms was that it was the end of the road for Howard Jones as their manager.

VII

Ian Brown has been more than frank about the Howard Jones era and the abrupt ending of his tenure, admitting: 'we did use him. Took him to the cleaners, really. I'm not too proud of that, looking back, but a lot of it was his own fault'. Andy Couzens was more direct: 'Howard had to go; it was as simple as that.'

Jones had used his contacts tenaciously, landing the Stone Roses a 'big-name' producer to work with in Martin Hannett and, it should be acknowledged, considerable interest from A&R people. He had however made some serious mistakes along the way, as well as having an unfortunate habit of rubbing the band up the wrong way. What is surprising is that he had a very different view of how things were going with the band, reflected in comments even years later, such as: 'I felt like a part of what they were doing. I thought we would go on and on.' The 'we' presumes a level of camaraderie with the Roses that was clearly not reciprocated, the problem being that they didn't particularly want him to be in their 'gang'. Couzens: 'Become one of the gang. No fucking chance, mate. He was miles away. Never came close.' Ian said 'We reckoned he was a bit of a dick, full stop, proper.'

So much, then, for Jones being part of the Stone Roses gang! Amazingly, for a seasoned businessmen such as Howard Jones, it was precisely this false belief in a strong bond between them that caused him to forego introducing any kind of contract. Thus, at the beginning of 1986, soon after the writing of "Sally Cinnamon", the decision to let go of their old sound meant letting Howard Jones go with it and the band were able to just walk away.

A short period of limbo followed, though the band continued to rehearse and shape their new sound. It wasn't until March of 1986 that they went out on the road, playing the latest set to anyone who would listen. "Sally Cinnamon" and "All Across The Sands" were debuted to a deeply unresponsive crowd, impatiently waiting for the headline act, at King George's Hall in Blackburn. So they were then treated to the band's old standby, "Love Missile" as a punishment.

On the 25th of the same month they played Warwick University, supporting Love and Rockets, which consisted of members of Bauhaus, minus lead singer Peter Murphy. The Goth curse had struck the Roses again, with the haughty attitude of these so called 'stars' getting on everyone's nerves. 'They were arseholes' said Pete Garner 'Would not talk to any of us.'

There was a sense among the band that they were losing direction: when, six months "So Young" had been released and disappeared, they were manager-less and still nowhere near completing an album, but then they came across an ad in the International looking for new bands to manage. Gareth Evans, the club manager Ian and John had met some months back, was responsible for this advertisement.

Gareth Evans' entry into the Stone Roses legend is another point at which our story becomes archetypal: it is a 'band -meets-mercurial-manager-bringing-them-major-success' scenario. With bells on.

Evans is the kind of rock manager that one could write a book about, a genuine maverick. Born in Wales in the late forties, he moved to Manchester when he was twelve and quickly got into Manchester popular culture, becoming initially enamoured of the nightclub scene at the start of the sixties, before deciding to become a full-blown mod, albeit scooter-less.

Evans was, of course, living through the first mod craze, 're-enacted' by Ian Brown and his mates in the late seventies, and, like Ian, had seen the violence that went with it – though he actually bore scars to prove it. At sixteen, his first proper job was that of runner at the Jig Saw Club in Cromford Court – eventually demolished to make way for the Arndale shopping centre. Due to staff shortages he unexpectedly found himself running the club one day and – whether by chance or design – doubled the usual profits for that night. So it was that Evans became a teenage manager of one the liveliest clubs of the era.

He went on to enjoy a relatively exciting early youth as quite a big fish in the Manchester music scene of the early to mid sixties. He regularly put on upcoming artists on his stage who went on to become huge stars in their own right, Elton John and Eric Clapton for instance. Like many nightclub owners, he inevitably found himself drawn into the orbit of the underworld, which he was duty-bound to deal with occasionally although he was never part of it. Quite by chance, he was even a witness to the 'deportation' of the infamous Kray Brothers, when they were put on a train out of Manchester and told never to come back.

As a mod Evans made frequent trips to check out the London scene. He did a bit of 'mod modelling' work for none other than Vidal Sassoon, who, with the young Evans tucked firmly under his wing, took it upon himself to show him how to cut 'n' blow – there's nothing like being taught by the masters. This proved the catalyst for the unlikeliest of career detours, and one that Evans himself has been unable to explain properly, in words other than 'I didn't earn much money but it was just great fun'.

But Evans, ever the entrepreneur, could earn vast amounts of money by having joint control of over 30 hairdressing shops, which is exactly what he went on to do. And just as the sixties gave way to the glam age, when cut 'n' blow, not to mention all the new styles, could be charged at a premium. Evolving into the shrewdest of businessmen, he created unisex hairdressing salons before diversifying into, first, sports retailing and then gold bullion. The latter, which involved regularly travelling between London and Manchester with huge stashes of cash on his person, was clearly his riskiest venture yet, and one that put his lifestyle on a par, at times, with the notorious Krays.

It was time to try a less dangerous way of making a living, and Evans decided to go back into the nightclub business. In 1985, along with a business partner, he inaugurated the International, instigating a 'state-of-the-art' playlist, and recruiting the legendary Roger Eagle, who had gone from being a Northern Soul DJ in the Twisted Wheel to a lynch-pin of Eric's in Liverpool, the breeding ground for bands like Echo & The Bunnymen and the Teardrop Explodes. Very soon the International was as hip, if not hipper than the Hacienda.

It was with a view to getting the very hippest of bands playing there that Evans circulated the ad that was swiftly picked up on by the Roses. Rather than send a tape along like everyone else, the band decided to present themselves in person at the club and request an immediate audience with Evans. Once inside his office, the band launched into the kind of self-glorification that Ian usually reserved for live performances.

Evans was possessed of at least as much self-belief and 'front' as the band and something instantly clicked between them, indeed their brash approach seeming to win him over without even having heard the music. He 'recommended himself' to them by dropping his trousers to display the novelty underpants he was marketing, as well as accidentally-on-purpose dropping a wad of cash at their feet. But what really sold them on the idea of a working partnership with this guy was the immediate package he offered of free entry and free drinks at the International every night – plus free rehearsal time. 'It was all so easy,' said John later, 'it solved a lot of problems at once. People immediately thought we were mad but we got in there and started rehearsing.'

The problems included the fact that they were all on the dole, only earning a crust here and there; John had even left his job at Cosgrove Hall (Reni was perhaps the most entrepreneurial of them all at this time, earning some money as a kissogram!). But now, not only could they save on paying for rehearsals, they could also live a bit of a 'lifestyle' into the bargain. It was plain to see that Evans was a born businessman and that he had a good chance of getting them a deal, a much better chance than Howard Jones.

When Evans presented them with a management contract two weeks later, hastily put together by his lawyer, and binding the band to him for ten years, they were probably being as legally naïve as Howard Jones had been in not binding himself to them at all.

A lot of people around Manchester were extremely wary of Evans, and as *Muze*'s Paula Greenwood (always one the band's foremost supporters and actually present when the contract was signed) recalls, 'When Gareth and the Roses linked together eve-ryone was totally shocked.'

The band were, however, happy for the time being to be rehearsing on a full-sized stage at the International rather than in the basement at Spirit, and threw themselves into extending their repertoire. They now even turned up armed with a guitar engineer to help John, an all-round vibemaster and unofficial fifth-mem-ber, (Steve) Cressa, a Manchester scenester, whom the band had known for years and who can also be credited with introducing the band to flares.

And now Ian and John had actually got into the habit of re-pairing to one or other's bedroom to work on songs, reconvening with the remaining group members for their input and fine-tuning. This was a much more productive arrangement all round and also resulted in a deepening bond between the two. Ian later said, 'I've never heard him talk to anyone else the way he used to talk to me'. The emerging song-writing pattern was to culminate in a sleeping bags and guitars journey to Italy – just the two of them – where they worked intensely on new material. Meanwhile, one of Evans' most urgent tasks was to get studio time sorted out for them at a reasonable rate, as the band were also keen, and now better pre-pared, to get back to recording.

Evans was firing on all cylinders, tirelessly pushing them on studios, until he alighted on one, the Yacht Club, whose owner Chris Brophy, he managed to barter down to an incredible £70 a day. It was to be an important session for the Roses, where they managed to impress Brophy both with their professional attitude and alluring sound, as they worked through "The Hardest Thing", "Here Again", "This Is The One" and "Sally Cinnamon". Brophy's comment says it all: 'I knew, right from the very first chord, that this band would be massive.' The only one Brophy was less than impressed with was Cressa, whose recently adopted role of 'guitar engineer to John' warranted, apparently, an unlicensed and infuri-ating twiddling of knobs. Bumping into them later at the Interna-tional he congratulated them on the session, and, in 'announcing' to them that they were going to be 'big', was typically met with stares of incredulity, as if to say 'Of course, we are.'

But it wasn't to be plain sailing from here on in, as a troubling series of events immediately followed the highly successful session. The momentum that was building up was not lost on any of the band members, least of all Ian and John. Now key songwriters and close allies, their thoughts inevitably turned to the eternally contentious question of publishing credits, should the band be signed. The pair were united in the opinion that since they were bringing Stone Roses songs to the sessions, regardless of embellishments from the others, any recording should credit the Brown/ Squire writing partnership exclusively. While Gareth Evans was not privy to these early discussions, his actions began to show that he was following a similar train of thought.

When Ian and John announced their intention just before a rehearsal – that they would take the publishing credits and royalties while the rest would earn merely mechanical royalties – the other, initially stunned members instigated a brief split. After some deliberation, however, they decided it was probably in their interests to accept the deal, although not without some bitterness.

Couzens has gone on record as saying 'A lot of it was John. Seizing power, y'know. John is a very selfish person.' Evans seemed to agree when he called later Squire: 'Very cold and calculating. He won't ever admit it... but he owes an awful lot to the other Roses, especially Reni.'

But this was one of the few things that Evans and Couzens ever did see eye-to-eye about. In keeping with rock managers from time immemorial (and just as Howard Jones had mistakenly done with Reni) Evans was already looking for a weak link in the band. Reni and Garner were safe from his scrutiny, but Couzens most certainly was not.

From day one, Evans had made it clear that he didn't want Couzens in the band, setting off on a classic divide-and-rule course. Never one to do things by halves, he piled on pressure, escalating from cheap slurs in passing against Couzens at first, to cascades of insults, 'hairdryer' style, within inches of the guitarist's face. The (largely concocted) insults ranged from being *faux*-working class to a drug dealer. The redoubtable Couzens stood his ground while the others looked on in bemusement with, apparently, Ian and John putting it down to some kind of psychotic problem Evans suffered from. Indeed, when the band heard from Couzens that Evans had offered him £10,000 just to leave, they all fell about laughing and considered getting him to agree to the deal and share the money out, before welcoming Couzens back the next day.

At the other extreme, Evans was showering a much more positive kind of attention on Brown and Squire. As well as giving the pair lifts all over the place, he started buying them gifts, drinks and meals and even dragged them into hairdressers, clearly grooming them for stardom. He was placing his money on the Brown/Squire partnership and it could be only a matter of time – or opportunity – before he made an even more decisive move to isolate Couzens.

If John was 'cold and calculating' one wonders what the attitude of Ian was at this time. He had always acted like a pop star with the Roses, but he was now being treated as one before it had actually happened. Evans commented revealingly to Mick Middles about his early days with the band, describing the mutual love between himself and the Roses (excepting Couzens, of course): 'They did, you know… Ian in particular… loved me!' While Ian's head may have been turned by all the attention, it seems that those 'feelings' were not as fully reciprocated by Ian as Evans would have hoped. He was using Evans as much as he had used Jones, knowing that he and the band were, for the time being, making progress with him.

Miraculously, after all this, there still remained some semblance of 'togetherness' amongst the band as they embarked on a trip to Dublin to play at a gig Evans had organised. The event in question was to take place at McConagel's Bar, something of a rite-of-passage venue in Irish rock, where artists including Thin Lizzy and U2 had come to make their mark on the scene. The band were definitely looking forward to playing here, but they arrived at the venue blissfully unaware that they had in fact been booked on to the wrong night and a hardcore heavy metal crowd awaited them! Their entrance onstage certainly wasn't helped by the attire John had pressed his band-mates into wearing (Beach Boys-style bowling shirts): then he blotted his copybook further by provocatively introducing the riff to Deep Purple's "Smoke On The Water" early on in the set – a signal for all hell to break loose. Unlike those that had occurred in Preston and Sweden, the riot that ensued was, this time, not one that Ian and Andy could casually observe from the relatively safe vantage point of the stage before strolling off. The band ran for cover, their backs pelted with beer glasses as they went – another legendary early Stone Roses gig, and for all the wrong reasons. It was also the last to feature Andy Couzens, as Gareth Evans took the opportunity that now presented itself to do what he had been intending from the outset of making his deal with the Roses.

Needing to get back from Dublin to do one of his odd jobs, Couzens paid his own flight home, rather than take the eight-hour ferry from Liverpool. The next thing he knew he was being summoned to a meeting of the band members, with Evans presiding over what was essentially a 'kangaroo court' at which Couzens would be 'tried'. The charges brought against him amounted, it seemed, to no more than his being 'above himself and not part of the gang'. While Reni and Garner creditably tried to calm things down from the off, Ian and John maintained silence throughout until Couzens asked them directly: 'Do you agree with this?' Now Couzens was met with the trademark blank stares from Ian and John and with no more ceremony than that, he was out of the band.

The new four-piece Roses took a little time adjusting to life without Couzens – but not that long. The fact was that John Squire was continuing to develop as a guitarist, inspired by Reni's consummate musicianship and, after the first couple of post-Couzens gigs, no one could justly have said the Roses *needed* any guitarist other than John. And though it must be admitted that Ian was never going to be the 'shouter-type' vocalist usually spawned by rock n' roll, his style of singing was also developing in a way that perfectly suited the Roses fast-evolving musical sound. The faintly psychedelic pop theme that was emerging was beautifully, and unusually complemented by a certain homespun charm in Ian's phrasing which, in contrast to the vast majority of UK artists' Americanised vocals, is heavily accented, with his Lancashire and Cheshire roots easy to hear.

But all this was pretty academic when, in reality, still not *that* many people were actually seeing or hearing the Roses at this point. Their career was evolving into a pattern of taking one step forward, only to go two steps back. Evans, boosted by the departure of Couzens, was doing his best to get record companies interested in them as well as land them gigs, but the relative frailty of their position (and with it Evans') is painfully revealed when one looks back to the events of July 1986, and the Festival of the Tenth Summer. Though the festival concept had emanated from the Factory folk, the Manchester G-Mex line up was not all Factory bands, and many local outfits were meant to play, along with New Order, the Smiths, the Fall and such like – but there was no room on the bill for the Roses.

Evans, indefatigably trying to turn things around for the band, was seen now casting about in all sorts of different directions at the same time. He got the band to play regularly at the International, running around town prior to each show, distributing free tickets, which admittedly resulted in an increase in audience numbers. The strategy here was to build-up home support before taking on the national arena. 'I knew they should just concentrate on Manchester,' he said. He also bought the entire print run of a local music free-sheet, so that 10,000 issues were dropped around the town with Ian's face seemingly emblazoned everywhere.

At the same time, though, he recruited local promoter, Sandy Gort, through a meeting at the Hacienda, giving him the task of arranging twenty nationwide gigs, while also appointing one of the bar staff, (a Stone Roses fan only by chance), as press officer! Gort, nonplussed by Evans as he was, decided to 'come on board'. Needless to say the press officer arrangement never came to anything.

At the end of 1986, the band recorded their first demo as a four-piece, one that included early versions of "Elephant Stone" and "Sugar Spun Sister". Though the end results were encouraging, with the Roses clearly developing a more serious interest in refining their sound in the studio, it was nevertheless, at the end of the day, just another demo – of which they had produced countless versions by now, but they still had only one single to their name.

Evans' awareness of the Roses' growing impatience may go some way towards explaining the impetuosity of his next move. In all probability however, it was just a case of 'Gareth the madman', as he went on to sign his band of indie hopefuls, with their emerging sixties psychedelia sound - to a heavy metal label.

FM Revolver were, at first, just one of a whole host of record companies who received a regular earbashing on the phone from Evans on the Stone Roses and their utter brilliance. They were notable not only for being a heavy metal label, but also in this context, for actually calling Evans back. Based in Wolverhampton, they specialised in plucking local, spangled heavy/glam rock bands from obscurity, only to condemn them to another kind of obscurity. Having wrenched an album out of a band, they packaged it in suitable form and peddled it furiously to the Japanese market, which would, apparently, buy more or less anything that FM Revolver threw at them. Not a good home for the Roses, then. Sandy Gort, for one, was incredulous when he heard.

Evans had secured what is known as a 'reverse deal' whereby the band provide something on signature, rather than the label forwarding an advance to make an album or pay for lengthy studio time – the label simply being committed to putting the product out through their distributors. In Evans' words, it was a 'vinyl demo', a promotional exercise aimed at getting the Roses into the indie charts. Even so, Evans had airily signed the contract on the band's behalf, confident that any future problems it held could be circumvented.

The band went along with Evans' idea and duly met FM Revolver's MD, Paul Birch. This audience was a 'facer' to say the least, as it brought a rather sullen and suspicious indie-dressed quartet together with Wolverhamton's answer to Steven Tyler, resplendent in leopard-skin trousers waist-length hair, and, you guessed it, Aerosmith boots.

With the meeting over, Evans' next move was necessarily a morale-boosting one. He pulled over during the drive back on the motorway and pitched every copy of "So Young" that he had on board into the road. Switching into reverse, he proceeded to smash every copy, while the band looked on, highly impressed. His last word on his self-styled Howard Jones exorcism was: 'The new era begins now.'

VIII

The 'new era' appeared for the moment, however, to be a bit like all the eras in the history of the Stone Roses to date: with a few positive events outweighed, invariably, by one too many negative ones. One of the former came about around this time, when Evans, with band in tow, door-stepped Manchester music journalist, Mick Middles, and proceeded to play "Sally Cinnamon". Middles was not only impressed but also touched at the sight of Ian singing, and blushing slightly, along to his own record. This encounter led to an encouraging report in the *Manchester Evening News*. Ian managed, however, to turn on the charm for only so long as during the photo session that followed, taking an instant dislike to the photographer and proceeding to ensure that the end results were pretty grim, so much so that the photos were unusable. A collage from the "Cinnamon" artwork was consequently put in place to accompany the article, at Evans' insistence.

Meanwhile, another local newspaper, taking note of their lighter sixties sheen, accused the band of changing their image solely to attract record company interest, something Ian fiercely denied: 'That's just stupid people talking rubbish. We haven't softened at all. I know they are stupid, these people. But they'll just have to catch up with us. And they will, in the end, because they will have to be in on the action. And we will be massive'. So overall, the press encounters and ensuing coverage were proving not to be totally positive experiences for the Roses.

The "Sally Cinnamon" single came out in May on FM Revolver, who pressed a thousand copies. With little widespread publicity, it was no surprise that it never got near the indie charts, but sold out quickly in Manchester, even though it was proving difficult to find: Ian himself was even spotted in the Virgin store on a fruitless search for the single! Despite his self-confidence and bravado, the Roses' audience was actually getting smaller, and Ian's on stage demeanour was being less and less well received. It was taken as sheer arrogance by a gathering of rockers in Sheffield, for example, while another audience of less than thirty, admittedly more receptive punters, simply didn't know how to respond when he climbed off the stage in the middle of songs and mingled with them.

Muze's Paula Greenwood described Ian's preening as an essential part of the Stone Roses 'aura', which they maintained even as audiences dwindled: 'Ian had an arrogance on stage. He demanded attention and he got it. He controlled the audience.' A *Sounds* live review around this time put it more crudely, while still allowing for his magnetism: 'He's whirling around the stage like a demented muppet crooning to no one in particular, he does fancy himself and you want to hate the guy'.

They played Liverpool in August of 1987, appearing at Sefton Park at the 'Larks In The Park' event, with town favourites, the La's. Like the La's, their melodious tunes went down well with a summer crowd, the biggest they had played to for some time. They also received far-sighted praise from *Melody Maker*: 'Next big things. Brattish pop in psychedelic clothes'. But the one-step-forward-two-steps-back pattern re-asserted itself once more on the band.

Clearly still nursing a grievance from the publishing split forced upon him, Pete Garner called it a day, having forewarned the rest of the band in June. The remaining Roses, cast down by his departure, tried another bassist almost immediately, but he was rejected after only a week of work. What they needed was some-one who, apart from being a formidable musician, was also capa-ble of being a true part of the gang.

The solution presented itself in the shape of the inimitable Mani, last seen being ejected from the Preston Clouds by Howard Jones. Mani seemed the ideal choice, a perfect rhythm partner for Reni. Mani's punk/Northern soul hybrid bass style had developed in parallel with the Roses playing. The punk influence had largely disappeared and his delivery was now much smoother and more fluid. As Ian and John became closer, Mani's positive nature and enthusiasm would be a complement for the irrepressible Reni as well.

The first gig he played with them was predictably at the International, and it was a showcase for, among others, "She Bangs The Drums" and "Waterfall". Once on stage with them, it seemed like a seamless transition for the band and now they were well on the way to creating an English psychedelic image. John splattered shirts, guitars and amps with paint, Jackson Pollock style and Ian later confirmed that they were always image-conscious, even to the point of dressing each other: 'The Roses were always about clothes. We'd buy each other things and say. "Look I got this for you – try this on" or "You're not wearing that."

Other aspects were by now also falling into place. Gareth Evans had been throwing all his energies into managing the band, with low-key help from his business partner, Matthew Cummings. He now made one of his shrewdest moves to date by bringing in a third person, Lindsay Reade, and forming a management group. Reade, who was the ex-wife of Factory records boss, Tony Wilson, had enjoyed a highly successful time at the label and had a strong working knowledge of the music business, as well as a calm, practical sense of all the mechanics, contrasting with Evans' bluster and extravagant nature. Pitched into the office at the International, she was taken aback by Evans' chaotic style and methods but, at the same time, undoubtedly won over by his enthusiasm. Also keen on the Roses, which did help, she got straight down to the job of winning A&R interest in the band and, unlike Evans' track history in this department, she got results.

With their regular gigs at the International and another booked at Dingwall's the band began, henceforward, to treat all performances as A&R showcases, where with any luck, labels would be fighting for the Stone Roses' signatures. Top of the list for Evans, apparently, was Rough Trade, the Smiths' label: Reade was able to persuade MD Geoff Travis along to the Dingwall's gig. She also managed to generate interest from another company, a curious outfit (though not as curious as FM Revolver) called Zomba, based in Willesden, London, who promised to send someone along to the International.

Zomba had on the one hand, page-three-lovely-turned-singer, Samantha Fox (with whom Ian, allegedly, was to get on very well) and on the other, a host of successful black artists in World and Rap music, such as Hugh Masakela. Reade had, in fact, infected their A&R man, Roddy McKenna, with her enthusiasm for the Stone Roses. So McKenna, among others, turned up at the International with serious intent.

On the night, the band's performance was all that McKenna had hoped it would be. Having been bowled over by the demos he'd previously heard, he headed back to London to notify his boss and a colleague to ratify his judgement of their live act. All three were due at Dingwalls, as well as Travis.

By the time of the Dingwall's gig, another integral part of the developing Roses image was well in place. Ian had now abandoned his increasingly unpopular walks into the crowd, but in their place had perfected a repertoire of on-stage moves. These amounted to a subtle mixture of grace, buffoonery and stone-cold arrogance that would one day earn him the nickname 'King Monkey'. His way of looking contemptuous of all that was going on around him did not, however, recommend the Roses to McKenna's colleagues who remained unconvinced overall.

Just across the room, they were able to see Lyndsey Reade with Geoff Travis from Rough Trade, who, after one song told Reade: 'That's it… I'll sign them.' All too easy, apparently, but while giving Reade the green light to open negotiations with Rough Trade, Evans also began talks with Zomba, having imposed himself on McKenna as the leading player and viewing him as the most 'persuadable'. There are conflicting accounts about exactly what happened that night, but the upshot of it all was that Rough Trade hedged their bets and agreed to finance a single as FM Revolver had done, while Zomba set about putting in a draft proposal for a record contract. Evans would later say that he had been waiting for a big label to come in all along right up until the time, in fact, that Zomba actually produced the contract. This might explain Evans' rumoured presence at a Rough Trade marketing meeting for the *next* Stone Roses single on *the* day that the contract with Zomba was finally signed. If true, Evans was clearly hedging his bets as much as Rough Trade, while holding out for his dream bid.

Meanwhile, he had got the Roses into the studio at no cost again. And, not only that, he was able to persuade New Order's Peter Hook to act as producer. Selecting "Elephant Stone", from the first four-piece demo, was a brave choice. An exhilarating kaleidoscopic mix of wah-wah, chiming guitars, driving bass and drums, with one of Ian's most uplifting vocals to date, it was perhaps at this stage, too brave a choice. "Elephant Stone" *is* a pop song, but arguably one with a few too many wide-open spaces, thus lacking the compact punch of many *breakthrough* singles. (Added to this, the b-side, "Full Five Fathom" was "Elephant Stone" recorded backwards – the Roses' first dabbling with 'backwards psychedelia' – and again perhaps not the most commercial of choices).

It was these nuances of the record, as well as stiff competition from a range of up and coming indie bands (including fellow local lads, the Happy Mondays who were beginning to make their inimitable mark on the musical landscape) which caused "Elephant Stone" to become, rather frustratingly, another 'failed' single.

This disappointment was offset by the still-keen interest of Zomba, who came up with a draft contract in March 1988. The Roses trusted Evans to do them a good service on this side of things, but maybe they placed too strong a trust in him, as this was a time when he was, in truth, at his most cavalier. His later comment, 'I knew that contract was no good. That's why I let them sign it', says it all really, although his qualification goes some way to explaining this rather staggering statement: Evans still maintains that on signing the contract on behalf of the band, he asked Zomba to provide an alternative one to cover the band once they got into the charts – which they apparently agreed to do. And Evans was confident that he would be able to get out of the contract if he needed to.

Essentially, Zomba's contract was still a draft proposal at this stage, one that covered the basic provisions for advance, royalty rates, time span etc, prior to being batted back and forth by lawyers from both parties to their mutual satisfaction. Evans had instructions from the band to obtain an advance that, after some haggling, was set at £27,500. Instead of handing the contract to a music business lawyer (which Evans didn't have to hand anyway) to deal with all the finer points, he signed and returned it himself once the magic figure for the advance was in place. This was clearly going to turn out as an act of either breathtaking folly or commendable *chutzpah*. With Evans there were no half measures.

As for the Roses, little else can be said except that they were undoubtedly out to get the money and the recording deal and were probably justified in thinking that they had waited long enough, so a sense of caution never really entered into their minds. As John Squire put it: 'We weren't interested in the business side and we weren't interested in business people. So Gareth would take care of all that and report back to us.' And later, in an interview with *Mojo* he stated even more frankly, 'We all passed around this telephone directory of a thing and said, "We ain't got a clue," and giggled and signed it.' So, like many a band before and since, they simply trusted their manager *too* far, because this was a contract that would come back to haunt them.

For the time being, though, everyone was happy. Zomba had slightly overpaid on the advance, but they were enthusiastic enough about the Roses to inaugurate a label within the label, Silvertone, to be run by their highly creative A&R man, Andrew Lauder, who had a strong background, having worked with Elvis Costello, for instance. The name, Silvertone, was well matched to the Roses and their sound too.

Soon after their contract was signed they played a gig which would always be special to Ian: 'I once said it was the perfect Roses gig… They didn't know what hit 'em that night. I felt really proud.' Rather than another night at the International, this time the Roses played at the satellite club, also owned by Evans, known, rather unimaginatively, as the International 2 and a much more cramped version to boot.

The event was organised by the renowned Manchester DJ and author Dave Haslam, whose book, *Manchester, England* is an admirable study of the city's story in music. An anti-Clause 28 gig (Clause 28 being part of a bill put forward by the Conservative government which was prejudiced against homosexuals), it was a prestigious night with the Roses second on the bill after James. Arriving on stage late – much to the annoyance of James – they played brilliantly while Ian gave one of his most fiercely arrogant displays yet. He antagonised some of the audience and fighting broke out during "I Wanna Be Adored", but he definitely inspired one local lad at least – Liam Gallagher, the brother of Noel – who stood transfixed by Ian's presence and authority.

Unknown to any of them, also watching the Roses for the first time in the shadows of International 2 was the producer who was to work for them on their first album. Ironically, in November 1996, John Leckie would be picking up a Best Producer award from Q for his work with the Roses – the same awards ceremony that was stormed by Liam Gallagher and Oasis. Leckie has an enviable pedigree as a music producer: Abbey Road was very much his *alma mater*, where he not only worked with Pink Floyd on *Atom Heart Mother* as an engineer, but had also collaborated with both George Martin *and* Phil Spector, something that possibly only John Lennon and George Harrison could also boast of doing. As a producer, he had helped create acclaimed work by XTC and The Fall to give just two examples. None other than Geoff Travis had first suggested his recruitment to Evans, when Rough Trade was still in the running for the Roses' signature. At first, the band was thinking about getting DJ Pierre, the acid house supremo. Ian said: 'I was on the phone to this kid for about an hour, telling him why we loved his records. He seemed to us to be the boy to do it. But he had three months' work so he couldn't.' Jamaica's renowned producers, Sly and Robbie were also apparently considered, but once John Leckie, with his outstanding credentials, came into the equation there really was no contest.

Having been confirmed in the role, and after seeing a couple of rehearsals, Leckie remained mightily impressed with his latest charges: 'I thought they were fantastic and I just couldn't wait to get them in the studio.' The album that he was about to start work on would become possibly Leckie's greatest achievement, and finally bring the Stone Roses a recognition and acclaim they richly deserved.

PART TWO

ADORED

PROLOGUE

One day in 1994, Noel and Liam Gallagher, the brothers from Oasis, were taking a short break from recording their band's debut album, *Definitely Maybe*. They were based at the Valley Recording Studios, in the small market town of Monmouth, where they happened to be walking down the high street.

As they walked by WH Smiths, they suddenly noticed none other than Ian Brown, bounding out of the shop, 'shadow boxing like Muhammad Ali', and making his way towards them. As they stood in astonishment Brown called out: 'You're the guys out of Oasis, aren't you? "Cigarettes and Alcohol", fucking hell. Great song.'

The Gallaghers were all amazement at Brown's magnanimous praise for their single. Noel Gallagher was to say later that there wouldn't have been any Oasis if the Stone Roses hadn't existed before them, while Liam was staring into the face of his inspiration for going into music.

And Ian Brown was staring back, and into the future of British music, if only he'd known it. That meeting represented a symbolic summation of the Roses' rise and fall. The release of the first Oasis album would dwarf the success that he had known with *The Stone Roses* and by this point, Ian Brown's band had long been living on past glories. With hindsight, the trajectory of the Stone Roses' career showed that, whereas Oasis were on the springboard of commercial dominance with *Definitely Maybe,* The Stone Roses had already known a beginning and an end. The beginning of the band had been the stuff of legends – a legend that survives to this day – of a band that became adored for making the greatest debut album of all time. It was the culmination of years of hard work, slowly building towards a line-up and a musical conception that was close to perfection.

The Stone Roses shot straight into the musical firmament like a blazing comet, but it was burning up all the time, with fault lines visible from the very beginning. The band descent began almost as soon as it had risen, careering off course, and, slowly dropping in the sky, it flickered and died.

This is how the Stone Roses ended.

IX

The band's first appearance for work at Zomba's Battery studios in London was an inauspicious occasion. Reni was late and rang the studio to ask John Leckie if he could borrow ten pounds for the cab. While Leckie was no doubt bemused, Gareth Evans was enraged, when he arrived to find Reni distinctly absent. Leckie recalls: 'When Reni arrived and asked for the tenner Evans shouted, "Don't ask the *producer* for money, ask me", and swiftly punched him. There were bloody noses, they were thumping each other against the wall, and then Reni just left. I thought, this is a good start.'

But any trepidation felt by Leckie was quickly allayed. From the beginning, and throughout, the whole band showed a commitment to the project that made a great impression on him. Contrary to the behaviour one might usually expect from a band who had just got their album deal, they displayed a highly professional approach – Leckie illustrated this by claiming that during the recording period, *he* actually drank more than they did. Ian Brown, he noted, never touched so much as a beer.

Ian's own words also demonstrate how seriously he took the work in progress: 'We had beginnings and ending for all the songs. "Sugar Spun Sister", for example, had to finish on a particular chord. We were absolute about how that should be – so well prepared. The Stone Roses never ever winged it. We never had to'

When not in the studio, the band was based at a flat in Kensal Rise where they slept during the day. They recorded through the night, leaving the studio at 7 a.m. so there was thankfully little time to spend the £10 a day allotted them by Zomba! They worked quickly and, by the end of the first session for the album, as well as feeling admiration for their work ethic, Leckie was beginning to realise the magnitude of what they were producing. His wealth of experience in the business meant he could spot something unique and musically important a mile off, and he was also inevitably becoming infected by the time-honoured Roses confidence: 'We had a few traumas... but there was always this fantastic underlying sense of belief. I thought I might just be getting carried away, y'know, losing my objectivity a bit. But it dawned on me that this was something special.'

Leckie encouraged them to scrap a lot of material and then pour their efforts into playing as a tight unit on what he considered to be the 'outstanding' songs. The Roses wanted the highest standards of production without sounding over-produced: one of the main aims was to recreate, as much as possible, the excitement of the Roses' live performances. This meant that Reni and Mani were recorded live throughout, with no overdubs whatsoever – demanding high standards of musicianship from the pair. And with this, the album gradually began to take shape.

"I Wanna Be Adored" is a portentous start to the album with a slow, almost growling build-up from John's dramatic opening riff. What is most surprising though is that, instead of a rousing vocal, there is Ian's understated, some would even say laid-back voice, which manages to convey infinite menace as well as sheer confidence that he *will* be adored. John rejects the traditional solo as a bridge, in favour of a series of bar chords, with a myriad of frills laid on top, reflecting the insistence of Ian's message. The grinding chords ending the song, along with Ian's final 'I wanna be adored', serve to add even greater emphasis to his powerful message.

This is followed by one of the brightest, most uplifting moments in the Roses canon: Reni's hi-hat jumps into life alongside Mani's bass before John's guitar rings out with a simple but sublime combination of notes that herald "She Bangs The Drums". The perfect backdrop to a love song, Ian cleverly and cheekily subverts traditional love song orthodoxies with, first a metaphor 'I feel my needle hit the groove' and then the plain rudeness of 'kiss me where the sun don't shine'. Even the typically arrogant words 'the past was yours, but the future's mine' seem not to suppress the charm of this song.

"Waterfall" is a breathtaking tune brilliantly woven round one of John's greatest creations, a circling, hypnotic guitar motif that hardly ever changes. The crystalline vocals from Ian and Reni (who provides excellent backing throughout) merge with John's guitar to give an effect that even suggests a waterfall – the pure sounds washing over the listener, as it were.

"This Is The One" shines just as brightly and benefits hugely from its brave stop-start arrangement, a clever build up to a thrilling fast-paced finale, showcasing John's surging power when, on a lot of the album, he is consistently understated, even restrained in his contributions. John is equally luminous with the laid-back, jazz inflected "Shoot You Down".

John actually digresses dramatically in his guitar accompaniment to specific tracks, rejecting most of what he had previously played live, and rewriting solo pieces to fit with the recorded versions. On "Bye Bye Badman", for example, which displays one of his greatest guitar lines, he wasn't sure of exactly how he would play it until a moment of inspiration just before the recording. Spontaneity indeed played a huge part in the making of the album, generating tracks such as Ian's personal favourite "Don't Stop"(the backwards version of "Waterfall") where John wrote the lyrics, working on what was suggested to him in the moment rather than himself or Ian composing something beforehand. The delicate re-arrangement of Simon and Garfunkel's tune, "Elizabeth My Dear", transformed in order to deliver a tough message to the reigning Queen, (Ian would back his views up later with a tabloid-baiting claim that he would suffocate the Queen Mother) also owed a great deal to this method of working.

But the spirit of spontaneity is best illustrated with the stupendous closer on this album, "I Am The Resurrection". Starting, according to Reni, as a 'reverse bass pisstake of Paul McCartney on "Taxman" ', it was soon clear this piece of light tomfoolery had the makings of a truly great song. And Ian was instrumental in assuring its greatness: 'It was me who coaxed them to do that ending on "Resurrection". Only prog. rock groups and players up their own arses did 10-minute guitar solos. But I kept saying to them, "Look you're great. Let's do a ten-minute song where you're just playing and playing and playing". For two days I watched them work out the ending of that song. It was just fantastic and it still sounds amazing.'

Ian has aptly described Reni's drum intro as 'Motown-influenced' and, indeed, as it kicks off it has all the stomp and swagger of a Stud Brothers classic. Again, Ian's singing is somewhat laid-back with a hint of a sneer that builds up throughout and, in another innovative arrangement, he sings verses and short choruses, broken up with some strafing chords from John. Stunningly, the *real* chorus is revealed at the end of three verses, a majestic, magical howl of triumph: 'I am the resurrection and the light' – taken from the Bible. Arguably Ian's greatest recorded singing moment, it is a rousing battle cry as well as a passionate, almost blood-curdling affirmation.

Not that this is where the song ends of course. After the second of these choruses, the sound appears to list to one side as Mani picks out a funk groove. Suddenly, Reni and John burst into life once more and work around Mani before they all skid to a halt. And then the song begins *again*. They all crash in once more, building to a climax where John introduces two guitar riffs warring against each other, one a Hendrix-like fuzz, the other the more familiar bright, up-beat Roses sound. In a case of what could only be described as musical welding, the three musicians create a rock/funk hybrid which is, at once, danceable, while at the same time appealing to any self-respecting air guitarist, such is the power, energy and precision of John's playing. Everything seems to be winding down again, when chiming notes from an acoustic guitar ring out, a slide guitar joins in, followed by Reni and Mani, who, through improvisational playing, draw the listeners' attention, miraculously back to the drum and bass pattern where we started "The Resurrection". And on this crescendo, the track and with it the album is brought to a dramatic close.

This song in itself could be defined as the musical equivalent of being carried on the crest of a wave, such is its unstoppable power – as a closing track it is almost unrivalled, an epochal triumph in rock. It would certainly have made sobering listening for many a diehard Smiths fans, for instance: while Johnny Marr was certainly John Squire's equal, the Smiths never came near to creating a musical improvisation as historic as this. The 'bookending' of this album with "I Wanna Be Adored" and "I Am The Resurrection" is equally inspired. To say both tracks are daunting affirmations of the Roses' unshakeable self-belief would be an understatement. And starting as well as ending an album in this way undoubtedly left them open to attack. The rest of the record needed to more than live up to the expectations produced by these accolades to themselves... which of course it did.

Of all the songs on the album, "Adored" is something like a character key, and obviously inspiration for the title to this book. Introducing the idea that Ian had no need of a pact with the Devil – 'he's already in me' – is chilling, but counteracted by the yearning that comes through his voice in the choruses. It's a perfect reflection of Ian's obvious hard edges, yet surrounding a real and genuine warmth, contained even within that infamous self-confidence, which again rears its head here when he whispers 'you adore me'.

In truth, each and every song is memorable on *The Stone Roses* and, within each song there are the brightest flashes of inspiration from all of the band members. But, surprisingly, in retrospect, the band was somewhat critical of the finished album and the press not unqualified in their initial praise, as many in the future would be. *Q* magazine suggested that it had a 'monochrome' sound, a view with which Ian had some sympathy, while John was disappointed in his guitar approach, which, he claimed, gave the impression of there being two guitarists, not just him. 'The album just doesn't have the stamp of a real guitar player to me – apart from a couple of solos.' Ian summed it up rather dismissively: 'As we were rehearsing, the bass and drums got you in the belly every time, but as it turned into a record, it sounded like another sixties thing.'

Despite their reservations on that front, word was beginning to seep out about this band and their 'sixties thing', and with it, slowly and surely, the Stone Roses were entering the most celebrated part of their career.

X

"Made Of Stone", a key track on the album, was probably the most obvious single choice after "She Bangs The Drums". Though, on the one hand, decidedly a pop record, and a very classy one, it is also a song of rare refinement. The restrained and even moody intro and opening verse belie the rousing chorus which follows, while a beautifully timed interval between that and the second verse allows John to pick out the gentlest of notes. As the second chorus finishes, John now cuts in with his most accomplished solo from the album, ending in a shimmering haze of flanged guitar. And, rather like "Resurrection" – though more directly this time – John uses his intro also as the 'outro', with himself, Mani and Reni brilliantly and gradually slowing down the beat until the final note.

In February of 1989, Silvertone released "Made of Stone" as a single. In contrast to the reception of their previous attempts, the press really picked up on this, the first single from the album. It became single of the week in *NME,* though that tribute was slightly marred by *Melody Maker*'s inexplicable comparison of them with Spear Of Destiny. This was somewhat compensated for later, by the fact that a journalist from the paper, Bob Stanley, 'converted' to the band after seeing them play live and became one of the greatest champions of their cause.

Quite how significant this was revealed itself when "Made of Stone" suddenly landed in the indie charts at number four, even appearing on the fringes of the mainstream Top 100. This was the kind of reaction that they had wanted for "Elephant Stone", but neither the Roses nor Evans were complaining about that now. From this moment, the Stone Roses were no longer just a band from Manchester.

Apart from recording the album, they had been playing gigs. In March they had played Bradford one night, Cardiff the next. Others were held at universities and polytechnics – nothing new in itself for the Roses, the difference being that this time people were really listening to them, and talking about them, and the band were able to build on their growing reputation, taking on bigger and bigger gigs.

At the end of February, with "Made Of Stone" still in the charts, they played the Hacienda. The club was, as ever, the fulcrum of the Manchester scene, but at that time had, of course, a secret ingredient to add to its appeal: ecstasy. First experimented with by American academics in the late sixties, the ecstasy/MDMA drug had made its long trip to the UK and in turn, to Manchester. It was rumoured that their old friends (and 'friendly' rivals) the Happy Mondays had a former ecstasy dealer in tow – in the shape of Bez, their resident dancer/vibemaster/ 'percussionist' (and, coincidentally, the son of a police officer).

Even though Manchester's streets were patrolled by police in the vigilant charge of the somewhat intolerant (and certainly not very drug-friendly) James Anderton – later immortalised in the Mondays' "God's Cop" – very few people were aware that the country's youth were on the verge of pretty much a revolution. Later that year New Order would feature on *Top Of The Pops* performing "Fine Time", where the normally rather wooden front man, Bernard Sumner, displayed a 'dance routine' that would tell anyone in the know, that *he* certainly had an enthusiastic interest in the ecstasy scene. He had also, of course, a business interest in the Hacienda who were welcoming ecstasy revellers through their doors.

It need hardly be doubted that the ever-streetwise Roses were aware of what was going on too. The issue for them, though, was whether, as a 'guitar band', this crowd would accept them. Despite their misgivings, their performance and the reception it received was, in a word, triumphant. Ian later commented, rather scathingly, that 'you had to play the Hacienda as a sort of homecoming gig'. But it must equally be acknowledged that this venue, above anywhere else, was where the crowd embraced the band wholly, not only as one of their own (i.e. part of the Manchester scene) but, more importantly, simply for being themselves. And it was impossible for the Stone Roses to be anything other than that.

The *NME*'s Andrew Collins was, like Bob Stanley before him, totally swept away by the band: 'I'm already drafting a letter to my grandchildren telling them... I saw the Stone Roses at the Hacienda... The Roses, comprising four unassuming boy wonders and a Happy Mondays roadie (Cressa) acting as 'surf' dancing accessory, playing thoroughly regardless brat-arsed guitar Pop, have taken four years off my age.'

The Roses embarked on a short tour of the UK as the album was released. The concerts were now carrying proof of the levels of excitement mounting around the band. At the Leeds Warehouse, people were seen dancing on tables, while spontaneous chanting of 'We are Leeds' from the crowd, may or may not have been a reference to the football team, sworn enemies of the Roses' beloved Manchester United. Where in the past this might have elicited an 'arrogant' response from Ian, he now smiled and responded with, 'This is Leeds' and the band carried on pouring out the tunes. They played at the ICA where they were seen by another music press opinion maker, Everett True who said: 'The whole f**king hype is justified.'

So, coinciding with growing acclaim for the album, was the kind of word-of-mouth phenomenon that the Roses had come to rely on in Manchester – but it was finally happening on a national scale. They found they had pockets of fans everywhere, including Liverpool, where traditionally it had been very difficult for a Manchester band to gain a loyal following. The Roses, of course, felt it was nothing less than they deserved, with the old 'one step forward two steps back' pattern only ever being viewed as a temporary thing by them. As Mani described it later: 'even at the warehouse parties before we broke through, everyone knew it. It was the worst kept secret in rock 'n' roll.'

But what, even with Roses-enthusiasts like Stanley and Collins behind the band, would the notoriously fickle music press make of the album when it finally came out in May 1989? Typically, there was a pretty loud dissenting voice in the shape of the *NME*. Giving it merely seven out of ten, Jack Barron cuttingly remarked that it was 'aural Big Mac laced with a psychedelic drill' and 'this is living proof that acid is good for you. Just.'

Bob Stanley at *Melody Maker* could be relied upon to redress the balance of course, with his opinion that the album was, apparently, 'God'. It couldn't get better than that really, but others certainly did try. A future biographer of the band, John Robb, who was writing for *Sounds* at the time, could not help himself as he called it a 'masterpiece'. 'Who'd have guessed that a gang of scruffy kids thudding away in a rehearsal room, could have come up with something this magnificent, beautiful and confident?' He had, in fact, often been next door to the Roses at these rehearsals with his own band, the Membranes, and it was (and is) hugely to his credit that he celebrated the Roses' triumph over that of the Membranes, who enjoyed little success by comparison.

This was a time in music history when bands were beginning to get serious coverage in mainstream newspapers. The *Observer* reported, rather quaintly, that the album was 'jangling in every sense', and in the *Guardian*, Robin Denselow sensed the band's ambitious streak, 'The Stone Roses seem to be the first to swap their massive cult following for international success.' And, rather unusually for a British debut, especially one of the 'indie' variety, the Roses were mentioned in *Rolling Stone* across the pond with the tribute: 'The Roses are blooming in Technicolor.'

The press were virtually unanimous in their reference to the sixties influence throughout the record, emphasised by John Squire's celebrated sleeve. The psychedelic Jackson Pollock style was one with which he had already experimented, and he was convinced would be perfect for the album cover. 'I knew exactly how it should look,' he stated, and soon he was being asked by the other band members to 'Pollock' their guitars, clothes and equipment. Ian Brown can be credited for introducing another important ingredient to the album sleeve – lemons – one of which forms the 'O' in Roses. The catalyst for this was something that had occurred on one of his European sojourns.

'I met this guy while I was travelling. He had carried this lemon about in his pocket for years. He'd been on the front line in

Paris. If you suck a lemon, some of the CS gas effects are eliminated so you could still do something.' The 'front-line in Paris' referred to the student riots of 1968, a flashpoint year for left-wing politics, where the Situationists (later to inspire punk) would be at the vanguard. Ian said: 'We admired these people – not just for their politics – but for their clothes and haircuts.'

Leaving aside fashion for a while, the Roses' album was then, if not a political statement in the way a Billy Bragg or Redskins album could be categorised, at least something which they felt reflected where they stood politically. And it was, handily, the revolutionary spirit from the sixties that they were summoning up. Incidentally, John, who had collected for the miners in 1985, was known as Red John for a time, while Ian had joined a number of marches, including the Anti Clause 28 one, following their gig played in support of the cause. As for Mani: 'we saw some of the spirit of Paris of '68 reflected in the acid house movement'. One mustn't forget "Elizabeth My Dear" too – of her and her family Ian was to add, 'we're anti-royalist, anti-patriarch. When the ravens leave the tower we want to be there shooting them'.

So, the music press, though they may not have recognised a Situationist symbol, even as it stared at them from the album cover, would have to have been deaf as well as blind not to have heard and seen the sixties influence coming out of the Stone Roses. There were, however two aspects that seemed to have totally passed them by at this point. Firstly, the Roses had created an image independently, the kind of thing that marketing people spend hours trying to come up with. It might have taken the band a few years to fine tune, but it was an image all of their own making. Just as the Ramones had done before them, the Roses appeared with a do-it-yourself 'brand', and it worked for them right from the off, Mani's faintly Perry Boy look and Reni's beanie hat (soon to be copied all over the country) fitted in perfectly. It wasn't, after all, just about what people were doing in Paris in 1968, it was also about what they were wearing, as elaborated on both by Ian and John. Ian: 'they had semi-flared hipsters and bowl haircuts'. John:

'a guy in a cord three-button jacket behind the barricades with a top fringe, throwing a rock at the police.'

Another significant press oversight came in the form of a total lack of recognition of the significant position held by the Stone Roses, alongside the emerging Happy Mondays, at the vanguard of the 'acid house movement' also known as 'Madchester'. Don't forget that this was an era well before the likes of *Mixmag* hit the stands, and the music press was still most decidedly centred around indie guitar bands, while – as Noel Gallagher so aptly put it – 'guys from guitar bands (were) going to clubs.'

The band members had always listened to and taken from an eclectic range of music, and as soon as the press did begin to pick up on what was going on Ian was quick to comment, 'Everyone is talking about indie and dance coming together. But everyone I know has gone into each other's scene and had dance records since they were little kids. You either get a good feel off a record or you don't – and there are as many bad house records as there are good rock records.'

As the Happy Mondays continued to break through, more and more stories of the scene in Manchester circulated, and in the end, when the Mondays put out an EP, Factory Records insisted on calling it the 'Madchester EP'. This was in spite of the Mondays' objection to the idea, which they saw as a rather cynical piece of opportunism. Very soon, Madchester became, apparently, a 'state of mind', and countless teenagers all over the country were to be seen walking around with the legend emblazoned on their T-shirts, many of whom became part of a stampede that drew to a halt outside the ecstasy-soaked Hacienda each week. As Ian told the *NME*, however, 'We might come from Manchester but we don't see ourselves as a continuation of any Manchester scene. The world doesn't begin and end at the Hacienda and we're interested in reaching the world.'

This attitude may be another aspect of the Stone Roses agenda that the music press failed to pick up on at first, but they were soon to be confronted with it full-on. Now that the band's limitless self-confidence looked to be justified by an overall positive response to the first album, and as they prepared for their next tour, the press were increasingly gathering in their droves to speak to the Roses, and they were to be greeted with some grand pronouncements from the mouths of the band.

For instance, no sooner had they got into the pages of *Q* than Ian was to be found giving archetypal '*Q*' band U2, a royasl dissing. 'U2?' he said of them, 'Drivel. Just crap. They don't sound like they mean it.' Bruce Springsteen was treated equally scathingly: 'He always sounds to me like he's having a shit.' At the same time he also alluded to the band's aspirations of chart success with the comment, 'I'll be severely disappointed if we haven't had a Number One by the end of 1989. 'Cos the time is right. Anything is possible.'

Ian, in the tradition of the best front men before him, was becoming a challenge for the journalists who were making tracks to see them. The others were happy for him to take this kind of lead. John, on the other hand, was well-known for not saying anything at all in some interviews – also a difficult scenario for reporters. Ian was adept at turning questions around to suit the Roses and with that intimidating stare he was, to say the least, a handful. But his overriding theme was, unfailingly, the size of ambition entertained by his band.

Speaking to *Melody Maker* he referred to their desire for an appearance on *Top Of The Pops*: 'I want to be on that show. I watched it last week and it was like *Junior Show Time*. I wanna shake them all up.' In another interview he confirmed this view: 'We should be on *Top Of The Pops*. I'd like to see our record going up and Kylie and Phil Collins going down. You've got in there to stamp them out. Because I believe that we have more worth.' He showed equal determination on the band's behalf when speaking to an American magazine: 'We are striving to be part of a new movement in rock, like the Beatles were to the 1960s and the Sex Pistols were to the 1970s. We've got it.'

Grand pronouncements indeed and, with hindsight, one can easily see how the Gallagher brothers, who were still to form their group at the time, were simply following in Ian Brown's footsteps when they claimed sometime later that they wanted to be 'bigger than U2'. Typically, Ian could even top that boast because he is also recorded as saying that they wanted to be 'the first band to be playing on the moon.'

Ian and the Roses can perhaps be forgiven for all this hyperbole to a large extent in light of the fact that they had, after all, just produced a stunning debut album, even if all the world didn't know it yet (for the record, *The Stone Roses* sold *only* 75,000 copies in the first year of release – but by 2002, it was up to 3.5 million). While they were still in search of a number one at the time, there were few people who would argue that they weren't *the* band to see at that moment.

The Roses had been, literally, playing out of their skins throughout 1989, with many of their gigs attaining legendary status. One, at the International 2 in May had been an indicator of things to come, with tickets sold out almost as soon as they went on sale. The band got a massive reception as they walked out on stage to the crowd's chanting of 'Manchester la la la'. With a 'Pollocked' Union Jack behind him, Ian held the audience spellbound – never speaking once. Shortly after, they returned to Leeds, playing to an equally enraptured audience.

Following the release of the album, and in keeping with their vaunting ambition, the Roses started looking towards more ambitious places to play. The first suggestion was, in fact, the brainchild of Gareth Evans, still beavering away in the background, attempting to land gigs in grander settings. He, of all people, was well aware that the band needed to move forward in this way, in order for them to solidify their reputation and also, providing the Roses played to the best of their ability, hopefully to spark envy in any rivals that they might have. His efforts were also a sign of Evans' supreme and continued confidence in his protégés. Everyone around them knew that there was a larger audience 'in waiting' for the Stone Roses. The venue that Evans came up with, to the band's enthusiastic agreement, was Blackpool's Empress Ballroom. His original concept was to do a tour of decaying British seaside resorts (an idea that would certainly have appealed to

Ian who claimed already to know most of them). The seaside tour *nearly* happened but for some reason the band and Evans decided to make it a one-off, and Blackpool was a prestigious symbol of the British seaside, so a date was duly set in high summer.

It was still a risky proposition. Sealing a band's reputation as a live draw is no mean feat, hence the number of relatively successful bands around with no reputation at all for their live performances. Some bands, admittedly, suffer fiascos that put them off playing at all, while these days, a band like the Manic Street Preachers can gain kudos (and fans) through supporting Oasis. Certain spots at Glastonbury are much-coveted as reputation-makers such as that taken by Oasis in 1995, followed by Radiohead in 1997. For the kind of event that Evans was proposing there were few precedents: Echo & The Bunnymen had enjoyed 'A Day Out in Liverpool' which included a fans' cycle ride (the route was shaped like a rabbit), culminating in a gig at Liverpool Cathedral; Queen had undertaken their *Crazy Tour Of London* in the seventies, playing in discos and even bingo halls. But these were essentially diversions for bands that had already reached a level of success they were happy with. For the Stone Roses, their Blackpool gig was meant to be so much more, a platform, in fact, to another plateau.

The attitude of the music press was to be crucial too, because for all the momentum that the Roses had built up, and for all their bluff and 'don't care' attitude, the press inevitably maintained great influence over the record buying public. And if the press chose to scoff, as well they might (and as they had indeed done when, for instance, Siouxsie and the Banshees announced a 'big gig' at the Royal Albert Hall) it could end in disaster for the Stone Roses.

When the day arrived – August 12, 1989 – it was clearly to be a red-letter day for the Roses (and 'Madchester'), from the off. Only an hour away from Manchester, there was plenty of time for the hardcore fans from the Roses' hometown to get to Blackpool and enjoy a day out by the seaside before the gig. It turned out a glorious summer's afternoon and, suddenly, Blackpool was full of people sporting, to use the newly minted phrase, the 'baggy' look. So, mingling with the pensioners and the Blackpool-day-out sightseers, was a sea of young men and women in flares, 'Madchester' or Stone Roses T-shirts, and of course, the now obligatory 'Reni-hats', as they had come to be known.

Far from scoffing, the music press flocked to the gig along with all the fans, though some were undoubtedly feeling thwarted by the stonewalling style of the Roses, who were, if possible, more alive to the gang mentality than ever before. They often closed ranks, frustrating many an interviewer at the time, knowing no doubt that they were pretty much unassailable. Despite the bad feeling created, a lone dissenting voice arose from Blackpool that day, in the form of the *Sounds* correspondent who called them 'just another bunch of dimwit parochials with nothing to say.' But even *Sounds* had put them on their front cover the week before! The ever-dependable Bob Stanley, in contrast described them effusively as 'Four blokes from the Stretford End with four teenage Jesus Christs. Pop perfection', while the *NME* simply and powerfully anointed them 'the future, the resurrection.'

Ian later summed the day up: 'We wanted to give people a big day out to finish their summer.' And, although they may have remained aloof with the press in Blackpool that day, they mingled happily, and very naturally, with their fans, echoing the style of their heroes the Clash. Ian also brought a bonhomie to the electrifying show itself, joining in with some of the chants, seizing a pair of bongos as "Resurrection" was played through and revelling in the musicianship of John, Mani and Reni – just like all the fans in front of him. And when a pint of beer was thrown at him, far from getting annoyed or lapsing into 'aggressive' mode, he merely moved his mouth like a goldfish, his great eyes staring out into the crowd. The band were on top form and they came off stage triumphant. And afterwards Ian even went as far as to perform a 'charismatic host' act backstage.

Blackpool is commonly acknowledged as the Roses greatest ever gig. They had followed what was later to be recognised by many as the greatest debut album ever, with the boldest of moves in planning to play at Blackpool. As soon as they walked on stage they sensed the atmosphere of anticipation. They felt the reaction to the opening notes of "Adored" and the frenzied euphoria amongst the crowd (regardless of whether they were on E or not), and they knew then that everything had paid off – what better incentive could there be to give your best show?

As the Roses and their fans left Blackpool, drifting out of a city that had been truly shaken by 'Madchester', none of them was to know that it was, in terms of live work at least, an absolute 'one-off'. The band and its 'home' fans could never be joined in such a communion again – they were too big for that now. It was what the Roses wanted, of course, but as Gareth Evans has said, 'To the people who knew them and had helped them build to this day, it was a thank you and goodbye.'

XI

How different the Blackpool event was from the first gigs in Europe. Instead of Ian having to pretend that the band was one of the biggest in Britain, a reputation was now beginning to precede them. Instead of stepping off a ferry, broke and hungover, they were being flown to Europe to play their first proper tour – six cities (Valencia, Barcelona, Milan, Ghent, Hamburg and Amsterdam as well as *Les Inrockutiples* Festival in Paris) and with no less than *five* coaches of fans following them. And, again, the Roses were generous and hospitable to any fans they met.

On the whole, the Stone Roses were received well by their new audiences and they took the opportunity to preview a new, unusual song at one of these gigs – "Fools Gold". In Paris, they were on a bill with the La's and, where the Roses had been somewhat overshadowed by them at the Larks In The Park festival, it was now most definitely the La's (going into an irreversible decline by this time anyway) who faded into the background. The Parisian audience bore witness to the furore around the band, as 'home-fans', intent on recreating the Blackpool spirit, poured out the Manchester chants. Surprisingly, Amsterdam was the one city where they didn't go down too well.

Ian may have had the fondest memories of the tour, as a highlight for him occurred through a chance encounter in a nightclub in Rome, which took him on a nostalgic trip back to one of his earliest passions. On the occasion in question, Ian spotted Marvin Hagler, probably the greatest middleweight boxing champion of all time, who had only ever been knocked down but never out in his career. Ian strode fearlessly over to this awesome character, who was, in fact, only too delighted to engage in conversation with this young English boxing fan.

Europe was followed by a short visit to Japan, where the Roses played two shows, in Tokyo and Osaka. As the band were aware, from their earlier encounter with FM Revolver, the Japanese have an insatiable appetite for Western culture. There was, however, no question of the Roses being cynically thrust on unsuspecting Japanese listeners. *The Stone Roses* had already sold 20,000 copies by the time the band arrived there and they were treated, if anything, more like major rock stars than they had previously experienced.

Back in the UK, the Roses had already announced another unusual gig, on a similar scale to Blackpool, this time in London. Evans had alighted on Alexandra Palace, to the north of the city. Sitting on top of a hill, the recently renovated historic building was famous for having the first BBC transmitter, the odd landmark rock concert (Led Zeppelin, Syd Barrett-era Pink Floyd, Soft Machine) and a lot of Ideal Home-style exhibitions.

As preparations for this show were being made, the Roses were back in the studio, working on their next single. They had earmarked a new song, aptly titled, "What The World Is Waiting For" which they were to spend four months working on in total. They also intended to use the number they had tried out live in Europe, "Fools Gold", as the B-side.

Silvertone's Andrew McKenna visited the studio following a trip to the States, just as the band had completed "What The World Is Waiting For" to their satisfaction. Quite by chance, he happened to hear "Fools Gold" and to McKenna, this song was an utter revelation. He, or anyone for that matter, could be forgiven for thinking that, at this point – excepting the extended finale of "Resurrection" – the Roses were still very much an indie-guitar band. He was floored by the mastery that was on display in this *funk* record, from what he had previously considered to be nothing much more than an indie gang of Clash fans from Manchester. What he heard would have made George Clinton proud, it was so authentic. Mani's plucked bass-line, which carried the tune, was simply extraordinary, sounding like the equivalent of the 'golden chord' for a funk guitarist, while John and Reni complemented beautifully – it was like listening to a 21st century James Brown backing band.

Of course, the band were well-versed by now in a wide variety of music, so they no doubt weren't at all surprised by their own accomplishment, but they *were* surprised by McKenna's enthusiastic response – perhaps not least because the track was nine minutes long.

Nevertheless, he fought to convince the band, Evans and Silvertone that this was the number that should be the A-side. He succeeded eventually, and even if it was released as a double A-side (as was suggested for a time) he felt confident that once the white labels went out, there would be little dilemma for the DJs as to which track got the airplay.

McKenna's enthusiasm swept through Silvertone and with the album still selling well, they were also setting about getting some serious television exposure for the band. The Roses had had a chequered experience with television up until this point. They had made their first TV appearance in January of 1989 on *The Other Side Of Midnight*, a Granada programme presented by Factory's Tony Wilson, playing "Waterfall" and "Don't Stop". It hadn't set the world on fire, though this was before the breakthrough, rather than part of it (the rear sleeve of *The Stone Roses* features pictures from this appearance). They had taken on pop digest *Music Box* as well and a performance from the Hacienda had also been broadcast. They had declined to take part in a feature made by Granada on the 'Madchester' scene, in keeping with their wider ambitions (Ian said: 'We support Manchester if you like. But we also support other places like Glasgow, Belfast, London, Liverpool, anywhere where people try and do their own thing') – they were, revealingly, the only 'Madchester' luminaries *not* to appear on the programme.

Silvertone had shown some lateral thinking by sending out the forthcoming double A-side single, with a press release, to arts shows as well as the usual chart offerings. *The Late Show*, screened on BBC2, they realised, would be quite a coup if the band could land a spot there, although they had no real expectation of doing so when they sent out their material. To their astonishment, an immediate interest was shown, with people from the programme calling, wildly enthusiastic about the funk track. Silvertone couldn't believe their sheer bluff had succeeded in getting the band onto a very useful programme indeed, in terms of exposing them to that all-important wider audience.

There's no way of knowing to what degree "Fools Gold" was helped by what can only be described as a legendarily disastrous screening – but provided one accepts the premise that all publicity is good publicity, their appearance is unlikely to have done them much harm! The band were, of course used to being feted by now, particularly following their Japanese experience, but their unwillingness to co-operate fully with the director and his team was at least in part provoked by their peremptoriness in manner, common to many a TV professional. Hours of wrangling ensued, with Evans being forced to get involved on a number of occasions. But these were *not* rehearsals for some pre-recorded programme – *The Late Show* was going out live.

As the band started playing in front of cameras any tensions that they may have felt were well disguised, as they studiously countermanded many of the directions that had been given – steering themselves away from cameras just as they were coming in for a close-up, to give just one example. The emerging sound wasn't too hot either, but the Roses must have felt, to some extent, vindicated when, lo and behold, the BBC's power supply proved far too fragile to withstand the band's amplification – resulting in a sudden and ominous silence. The presenter leapt out to explain to live viewers what was going on, but she couldn't disguise a grimace as Ian was heard shouting behind her: 'Amateurs, amateurs... we're wasting our time here lads.'

This certainly made riveting viewing, whatever your politics. To a nation of music fans used to mimed, or strictly choreographed performances (as this was clearly meant to be), it was fascinating, to say the least. To Roses fans, it evoked something like a source of pride. Gareth Evans has since claimed that it was all planned to be that way anyway: 'The entire thing was completely, utterly, engineered by us. By me... The BBC Arts thing was horribly patronising towards bands like the Roses. So we just wanted to stir things up.' This was news to Ian though, who would undeniably have had to be a very good actor indeed, to have produced such anger on demand, or for that matter, to have played the kind of active, premeditated part in proceedings that Evans was suggesting. Talking to *Mojo*, in 2002, he confirmed this viewpoint: 'There are some amazing things that he tried to take credit for that are just bullshit. Like walking off *The Late Show*. He claims it was a scam but it wasn't. The power just broke down and we reacted to that.'

However it happened, this proved to be well-timed exposure, immediately before the single was due for release on November 1st, 1989. The seven-inch, "Fool's Gold", now pruned to just over four minutes, went to number fourteen in its first week, climbing the next to number eight. A leap into the top ten in the second week could only mean one thing – Ian was finally going to get his long awaited appearance on *Top Of The Pops*, duly booked for 23rd November.

But before that, there was the gig at Alexandra Palace, to take place on the 18th. Where Blackpool's Empress Ballroom had a capacity of 4,000, the Palace, or 'Ally Pally', could almost double that, at 7,000. The fact that Evans and his team were still not sure of the fanbase situation in London, made this a bit of a worry. Their concerns were only added to upon finding out that the Happy Mondays were playing at Manchester's Free Trade Hall on the same night, meaning there were bound to be less hometown fans travelling down. The ensuing poster campaign around London, attempting to counteract these possible hiccups proved, in the end unnecessary, as the tickets sold out straight away, and it was, no doubt, with some relief that Evans and Co. observed multitudinous 'Reni hats' bobbing up the long hill to the Palace.

Despite this promising overture, the day was jinxed in a whole host of ways. A lengthy problem with the lighting in the hall meant that all other aspects of the preparation were delayed, inevitably rendering them hurried affairs, including the soundcheck, which was completed in less than two hours. The warm-up DJs encountered technical problems throughout their sets too, with records jumping out of control.

And then, when the fans were at last allowed in, another serious problem quickly became evident: the people hiring the hall out had grossly underestimated its capacity, having not, after all, held a music event in years. Once on stage, the band would immediately have been able to see great wide-open spaces at the back of the hall: 4,000 people's worth of space, in fact. This was not only intensely annoying for everyone making money from the gig, but also for some of those who had actually paid that money. When the music started, fans at the back were instantly hit by echoes from these huge cavernous spaces, making it impossible to hear the music they were aching for, being played at the front. And it took too long for the organisers to realise what was happening to be able to find a solution to the problem.

Despite these sound catastrophes, the gig did improve as it went on, and Ian later went as far as to say that 'the atmosphere was great'. Thankfully, not many reviewers present happened to be standing at the back where all the sound problems were, and overall response was fairly positive (apart from that of *Melody Maker,* who had failed to send Bob Stanley along this time!). But it was a disappointment to the band, as Ian admitted, 'We made the mistake of using our mate as the sound engineer. He'd done the tour but the place was too big for him.' The band's awareness of the problems may have led them into doing something generally disapproved of these days – they actually played an encore. And then, of course, it was *Top Of The Pops*-bound to perform "Fools Gold".

Just five days later, the band were getting out of a cab at the BBC studios, asking the driver to wait, in case they came straight back out again. Ian's enthusiasm for the programme had clearly waned since being questioned about his goals earlier that year. BBC crews were to experience the Roses awkward ways again, as a battle ensued over whether they would be allowed to get their amps on stage, appalled as they were at the thought of having to mime their song. It's difficult to believe the Roses weren't already aware of this well-known practice, enforced for years by the now out of favour programme. Only very rarely had exceptions been made to the miming rule, such as with Kate Bush's historic performance of "Wuthering Heights". No doubt having heard all about the *Late Show* debacle, the *ToTP* producers were ill-disposed towards giving the Roses special treatment, and sharply told them they would have to go along with the tradition.

Many highly acclaimed bands have accepted the *Top Of The Pops* miming charade, blissfully happy just to be on the show, and a few have agreed with it but moaned about it afterwards. While it doesn't take much of a genius to work out that the instruments aren't actually being played, it does take a trained eye, as it were, to notice a 'subversion'. Robert Smith, for instance, had woollen guitar strings for one of his performances, yet aroused very little comment.

But the Stone Roses' 'subversive' *Top Of The Pops* perform-ance of "Fools Gold" has most certainly been more than com-mented on, it has, in fact, been eulogised as an insurrectionary act no less, and only recently, by John Harris in *The Last Party*, his definitive account of Britpop. In fact, nothing like it had ever been seen on *Top Of The Pops* before. To watch Ian cavorting around the stage with the microphone way above his head and some dis-tance from his mouth, as he blasted the lyrics out into the studio, was indeed to witness history in the making and tantamount to anarchy as far as the show's brief was concerned.

Joining the Stone Roses on *Top Of The Pops* that night, were their old friends and sparring partners the Happy Mondays (and according to John Robb, being kept well away from his band by Evans, in case the notoriously mischievous Mondays tried to spike their drinks). Spiked drink or not, a sublime moment in pop TV history occurred that night, and one that couldn't be matched, even by Shaun Ryder's on stage antics.

This edition of *Top Of The Pops* was an equally seminal one in the annals of 'Madchester', for showcasing the Roses' defini-tive song of the era, as well as featuring the Mondays. It also con-tained a chart rundown, which read like an indie/dance roll call, including 808 State's "Pacific State", Bernard Sumner and Johnny Marr's "Electronic", and the Inspiral Carpets in number one spot. It was a *Top Of The Pops* broadcast that encapsulated the ascend-ancy of the Manchester scene, which has never been bettered, before or since – notwithstanding New Order's sly suggestion of the prevalence of a certain drug throughout the land, with the 'E is for England' chorus in their "World In Motion" World Cup single (topping even their "Fine Time" performance).

Soon after this Ian would speak positively about the Happy Mondays to legendary rock journalist, Nick Kent for *The Face*. Kent had been present at the *Top Of The Pops* show and his piece was intended to be an assessment of the 'Madchester' scene among other things. 'They're the only other group we can just sit down and have a drink with, like,' said Ian, sounding almost like that other Manchester icon, Albert Tatlock. Ryder was equally effusive when Kent spoke to him: 'Y'll find no rivalry here, pal, Well the only rivalry between 'oos and the Roses, like, is, over clothes, really'.

With Gareth Evans, and Tony Wilson of Factory close by, Kent also asked Ian about where the Roses wanted to go. 'Being bigger than U2? Well, they're empty anyway. But yeah… I think we can deliver on that.' The article that followed did indeed relay this message to the reader, as well as conveying the bond that existed between the Mondays and the Roses, but it also tried to portray the Roses and the Mondays, rather stereotypically, as dim Northerners. Just as in his piece on Shane MacGowan, Kent had littered the text with 'Kssshhh' (a cruel approximation of MacGowan's toothless laugh), his text in this article was festooned with 'fookin', Viz-style quotes, all-too-clearly intended to make them seem like yobs.

To make matters worse, he went on to make a claim that Tony Wilson had joked about the death of Joy Division singer, Ian Curtis, which caused great upset and was also, incidentally, totally untrue. Though Kent unquestionably has a huge talent, bringing him justified respect, both from his peers and many figures in the rock world, (Evans being one, who presumably leapt at the chance of the Roses doing an actual *Nick Kent Interview*) his style of journalism is well known for this kind of sniping and, let's be honest, pretty low tactics.

In brief the Nick Kent 'Madchester' article did neither band any favours at all, and for the Roses, and Ian in particular, it must have been a sobering experience. Kent had been the one person capable of finding a chink in his band's armour – something not readily forgiven. The next year, taking questions from journalists, Ian said 'we don't have a grudge against anyone apart from Nick Kent because he's a liar.'

And the former confidence returned as 'news' came through that a certain Mick Jagger was bowled over by the Stone Roses and that some support spots on the Stones' forthcoming world tour were in the offing. Though the offer was given short shrift by Ian, 'The Rolling Stones? They should be bloody supporting us. Not that we'd let them.' Later, he admitted: 'We said no (to the Stones) 'cos everyone else'd say yes.'

If only he had known, then, that the stories about the Stones wanting the Roses to support them were a scam – of Gareth Evans' making. Of course, it provided great copy for the band and kept them in the papers, which was just what Evans wanted. If anything, he was becoming more passionate about achieving huge success than Ian Brown himself, 'I would have done *anything*... to keep the Stone Roses in the press at the time,' Evans later confessed.

And by the end of the year, Evans had certainly achieved his objective. In the press, the Stone Roses most decidedly were, their pre-eminence reflected in the polls. *Sounds* made *The Stone Roses* the album of the year; they achieved three out of the *NME*'s top four singles, while, even more significantly, *Melody Maker* readers voted the record into its top twenty albums of the eighties. Bearing in mind that it had only been released six months earlier, this accolade was undeniably an incredible achievement. As they entered the nineties, already with a classic album and an era-defining single to their name, the Stone Roses moved into their next phase: consolidating the success with that all important 'second album'.

XII

Looking back on such a mind blowing year as 1989 had been for them, the Stone Roses could well be forgiven for barely giving a thought to the period early on, when they had first encountered FM Revolver while releasing the "Sally Cinnamon" single. The same could hardly be said of FM Revolver, of course, who must have watched the Roses in their ascendancy with much gnashing of teeth.

Though the profits from Japan-bound heavy rock CDs were still coming in, the idea of not trying to cash in on the Roses' success was, evidently, becoming increasingly ludicrous to them. And the irony of Gareth Evans not returning their calls after the single with them failed, when they had religiously returned all of his when he needed their interest, would not have been lost on them.

So it was with a sense of dismal inevitability, then, that the still-growing band of Stone Roses fans were offered, by FM Revolver the chance to buy their second single. Accompanied by a very hastily put together video, it was the most blatant piece of opportunism, which no amounts of 'giving people what they want' mantras ought to have excused. But the Roses saw the whole thing in even starker terms.

To them, it was a travesty. The fact that it didn't trouble 'the charts' that much was by the by: it was sub-standard, unrepresentative and they felt that they had been well and truly betrayed by FM Revolver. Their anger failed to subside throughout a meeting, arranged to thrash the situation out, at the International; in fact, it got worse. The course of action that they decided on was one that was quickly approved of by Evans, to the extent that it could have come out of his own mind.

On January 30th, on route to Wales for a recording session, they made a slight detour to Wolverhampton to pay a visit to FM Revolver. As well as making an artistic statement, the band and Evans were, clearly carrying out a PR stunt as they 'Pollocked' the FM offices including that of MD Paul Birch – causing £23,000 worth of damage all told. One might argue that, although with some justification, and certainly with some incitement from their manager who should have known better, it was nevertheless, a pretty juvenile act from the Stone Roses.

It was also a criminal one and the four streetwise kids (the fact that they were now pop stars didn't really enter into it) were promptly to be found at Wolverhampton Crown Court answering charges. 'Ian Brown Is Innocent' T-shirts were on view but, in actual fact, he wasn't and nor were any of them. Each member was fined £3,000 plus £95 costs, the judge preferring not to pass jail sentences that would give them more 'notoriety'. They had, nevertheless, saved a small fortune in PR costs. The act had well and truly got them in the press, and not just the music press this time, making them the most recognisable face of 'Madchester'.

The tabloids had, in fact, been alerted to the Stone Roses for a while. *The Sun* had actually shown a prurient interest in "Elizabeth My Dear", on the realisation that the song carried an anti-monarchist message. They spent weeks ringing the band's associates and former girlfriends, a trail that led them to Ian's parents' front door, where they ran into his mother. 'It's his opinion,' she said gruffly before turning them away. Coverage from *The Sun* and the *Daily Star* led to Conservative MP Geoffrey Dickens (who also avoided paying a company for his PR) making a stand: 'Ban these pop idiots,' the *Star* reported Dickens as saying.

The band were duly greeted by this level of press in Wolverhampton but Ian remained sanguine, knowing the coverage could only ultimately do them good, showing them as heirs to a certain punk spirit, often overlooked as part of the whole 'Madchester' thing. 'Trial by tabloid,' he said to *Sounds*, 'that's ok. We're already in the tabloids last week. "Pop nutters the Stone Roses." It came from that *Sounds* interview a while ago where I fantasised about putting a blanket over the Queen Mother's head. That was our first tabloid press. The more the merrier. Front page every day. Forget the Sex Pistols, forget everybody. I want to see our band in the tabloid press. *News At Ten*, whatever. I'm big headed enough to think that we're more interesting.'

And, some would argue, Ian and the Roses *were* more interesting than a lot of other news around. Showing a depth of knowledge that surprised many during an interview in the *Observer* Ian spoke admiringly of a man called Benny Rothman. Rothman was as far removed as possible from music, being a political activist of the Thirties who made a stand against common land being appropriated by the aristocracy – his successful stand leading to the setting up of the National Trust. In *Select*, he discussed subjects as far ranging as the Boer War and Martin Luther King, showing himself and his band to be much more than a symbol of a city that had inspired the rave revolution.

They also got the unlikeliest of votes of support – for their music that is – and this time it wasn't something that Evans had made up. Roger Waters, late of Pink Floyd, provided this accolade: 'The Stone Roses reminded me of us twenty-five years ago. They've got loads of bollocks and arrogance and they won't take any shit.'

In the spring, during an interview in *Sounds*, Ian made note of the scene changes that had occurred since they had seriously started playing: 'Everyone's dressing up again – 1986 seems like a lifetime ago. A few skins have been shed since then.' The last comment was more pertinent than he might have known. In 1986, no group with the Roses' kind of background would ever have got near the kind of coverage that they were now receiving (the nearest the Smiths ever got was a *South Bank Show* special, broadcast just after they had split up). The media was also slowly becoming more aware of the ecstasy scene, and what the Roses were experiencing was what can now be recognised as the slow birth of a celebrity culture, driven by the press, especially the tabloids. This media glare would become an increasing source of annoyance to the band – and their next 'big' gig, that summer, would inadvertently cause the band's worst encounter with the press so far.

Evans and his team had been working hard on finding the next venue, keen to improve on what had ended up being a troubled gig at Alexandra Palace. The only vague criterion they had given themselves was 'somewhere within an 80-mile radius of London'. As their quest for a site unfolded and people got wind of the fact that the Stone Roses were looking for somewhere to play, the range of possibilities became rather surreal. Speedway tracks, caravan parks, gypsy sites, deserted quarries and many besides, were visited or at least put on offer.

The team hadn't got very far when the band decided that they wanted to 'hold their own festival, not near London but somewhere between Manchester and Liverpool.' Evans agreed to the idea and the spot he finally hit upon was a place called Spike Island, on Clywd Hill in Cheshire, which held views of both Manchester and Liverpool –important symbolically as *the* two dominant cities in musical culture (as far as the Roses went, at any rate) – as well as glimpses of the Peak District and Cumbria.

But, arguably the most eye-catching view of all, was the one right in front of the hill. Almost inevitably, considering its location right in the heart of the industrial north, and notorious among the locals, was the mess of machinery that clouded the eye: plants, pipes, chimneys and cooling towers, and with naked flames coming out of, it seems, every orifice. As Evans claimed later, and almost with a hint of pride: 'It was the biggest polluted area in Europe. Saddam Hussein bought his gas to kill the Kurds nearby'. Having rejected the speedway tracks and caravan sites as too bizarre, it was as if Evans had now decided to go one step even further into obscurity and contentiousness.

Later, though, Evans linked the decision with the Roses' political stance, claiming it was an attempt to draw attention to the ecological issues surrounding the area: 'I hoped we would get loads of press on it all. I wanted it to be the biggest issue of all.' They wouldn't be the first to link themselves in this way as, presumably, it had also been an issue for the people who organised and attended the Halton Annual Fair there, a 'weird, folksy, hippie-type fest' that attracted large numbers.

The band was in agreement with Evans' venue suggestion, and his team set about getting the necessary permissions. The nearest town, Widnes, (also with a music-history connection as being the place where a homesick Paul Simon composed "Homeward Bound") whose council presided over the area, were in favour – some members being Stone Rose fans certainly helping the cause – and things progressed smoothly at first, but once the press got to hear of the plan, all hell broke loose.

The *Runcorn Observer* managed to create a storm worthy of a tabloid, when it ran stories guaranteed to alarm its readers, relating to the size of the proposed concert and the level of disturbance likely. Objections flew in, first from the local community and then the police and each had to be dealt with methodically before the gig could go ahead. Some of the concern was justified. The capacity for this gig was far in excess of Blackpool or Alexandra Palace – almost 30,000 – so they were talking very big numbers. And in spite of precedents having been set by previous large events, such as the Halton Fair, the logistical requirements of exits and entrances *et al* also needed consideration. But the team managed eventually to sort out these worries, and the gig was finally announced via one advert in the *NME*.

Any fears that the site was too large to fill were swiftly allayed when 29,500 tickets flew out almost as soon as sales began, and the first thing Evans did, on hearing this news, was to take the band to see the site for the first time.

They were collectively blown away by the surreal nature of Spike Island: Wembley Arena it wasn't, which suited the Stone Roses down to the ground. 'I don't know how you fucking pulled this one off, Gareth,' said Ian, 'but it's just perfect.' Little did they know that rather than Evans excelling, he was in fact in the process of creating yet another disaster – in a disaster area.

The roadies that had made their way down to Spike Island on behalf of the Roses found themselves working in brilliant sunshine, and so stripped down to as little clothing as possible. When some of them were forced to visit a doctor in Widnes for their 'sunburn' (which was itching and blistering to an alarming degree), the first questions raised were about the wisdom of performing in the exposed area of Spike Island. Then other questions began to emerge, when a strange colour in the sky and haze in the air was noticed, as well as some unpleasant smells drifting around the site.

How aware the Stone Roses themselves were of these misgivings prior to the concert is unclear. Neither is it known whether they were party to the shenanigans surrounding the PA system ordered for the gig, which nearly didn't arrive at all. The cash payment for the gear was in fact, held up by Evans right until the last minute, when £30,000 was finally handed over in a plastic carrier bag, at a Widnes bus stop! The band were, however, most definitely aware of an impending press conference that Evans planned to stage, the largest gathering of press to date, and with representation from all over the world.

In keeping with the stark nature of Spike Island, Evans had earmarked Manchester's Piccadilly Hotel as the venue for the conference, and set it for the day before the gig. The hotel at that time might as well have been called 'Grim Reminder of the Seventies'. Pictures from the press conference show a featureless ante-room with striped wallpaper, and who knows to what extent this uninspiring setting caused the Roses to sink into boredom the moment they sat down?

Evans' hopes that the band were going to make a political (and newsworthy) stand were summarily dashed and, if anything, he ended up being the one to show most enthusiasm for the event and its location, when a couple of questions came his way. But the journalists themselves were also curiously quiet from the beginning, so much so that Ian felt the need to take on the role of a schoolteacher, telling them off: 'Why don't you ask summat? You've flown here from all over the world.'

What followed was as surreal as playing at Spike Island itself (and hardly anyone asked about that), never really a press conference at all and very nearly a brawl. Ian went on to do most of the talking, as usual, with Reni interjecting a bit and Mani showing the most enthusiasm of the four. John, typically, barely uttered a word, though he did provide the best laugh when someone asked him who his favourite painter was, to which he responded: 'Ronnie Wood.'

There were few other laughs to be had however, as trite questions were batted away by the band's proverbial mordant sarcasm, to which one journalist at least, Frank Owen from *Details*, took great offence (claiming that the Roses were trying to wind everyone up) and with another nearly instigating a fight. The latter journalist, having helped himself to more than his fair share of the free drink on offer beforehand, ended up heckling and goading Owen before getting up and lurching his way to the Roses' table, as the whole room visibly stiffened. The band's blank stare greeted him – mainly, it has to be said, because they didn't understand his question – and Ian actually asked if he was all right. Frank Owen's getting progressively more annoyed, and continuing to shout from the back, certainly didn't ease any tensions.

The whole conference came to a most unsatisfactory end when a photographer joined in, grabbing one of the Roses' mics and berated the journalists: 'You lot haven't asked shit for questions.' He was quickly manhandled off by one of the management team, who then took it upon himself to add: 'You come all this way. Drink all the free beer and you haven't asked fucking shit! You're all a bunch of wankers in whatever language you speak. If I was them (the Roses) I'd fuck off now!" And so they did, with only Evans seeing the conference as having been useful in any way. If only they hadn't been on their way to Spike Island!

With 30,000 tickets already sold for the gig, and with hundreds more ticketless punters making their way up Clwyd Hill to try and get in, the danger of overcrowding was becoming a serious possibility, and adding in the toxic air it looked as if everyone would be forced to breath, the now imminent event began to feel like a disaster waiting to happen.

As the band prepared for the day there were increasing concerns that, if the Roses had slightly over-reached themselves at the Ally Pally, then Spike Island really was simply going too far. *Sounds* were to describe the setting as 'a grassy knoll in the middle of the rusty, shitheap cement factory death belt of the Mersey.' In fact, it was as if it was only now, when everyone had taken so much trouble to get them there, that it finally began to dawn, on some at least, that this was no place for a 'festival'.

Even Bob Stanley was glum: 'I'd driven up from London and it was a bit depressing to find yourself in a horrible field, surrounded by huge electric pylons, factories and chemical plants.' By the end, 'your hair felt very odd and greasy, like it was totally coated with chemicals from the factories.'

To Phil Jones, whom Gareth Evans was using as promoter for the show, the toxic air (which the road crew had rightly been complaining to him about for four days) was the least of his worries. With the island already over capacity, it was brought to his attention that the nearby Mersey was not only in full flow, but rising rapidly. Somehow, he managed to get a team of frogmen into the venue to investigate the river, all of whom emerged from the water as concerned as he was. 'I was worried that we might have to evacuate... I thought we were going to have to start pulling masses of bodies out of the river.'

But Jones had to keep his eye on the rushing river for more than one reason: for sailing on those choppy waters was an enterprising rowing boat captain who was helping, for a fee, Stone Roses fans without a ticket to get into the concert for nothing. Jones and the security guys spent a lot of their afternoon and evening chasing him away, only for him to reappear on the horizon again half an hour later. Finally, having lost all patience, the ad hoc Spike Island charter service was brought to an end as Jones and his men put a very large brick through the bottom of the boat.

For people who had already got into the gig, the organisation (or lack of) was found initially to be more of a concern than the setting itself. For those who had their food snatched from them by over-zealous security guards at the gates, it must have added insult to injury to find that two burger bars – and one beer tent – were all that had been laid on in the way of catering, for more than 30,000 people. Even more seriously, the ground beneath them was very dry so everyone was kicking up a dust cloud which was 'toxically polluted', to quote the site manager. This would have some serious consequences.

As for people in the immediate vicinity of the stage, things were no less shambolic. The Roses had been supposed to arrive at the island by a helicopter, specially laid on by Evans. As the band weren't due to get there till an hour before the gig started, Evans decided to use the helicopter to bring in himself and his friends.

This 'trial' helicopter journey proved to be a perilous one, nearly causing a riverside crush. With already more than enough to worry about, Phil Jones insisted that the band come in by bus. Waiting for them backstage were their 'guests', all 5,000 of them, almost certainly proving Jones was right in his description of it as 'probably the biggest guest list in the history of rock'. It also made the backstage area a complete mess, precipitating serious danger of overcrowding there too, and a growing mood of disgruntlement was exacerbated when beer stocks ran out in the guest bar.

As the DJs and support began building up the entertainment for the throng, Jones was also forced to keep a watchful eye on one particular guest who wasn't there simply to enjoy the beer (if he was lucky) or the music. An official from the council, he was actually there to monitor the sound and, if it strayed into the higher levels, was fully authorised to close the gig down – and in this eventuality, there would be nothing anyone could do about it. He was in communication with his colleagues in Widnes who were wandering around with sound metres held aloft, all poised and ready to strike – as, indeed, was he. With a ferocious sound system in place and the shuddering thud of Jah Wobble's bass guitar kicking off the support acts, it's not surprising that Evans *et al* were immediately served with two warnings – one more strike and they would be out – the music would have to be stopped, and an audience of 30,000 would have to make their way home.

Of course, the vast majority of that audience was oblivious to all of these behind the scenes rumblings, and not only because many of them had been taking copious amounts of drugs. Yet what better drug could one take than ecstasy, when you're being robbed, poisoned and starved at one of the most badly organised events ever? With all the odds stacked against it, this little 'wonder drug' could literally be said to have saved the day.

However, there were still a couple of nasty shocks in store. As the Roses finally came on to the stage, Phil Jones lurched into the bar to have a relaxing drink. He'd not been there five minutes when someone from the ambulance crews found him and told him that a boy had died in front of the stage. Mercifully, the information had come second-hand and, though the boy had had a serious heart attack, news came through later that he had survived the night after all, to Jones's huge relief. All round the venue, though, people with asthma conditions were suffering, some sustaining quite serious attacks, and a lasting legacy of the Spike Island concert has been the introduction of routine Health and Safety checks at all venues, for dangerous dust levels.

And what of the Stone Roses, the actual reason everyone was there? They came on to a rousing reception on their largest ever stage and delivered a decent set, though they were the first to admit, by no means a blinding one. Reliving their Ally Pally experience, there were problems with the sound, showing that little had been learned from the earlier nightmare. It was lucky that so many there were in a drug-fuelled party mood.

Ian was in enigmatic mode on the day, making only one mysterious statement during the entire gig ('The time... the time is now. Do it now, do it now'). He carried an equally mysterious large plastic globe with him throughout the set, as well as his beloved bongos and, with his swaggering, pimp-rolling stage walk now honed to perfection, he was clearly in a gig that he was enjoying in his own way, and in many other ways, he was the best thing in it. Most people also remember the lighting show as a highlight, but the fact that the 'Madchester' anthem, "Fools Gold" ended, to say the least, chaotically, (or, as *The Guardian* put it, 'landed off key') was symptomatic of what was overall rather a jinxed day.

Once the band had come off stage, they certainly had plenty of guests to party with: Ian McCulloch, Peter Hook, 808 State and even Nigel Pivaro from *Coronation Street* were among the 5,000. They observed the £5,000 worth of fireworks also seen by thirty-odd thousand people now trailing away from the island to the coach centre, specially laid on to minimise disruption to the good folk of Widnes.

At the end of a long day, Phil Jones stood in the production office with the Roses and some guests, including the redoubtable Shaun Ryder. Later, he clearly remembers Ian turning to Ryder and saying: 'So Shaun William Ryder, what did you think of that?' Ryder's reply was: 'Well, it was alright, man.' His statement was probably spot on, in summing up the show which, let's face it, could have ended up so much worse.

But in a wider context, the most perceptive comment on the Spike Island fiasco came later from Bob Stanley. 'It should have been brilliant but, in retrospect, the best thing about it was being able to say you were there. In some ways, it was the beginning of the end.'

XIII

As with ecstasy, the comedown after Spike Island was a long one. It seemed to have had a positive effect for the Roses at first, when the following week saw a spate of articles in the broadsheets which, though they had covered the Roses' music before, had only recently caught up with the wider 'Madchester' phenomenon, in turn creating a lot of anticipation about the single, due out in July.

The Roses had, by now, learnt about the debacle at the gates, which caused a lot of anger. While Evans could point to the snow-balling press interest as a positive and direct result of the Picca-dilly Hotel conference and the Spike Island concert, reports that began to come back about the concert itself caused the band to look on their manager less with indulgence and more with a cold and resentful eye.

Looking back later, Ian's feelings were clear. 'We had a wanker running it. We trusted him. We are not the kind of people to put on a show where people have their sandwiches taken off them at the gate. That reflects on you. The kids think, 'Oh, they're doing that.' The way people were treated that day was despicable. The sound wasn't any good because he didn't spend any money on it'

Still, the band did indulge Evans in one last fantasy when his next wheeze for live gigs turned out to be putting them on in big tops. Two resulting shows, in Belfast and Glasgow, proved to be successes, attended by many who may well not have been able to get to Spike Island, enabling them to see the band when they were receiving almost universal acclaim. In many ways it must have felt like they couldn't fail at this point, as reports also came through that they were being played on American radio a lot more frequently.

But it turned out to be all part of the comedown. There was a strange sense that there were no more highs to be reached: every-one was waiting for the next single, of course, but from here on in, Evans' ever-evolving ideas to progress the band would become increasingly cranky and would be, ultimately, anti-climactic – they had already peaked.

The single, "One Love", when it appeared in July, was an indicator, being horribly anti-climactic itself. Its status as the best-selling Stone Roses single ever, as well as it being installed as the *NME* Single of the Week, are measures more of the overwhelmingly positive coverage of the time, than of the quality of the music. For this was a distinctly sub-standard Stone Roses track. The *NME* was, undeniably, doing nothing more than running with the pack, reflected in the review running alongside their so called 'single of the week' where, almost incredibly, they wrote, 'there is something a bit inelegant about its structure. It sounds like it evolved from a very loose jam the band had one afternoon.'

Though hardly an awful song, the *NME* reviewer did, in fact, hit the nail on the head with this comment about "One Love". It sounds a bit like a warm-up for "Fools Gold", with a lot of similarities in arrangement, but frankly none of the magic. Even "Ten Storey Love Song" from *The Second Coming*, is remembered more warmly than this hurried single from their golden era. Ian later admitted: 'We were trying too hard to write an anthem.'

The delaying tactics, employed by Evans for the song's release, by which he meant to build anticipation to the extent that the band got their Number One, were in the end a waste of time, as it 'crashed' in at number four instead. But there were other reasons why the record was delayed which provide a disturbing footnote to the tale of "One Love".

John was commencing work on one of his trademark 'Pollocked' covers, when Evans paid the guitarist a visit. One of Evans' redeeming features was his oft-displayed energy, best exemplified by his commitment, despite all the work with the band, as a single parent. Moreover, his son, Mark, had Down's syndrome, so along with everything else, Evans spent a lot of time fighting against all the stigmatism such a condition carries with it. The band knew all this of course, and Evans had hitherto felt their respect for him because of it.

The scale of his shock can only be guessed at then, when, on this apparently pre-arranged visit, he found John watching some disturbing footage of Nazi atrocities – including that of Down's children being escorted into the gas chambers. Evans is supposed to have berated John, naturally, asking, 'How can you have it in your home?' to which John is said to have replied 'Oh, there's a lot you don't know about me Gareth' before returning to the screen.

Imagine Evans' feelings then, when John submitted "One Love" artwork containing the image of a swastika. Such artwork simply couldn't be distributed. Putting his personal repulsion aside, Evans knew it was hardly in keeping with the sentiments expressed in the song's lyrics for a start, and certainly not with their previous political image. Some prints had already been made – one Roses roadie was even barred from a club because his T-shirt depicted the offending image – so John hastily re-designed the sleeve. John has always maintained that it was an accident (and Ian has backed him up on this) but the incident goes a long way to explaining Evans' later comments about John, many of which are far from generous.

For the time being though, Evans had to put all this out of his mind as he tried to move things along. One of his crankiest sug-gestions yet was to send Ian and John off to the Mull of Kintyre to write songs. To make things crankier still, he favoured staging an accident, so that the papers would run an 'Ian Brown Lost' headline, only for him to reappear sometime later, unharmed. Ian refused to go along with it, correctly realising that the risk of them being found out and looking ridiculous was too great a one for them to take.

There were more serious plans for the band to play on the *Wogan* show. The Radio Two DJ was then enjoying a tenure as TV's top chat show host, even though it is a series often best re-membered now for the show in which a pissed and raving George Best caused Wogan huge embarrassment.

For rock bands, it remained a very useful PR exercise to sing a song or two for Wogan's TV peak time viewing audience. Evans would, presumably, have been happy with just a song but the Roses were also angling for an interview slot with the genial host. Negotiations did ensue on this, and John Robb has suggested that the band were actually planning an act that would have knocked the Pistols/Grundy stunt into a cocked hat – to pull Terry Wogan's wig off live on air!

While the BBC people might not have suspected the actual plan (though *Sounds* did report BBC sources as saying that Wogan was apprehensive that the Roses would pull some sort of stunt), they would have been generally wary of the Roses, having been warned by their colleagues over on BBC2 about how 'difficult' the band could be. Though occasional exceptions to the 'performance only' rule for bands were made on Wogan shows, they were certainly not about to extend their exceptions to the very un-chat-show-like Roses.

When this story leaked out to the press, Evans, at least, would have been gratified by the tabloid mini-storm generated, where the failed negotiations were transposed into 'Roses Boycott Wogan!' and the *Daily Mirror* quoted Ian as saying 'Terry obviously doesn't have the bottle.' The Roses went on to knock back Jonathan Ross – whose *Last Resort* show would have been a more trendy option – by imperiously rejecting any coverage via that route when he ventured to say something disparaging about them.

A report in *Sounds* soon after these events, announced that Evans was planning to stage a Roses gig in Beirut. Not only was this testament, once again, to his lateral thinking, but also carried that distinct air of 'floundering' about it, which lately seemed to surround the band. In the Roses fanzine, *Made Of Paper,* Bob Stanley, though ever the fan, pointedly mused on where the Roses were going. First saying 'I see the Stone Roses becoming the most successful band in the world', but immediately qualifying the statement by adding 'how can such a cosmic claim be backed up?'

He wrote this while a tour of America was in its planning stage, the continuing American airplay making it an almost essential next step. But the Roses then unceremoniously ditched the

Captured relaxing with friends on a 1983 scooter rally in Morcambe Bay, one cropped and Krazy-Kolored Ian Brown

softly spoken singer with The Stone Roses. To his right is Cressa (the Roses' on-stage dancer), to his left is a man whose career in pop was apparently stymied by his appalling taste in underpants. (Inset) Ian Brown and Cressa - natural hair-colour mercifully restored - on offical Roses duty in 1990.

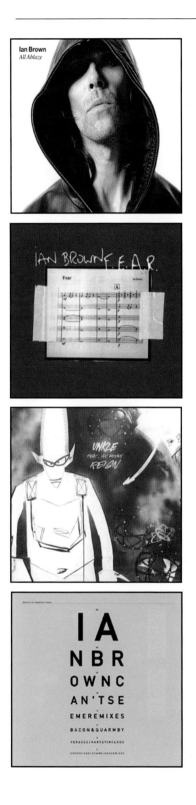

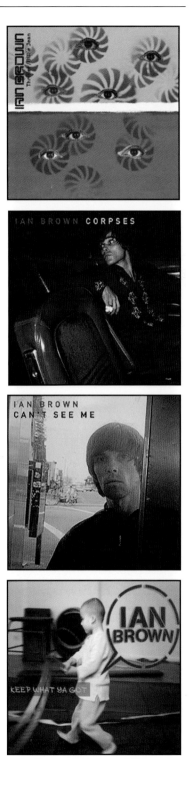

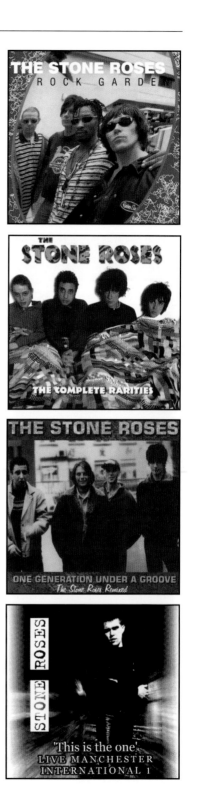

Ian Brown (The Stone Roses)

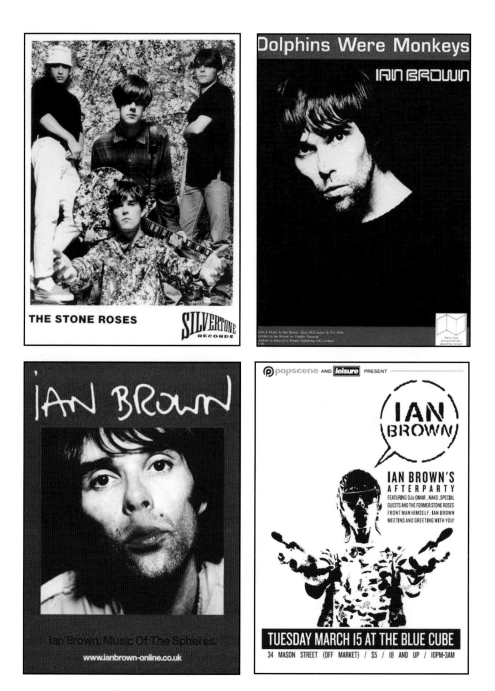

idea, to general surprise and reinforcing the sense of a lack of direction. John justified it thus, 'We're just naturally stubborn. If we get pressurised into going into America, which we have been, we'll turn it down.'

Ian went even further, saying: 'America doesn't deserve us yet.' A bold statement too far, perhaps, as a trip to America at that time could have provided that vital next step to 'world domination', as well as giving them a renewed sense of direction.

Having played to 30,000 plus at Spike Island, being consistently featured in the tabloids, and having enjoyed a reasonable amount of TV interest, one could argue that there was little more for them to achieve in this country, for now at least. As 1990, which the Roses had stormed into with a vengeance, drew to a close, their old friends the Happy Mondays appeared back on the scene, with the release of their hit album, *Pills, Thrills and Belly-aches*. Was this going to mean the end of the Stone Roses' reign as the leading lights in British indie music? The possibility seemed increasingly likely, if one takes into account the mindset of the Roses and their manager at this time.

Pills is undoubtedly a great album, though maybe not reaching the dizzy heights of *The Stone Roses*. It was certainly more than a mere continuation of the 'Madchester' vibe, and the Mondays' near-mindless hedonism (which was not without its charm) slowly became an integral part of the zeitgeist. The Mondays were defiantly 'Madchester' but their album also provided a bridge into the 'lad' culture, which – now alongside celebrity culture – remains a dominant force today. And let's not forget that by the time the Happy Mondays released *Pills, Thrills and Bellyaches,* the country was only a few years away from *Loaded*, the rediscovery of football and, of course, Oasis.

The Roses, with all their references to art and politics, despite being ordinary lads themselves, had a different, finer quality than the Mondays. The Mondays' *Pills* cover bore as much resemblance to art as a circus poster does to a Van Gogh, whereas John's first album design *was* art. Similarly, Ian's real knowledge and passion for politics was in sharp contrast to the comical politi-

129

cal insights of Shaun William Ryder: 'Thatcher? She's all right. Yeah, she's a heavy dude.' The Roses had undoubtedly foreshadowed and reflected a spirit of the times which could be dated to as far back as "Sally Cinnamon". But now it was the Mondays' turn – the Roses were no longer emblematic of the age.

But for the time being, the Stone Roses remained a huge band, with plenty of furore still surrounding them, as well as a decent history of chart success. Consequently, the eyes of the big guns in the music business remained fully trained on the Roses camp, who were certainly not about to ignore outside interest, despite having a contract with Silvertone.

Following Spike Island, Evans has said that he was waiting to hear from Silvertone, expecting them to be looking towards renegotiating the existing contract, in order to give the band improved terms. Apparently, all the while he was busy fielding calls from the major record companies, trying to tempt the Roses away, Silvertone simply didn't call.

Part of the problem was that the man who had been instrumental in their signing, Roddy McKenna, had left to work in the US. McKenna had been the key contact between the band and Silvertone, who were foolish enough not to install someone to keep the lines of communication open. The press were, of course, swift to pick up on the discontent emanating from the band's side, and in September of 1990 the *Melody Maker* reported that the Roses were indeed trying to get out of the contract. Whether this view came directly from the band or not, it led to a warning shot across their bows, as Silvertone immediately got an injunction preventing the band from recording for any other company.

This was balanced by an expression of good faith from Silvertone when they roused themselves to give the band a Christmas bonus, which was reported to be somewhere between thirty and forty thousand. It was after Christmas that Roddy McKenna was brought over from America, his main task being to try and sort out the problems that existed between the company and the band. According to Mick Middles, during a meeting with the band McKenna enquired as to whether they had been happy with their bonus: they said they were more than content – with the £500 each of them had been given. Though incredulous, McKenna didn't see fit to inform them that the monies Silvertone had handed over (to Evans) amounted to a considerably larger sum. Curiously, Evans allegedly told Middles that he had given the band £10,000 each!

Meetings between Evans and McKenna continued. As a prelude to one, Evans took McKenna on a drive with posters, two brushes, a giant pot of paste and, for reasons still unclear, a semi-comatose Shaun Ryder in the back of the car. Presumably, Ryder was not along to help with putting up the posters in Manchester as he was still at the fag end of a three-day bender. It may however, have been a typically wacky diversionary tactic on the part of Evans, because at the eventual meeting he made it all too clear that he was going to try to get the Roses out of the contract.

It wasn't until March that Evans finally announced what everyone had now come to expect, that the Stone Roses were going to court to free themselves from a contract which, they argued, was unfair and an unjustifiable restraint of trade. Between the 18th and the 22nd of March, the band members appeared in court themselves and Ian told *Melody Maker* that if the case went against them they would give up music and go on the dole. Of course, their fans were far more keen to hear about them making more music. Continued updates on their progress in the court, rumours of a concert in the summer and a string of re-released singles from Silvertone, (that had started in May 1990) weren't going to satisfy their craving for new product or live appearances. In fact, the wilderness years for the band had already begun, heavily symbolised by the image of the four of them sitting in court – when they should, undeniably, have been working in the studio.

Meanwhile in court, while it soon became clear that the case wasn't going to go entirely Silvertone's way, it nevertheless threw up some uncomfortable questions for the Roses and Evans about their dealings with Silvertone. They were, of course, by now, well aware that in the 'telephone directory of a thing' they had signed so glibly, the band were contracted to record for seven years with Silvertone. An extraordinary amount of time had been promised here, though Ian's sarcastic comment to the *Melody Maker* – 'Silvertone have got us for thirty-five years, we'd only have got ten for armed robbery' – was perhaps overstating things.

The foolishness of Evans' commitment on their behalf no doubt struck the band members between the eyes during those hearings. But when Evans stood up in court to explain, with his usual bluster: 'I wanted to be with this band for a long time. We'd been at it for five years and a lot of bands were following what we did,' they must have been equally confused, because it still didn't explain *why* he had signed the band to seven years with Silvertone, it was more an expression of *his* faith in the band. But if a seven year signing to Silvertone was too long, wasn't a ten year one to a management deal with Evans overstepping the mark even more rashly? And when Silvertone revealed the length of that management deal in court, it must have made things extremely uncomfortable for Evans, as was Silvertone's intention. Further pressure was applied by pointing out that he didn't give the band any accounts of his company. And it must have been excruciating for the flamboyant Evans when the Roses' very own QC added insult to injury by describing him as 'inexperienced in the music business.'

As the case wore on, it was almost impossible not to feel some measure of sympathy for Silvertone. The case swung in the band's favour as the court heard of some severe clauses in the contract, such as the fact that the label *wasn't* obliged to release Roses' product anywhere in the world and, in the event of a greatest hits album, the band would only receive half the royalty rate. The fact that Evans should have struck out or re-negotiated such clauses was clear, but didn't enter into the judge's eventual decision that the contract was 'unfair' – a decision that was taken without any pondering on the manager's skills.

When that judgement was passed, in favour of the band, Judge Humphries spoke of an 'immense inequality of experience between the record company and the group *and its manager.*' (author's italics). Moreover, he said that it was 'unlikely that any competently advised artists would have consented to sign it.'

Whether the Stone Rose were 'competently advised artists' was and is a moot point but, for now, Evans was celebrating having extricated the band from the contract, as well as securing the safety of his position – for the time being. The band had got bored with the court case long before this, although they were, of course, delighted with the verdict. Ian and Mani were in Manchester when Evans phoned the result to them and it was a case of a double celebration for John and Reni, who had just seen Manchester United beat Barcelona in the European Cup Winner's Cup Final.

The rest of the year would be frittered away by the Roses, but Evans was now free to follow up business that he'd continued working on all the time, when he wasn't in court. As has been noted, record company interest in the Roses had been intense even before the case commenced and Evans hadn't waited to see how it all panned out before flying off to America to meet one of the band's many suitors.

This turned out to be none other than David Geffen, one of the top moguls of this era (and others). Geffen was still to release Nirvana's grunge blockbuster, *Nevermind* in November 1991, but his wide taste and interest in music, as well the favourable reports he'd been getting, made signing the Stone Roses a top priority. Evans received two tickets to fly out to Los Angeles, for himself and his business partner Matthew Cummings. These two doyens of the Manchester music scene, who'd been driving around in a Ford Escort putting up posters in between devilling away at the International for years, were about to experience the L.A. way of 'doing business.' It started as soon as they got off the plane, when they were greeted by a fearsome looking driver who doubled up as a personal bodyguard. Fierce looks aside, he was also there to indulge their whims, happily whisking them off on a 180-mile round trip to a San Diego golf club.

On their return, however, Evans was handed a message from David Geffen, inviting (or was it summoning?) him to dinner that night. During the dinner, at one of L.A.'s top Italian restaurants, Geffen was happy for Evans to fill him in on the 'Madchester' scene and equally keen to hear what was going down in the court

133

case. Geffen would have been aware of Silvertone's £27,500 figure advance, which paled into insignificance when he handed over a cheque for more than ten times that amount (£350, 000) to Evans. And this wasn't even the advance.

Ostensibly, it was to help pay for the Roses' legal costs but, as Evans well knew, it was a gesture that said 'we are signing the Stone Roses once Silvertone are out of the picture.' Geffen's right-hand man, Ed Rosenberg, who was also at the dinner, made this abundantly clear to Evans, who, as they left the restaurant talked about getting the band's approval. 'You don't understand,' Rosenberg retorted, 'We *have* signed the Stone Roses.'

If these hard-ball tactics unnerved Evans he never really let it show because once the court case was over, there appeared to be four big record companies, including Geffen, who were confident of getting the Stone Roses' signature. On the day that they did sign to Geffen, there were representatives of all four present at the Halcyon Hotel in Holland Park, as well as the Roses themselves, summoned back for the big event. Evans later commented to Mick Middles: 'I didn't know they were all going to turn up.'

Whether that is to be believed or not there is yet a further twist to the tale. Supposedly, Evans met Silvertone's Roddy McKenna near the High Court *before* the judge ruled in the Roses' favour and offered money to concede the case, on account of the fact that he didn't want to appear in court any more.

Clearly, Evans had been playing a risky game with all parties, but his most heart-stopping moment to date might well have come as the Stone Roses dragged him into a room at the Halcyon Hotel demanding to know whom they should sign to. His nerves might have increased if he'd known that, following the court case, they had secretly resolved to distance themselves from Evans once they'd got a new deal. As he told them to sign to Geffen, he may well have been visualising their wrath had they been party to the fact that £350,000 had already been paid, and they were, in all but name, a Geffen band already.

And like history repeating itself, they again trusted Evans' advice. The signing of the contract actually took place on the top deck of a London bus, which they'd picked up outside the hotel (the chosen venue for such a major decision all too clearly reflecting the lack of solemnity involved). As the flurries of paper and pens commenced, there remained, with hindsight, only one more forehead-slapping moment of naiveté from the Roses. Needing a witness to all the signatures, and being rebuffed by one of their fellow passengers, they turned to Evans. The contract was solely between the Geffen Company and the band, but to have Evans' signature would make a mockery of any future claims that they were no longer close to Evans when signing this contract – a crucial point if they were to escape their contract with *him*. Once again, such artlessness would come back to haunt them.

XIV

The Stone Roses' contract with Geffen was certainly a lucrative one to be signing, as once again David Geffen's deep pockets conjured up a sum that dwarfed any previously paid out by Silvertone. This time £27,500 was multiplied by nearly a hundred and they handed over a whopping £2.3 million. Not only that, the band were to receive an increased royalty rate as each new album appeared. Though the record company had the option to renew the contract or cancel it every year, they showed their commitment by making it, ironically, a ten year contract – three years more than the one that the band had signed with Silvertone, and the same length as their one with Evans.

It was a shame for Geffen that the Roses' commitment to this contract was not enforceable by them in some way, as each band member, far from rolling up their sleeves and getting down to work, embarked on an era of pointless meandering, almost without parallel in the annals of rock. Almost (but not quite) making John Lennon's 'Lost Weekend' look like a spell in a boot camp.

The rum business of large record company advances does, in some cases, result in bands actually getting on with the job in hand. The first item on the agenda for the Roses, however, was indisputedly buying themselves homes at last, after years of devilling away on tour or in the studio, with admittedly nothing much to show for it. It was typical of Ian, in his true spirit of wanderlust, to go the furthest afield, settling into a bucolic lifestyle in a North Wales farmhouse and, though he was in fact to start his own songwriting there, he spent as much time indulging a new passion – for gardening. John also opted for the country, buying a place near the sea at Morecambe. Mani and Reni stayed firmly within Manchester (Reni actually had three properties in the city at one time) as Mani explains: 'Me and Reni, we are big townies... always will be, I reckon.' It may well have been a safer bet for Reni to have opted for the country as well.

Removed from close proximity to each other for the first time in some years and, no doubt, prey to boredom now that their lives weren't moving so fast, the band members got involved in other activities. While Ian and John enjoyed the country lifestyle, Reni now chose to play football rather than drums. He actually played to a high standard in physically demanding games in the Moss Side area and, when he was in town, Ian would join him. If Reni had confined himself to football, things might have been fine, but he also started to get into trouble with the police.

In September of 1991, Reni was found guilty of disorderly behaviour as well as a couple of minor parking offences, and he claimed in court that the police had physically abused him. This should have been a happy time for Reni: he was financially secure, not only having shared in the advance from Geffen, but also now bringing in a steady income in the form of rent from two valuable properties. It was reported that he had become a father too.

The whole set up was becoming less and less conducive to the band settling down to write more songs together. The fact that they all lived miles from each other now meant that it was almost impossible. The last month of the year was spent at rehearsal rooms in Wales, near Ian's place, but it is rumoured John Squire presented the band with songs which the rest of them wholly rejected. What is certain is that he and Ian were no longer writing together – by far the worst casualty of the band's separation. John was, as we shall see, turning inward and away from the rest of the band, his solitary nature re-affirming itself, while Ian absented himself from his front man duties for the first time. He was, it seems, content to be holed up in Wales most of the time now, barring a single visit to Manchester in September, specifally for the purpose of buying up the master tapes of the tracks recorded with Martin Hannett. This was done in order to pre-empt the bootleg tapes that he had noticed appearing. While this act in itself had its merits, showing some commitment to the band's catalogue, he was evidently in no hurry to build on the Stone Roses legacy, and neither were the others.

The fact that this legacy was being blighted to quite a degree made it even more important that they expanded their repertoire now. Silvertone obviously bore a hefty grudge against the group, as they peddled more Roses product relentlessly, generating revenue for themselves, while considerably denting the band's credibility. They released four separate versions of "I Wanna Be Adored" in September and far from being the last Stone Roses single through them, it was part of a long, long line stretching right up till 1995. Silvertone also reformatted the album, one of many incarnations, with "Elephant Stone" bizarrely added. To make matters even worse, they went on to release a video of the legendary Blackpool concert, with very poor production values and providing precious little confirmation as to why this had ever been dubbed their greatest gig.

Of course, what would have been beneficial for Reni and the rest of the band at this time, was a handful of gigs, but that would have meant dealing with Evans who they were increasingly intent on getting rid of. But even in this, they didn't seem to be in a particular hurry. One of his last acts as a manager was to arrange a meeting between the band and the Geffen people, who were keen to know what was going on with the next album. They had been generous enough to accept that the Roses were not the sort of band to embark on grinding tours to win over the US, so prestigious gigs at Madison Square Garden and the L.A. Forum were at the early planning stages. Despite Silvertone's best (or worst) efforts, the first album's reputation remained high, and growing still, so when the Roses rejected the US dates, everything was banked on a killer follow-up. For the band's part, they expressed keenness to get back into the studio, though determined not to do so until they were 100% happy with the songs they were bringing in. No doubt they neglected to mention that their most recent rehearsals had got them precisely nowhere.

In February 1992, the Stone Roses finally fired Gareth Evans. In consultation with their lawyer, John Kennedy, they had learned that the contract signed with Evans held an additional nasty surprise. As well as signing them for ten years – to which the band were supposed to have jocularly remarked at the time 'Make it twenty, Gareth!' – which they already knew about, they were also locked into an agreement to take Evans' business partnership with

Matthew Cummings into account within the contract and thus, 'the management team' were due to take 33% of band monies, later reduced to 20%, but even then, twice the normal rate for management. They gambled on being able to show in court that the contract was unfair, just as Evans had done with Silvertone. Evans, for his part did nothing – for now.

Evans and the Roses may well have parted ways agreeably, despite their differences, if the following events hadn't 'allegedly' taken place. Passing by Evans' home one evening, the fired-up band supposedly broke in and berated him about the contract. Evans claims he threw them out, only to have Ian return the next day, to relay the message that the band refused to pay him and Cummings their 20% fee, apparently running after Evans' car as he drove off, yelling at him to stop and discuss it. If indeed this incident did take place (the band themselves have refused to discuss it), it was the last meeting between him and the Roses. Either way, Evans was no longer their manager, but in his mind he had already resolved to see the Roses in court, when the time seemed right.

And whether the 'break-in' occurred or not, it's easy to see why Evans has later criticised the band for their arrogance at this time. For one thing, it's undoubtedly true that they 'upset a lot of powerful people' with their peremptory dismissal of the US dates. The Roses had, to be sure, proved themselves to be a great band with their first album. But they were just on the cusp of something bigger – a chance, as so many have claimed, to make the biggest impact on the music world since the Beatles or the Rolling Stones.

Ian had been proved right in that they didn't need to support the Rolling Stones at all, and the deal that Geffen struck with them reflected this. But not to consolidate the formidable reputation they had built up with their debut was, to be honest, to well and truly let themselves down.

Many a reader will have already noticed the parallels running between the stories of the Stone Roses and the Beatles. Now without a manager, no longer touring, nor the close-knit group of old, the writing was on the wall for the Roses, just as it had been for the Beatles when Epstein died, as they embarked on their (largely) separate lives.

But the parallels are not that neat. Evans, unlike Epstein, had been sacked, and the threat of court action from him hung over the Roses. Where it had simply become 'no longer viable' for the Beatles to tour, the Roses *chose* not to. The separate lives parallel, undermining their unity, certainly works in principle, except that by the time the Beatles reached this stage, they had amassed a huge catalogue of recorded material, had many world-wide tours under their belts and had well and truly cracked America, as well as producing several highly successful films. They also retained their work ethic for many years before their eventual split. In contrast, the Roses appeared to have mislaid theirs entirely – after one album and a handful of semi-important gigs. Where the Beatles threw themselves into studio innovation and worked hard to retain their pre-eminence, the Roses (well, three of them anyway) got into Led Zeppelin in a big way – as well as much besides, of even less relevance.

The Roses' 'Led Zeppelin' era was instigated by John, who immersed himself in this band and their style in the same obsessive way he had previously studied the Beatles and the Byrds, both of which had become major sources of inspiration for the Roses' sound. But then the rest of the band had counterbalanced things with their own tastes and, playing together as regularly as they did back then, the band were naturally more influenced by the contemporary sounds around, most notably, that of 'Madchester'.

Now, as they gathered in Wales, rehearsal sessions it would seem, amounted to repeated screenings of Led Zeppelin's *The Song Remains The Same* video. Over time, Ian was appalled to find his band-mates doing little other than watching this and other Zeppelin footage. 'What are you listening to them for?' he asked. 'They haven't got what you've got.' Later he said: 'I felt I was the only member of the band who knew how great we were, how much we meant to people. It was stupid, sitting around worshipping lesser bands, really stupid.'

One can sympathise with Brown's frustration. The Roses were, after all, supposed to be recording a convincing follow-up to the first album, and while it might have been perfectly acceptable for the likes of Primal Scream to mimic their idols – their *Give Out, But Don't Give Up* record, released at this time, being an unashamed paean to the Rolling Stones – this kind of scam was out of the question for the Roses. The stakes were so much higher – and only Ian seemed to realise it.

Nevertheless, what began to emerge from the ensuing protracted and often abortive sessions, was what Ian would call 'The John Squire Experience', where heavily riff-driven new material clearly foretold a 'Rock Roses' of the future. But this, in reality, was just a surface problem for Ian and the band.

Just as Lennon and McCartney had stopped composing together, the Roses song-writing duo had now collapsed, with Squire increasingly imposing his songs, and his will on the others. And other fissures were developing in the band's structure that would undermine everything. For one thing, there had been a long-term problem between John and Reni dating as far back as "Fools Gold" when John had opted to lay down his guitar track over a drum loop, rather than having Reni playing live. This had happened again with "One Love" resulting in friction between the two that any amount of time-honoured horseplay failed to disguise.

And there was certainly plenty of horseplay going on, as some of the wildest rumours attributed to this era in the Stone Roses history are testament. For a start, there are stories of a Roses tradition of throwing eggs at each other, dating from this time. There was also an increasing amount of drink being consumed, though Ian rarely indulged in alcohol, being the most keen to keep studio lethargy at bay. That he is reported as having done lots of skipping and boxing to keep the energy high, begs the question of how seriously he took this role, and in fact how much real work was actually being achieved.

An article in *FHM* in 1995, described a typical day for the band as follows: 'The band apparently spend most of the day in bed, smoke about an ounce of weed, get the £250-a-day programming guy to loop up a beat from a King Tubby record and then decide they don't like it.' The press of the time, evidently bored with waiting for news of the forthcoming album, became preoccupied with the ever more outlandish Roses rumours, not to mention adding their own kind of fuel to them, embellishing as well as creating a few stories from scratch.

The band were said to have become, first, heroin addicts and then, in an unprecedented departure from rock 'n' roll mythology, *golf* addicts. Presumably, they had become motoring fanatics too, as further rumour had it they had hired a fleet of Ford Fiestas and now spent all their time roaring around the North Wales countryside as if it was a go-kart track, instead of working hard on the next album. While Ian surely *didn't* lapse into a Brian Wilson-like inertia, ballooning in weight to eighteen stone, it is nevertheless true that entering one rehearsal room, he signed in as 'The laziest man in show business.'

And the press did actually try and get to see what was *really* going on too. The *NME* inaugurated a running feature, poking fun at the delay and sending one reporter along to smoke them out. They refused to be interviewed which was no doubt the best course of action under the circumstances – they were still nowhere near making another album and to be prefacing it now would have been a disaster, even if a continued silence was going to lead to more lurid stories of studio madness.

John's contribution to whatever madness *was* going-on was rather too predictably 'rock 'n' roll', as has been well-documented and confirmed by him and others, with Ian admitting: 'John was on cocaine all the time during the recording of *The Second Coming.*'

The drug use of the Stone Roses only really needs to be mentioned more fully now, as it was, remarkably, never a significant problem up to this point. We have seen many examples of the Roses' capacity for hard work and the fact that drugs were never in heavy use, despite their springing from the 'Madchester' scene, is testament to their single-minded determination to succeed.

All of them had a fondness for weed and in their scooter days, Ian and John would certainly have dabbled with amphetamine. The one with the keenest interest in drugs was Mani. Ian said of him: 'Mani used to take all kinds of drugs. Anything going really.' All of them were quite relaxed in talking about their experiences with ecstasy once it became widely available, but confirmed that it didn't in any way lead them to stray from the musical path. 'None of us were strung out at the time,' said John, 'I can't remember my first E. Probably on tour somewhere when the band was breaking. Did it have a profound effect on me? If you go insane you've always gotta come back down. Ecstasy wasn't the band's fuel. That was a desire to succeed and create.'

Of the ecstasy craze that coincided with the Roses' rise to dominance, Ian described the phenomenon in a *Q* interview: 'At the start of 1988 E was only available in London. By the end of the year you could get it in every small town.' His own use of it was recalled in the interview with Nick Kent.

'I was in touch with my own spirit before,' he said, 'so I don't believe E's changed me. But I can see it's changed a lot of other people. Only last year, people were taking it to extremes using it to dance themselves into a trance with. Fuck that. You've got to stay conscious, stay awake. Or else you're just some old hippie. Right?'

John Squire's immersion in cocaine *is* surprising as he'd always seemed in many ways the most controlled of the four, and at this time especially, his personal life was fairly settled, having just become the father of twins with his long-term partner. Often seen as the 'disco drug' of the seventies, John's heavy use at this time, between '92 and '94 foreshadowed its massive resurgence later in the 90s, in the 'blizzard of cocaine' Blur's Damon Albarn bemoaned at the height of the Britpop era

Ian was aghast at this development, having a very negative view of the drug, as he revealed later: 'You give nothing if you are on coke, all you are doing is taking… I loathe and detest coke. If you are on coke you are busted… there's something the matter with you. It could be that that (John taking cocaine) killed the

Roses. It was certainly a contributing factor.' Somehow, though, Ian could not rouse himself – or possibly he just didn't know how – to deal with the problem, as John's behaviour started to change. And clearly he had little support from the other band members in trying to deal with it, as suggested when speaking to *Uncut* a lot later, when he recalled leaving Mani and Reni with John around that time: 'I'd go away for a week and come back and no-one's talking.'

John has admitted: 'I made the mistake of using cocaine, thinking it would make me more productive. But it just made me more unsure, more paranoid.' Very soon, he was in the grip of it: 'I knew it was wrong but it seemed like the only way to get the creative juices flowing. You fall into this trap and the only thing that gets you up and running is another line.'

At one point, Ian tried to make it clear that it couldn't go on, as John reflects, '(Coke) really pissed Ian off because he was always against it, but it wasn't ever quite as dramatic as many people have made it sound. And, yeah, I got off it by cycling around Monmouth, sixteen miles every morning after doing the Charlie the night before. My heart would be pumping like crazy, but slowly I pulled away from it. It would return, I'll admit that, but never out of control.'

John's drug taking would cause a dramatic development in the band's music at least, the most glaringly obvious effect in relation to the music being: once upon a time, John's solos had been very rare (at the heart of the Roses lay the very antithesis of the kind of music that countenanced indulgent solos) and where they did occur, they were masterpieces of economy as well as innovation – the solo on "Made of Stone" being the shining example. But now, as, no doubt, yet another Led Zeppelin film was being fed into the video recorder, John seemed to be finding more and more excuses to include solos.

A gestating song like "Love Spreads" would now be Zeppelin-ised to the utmost degree, so that during these drawn-out sessions, the Stone Roses mutated into, of all things, a Seventies rock band – ironic when you think of their (and especially John's) shared passion for punk, which had set out to single-handedly destroy Seventies rock. It was little wonder that the Roses were putting off *NME* reporters for the time being, because they would have had a field day had they known what was going on.

The David Geffen Company were certainly not thrilled as they waited as patiently as they could for class material to emerge from the host of studios the Roses had reportedly been ducking in and out of. A Geffen representative, Gary Gersh, visited the studio every six months for two years and told *Vox* in 1995: 'We heard the beginning of this album a couple of years ago and it was a case of being patient until they were ready to let it go.'

The producer of the first album, John Leckie, had naturally been welcomed back into the fold for the follow-up from the off, but his involvement, also stretching over two years, would ultimately prove fruitless. It was during his first visit to see them in North Wales that the first egg-throwing session occurred, and, where he had been greeted with a full album of timeless songs when he met them to work on the first album, he was disappointed to find that this time there were just six songs awaiting him, none of them really complete – accompanied by a lot of larking around in place of the serious attitude that had so impressed him previously.

He paid a further call in March 1993, following prompting by Gary Gersh, which proved more promising. This time he was presented with three tracks, one of which, an early version of "Ten Storey Love Song", he was particularly excited by, feeling that it bore all the hallmarks of the 'old' Stone Roses – including a refreshingly economical solo from John. Leckie was able to send a favourable report back to Geffen, but he remained concerned that the band had generally given the impression of being in a weird contradictory state – a mixture of tension and lethargy – and though there was talk of a "Ten Storey" single at this point, it never happened.

In May 1993, it was the fourth anniversary of the release of *The Stone Roses* and almost a year before *Q* had listed its successor as 'imminent', and still there remained no sign of serious work being done on it. Leckie was getting more and more frustrated and, to Ian's irritation, was critical of most of the songs that they were playing to him. 'When it came to the proper recording Leckie said he didn't think we had the songs. We'd given him three of the best tracks on the album! I thought "Daybreak" was fantastic as it was.'

When Gary Gersh left Geffen, they didn't send a replacement along to make regular visits, and it became all too clear that the Roses had slipped down their list of priorities. Even so, as Ian confirmed later, 'they just kept sending the cheques over.' John Leckie, however, did not have the staying power of Geffen and, as his later comments to *Guitar* magazine showed, when he abandoned the sessions for good, he left a very frustrated and disappointed man.

'I'd tried, I really had, and contrary to what Ian says, I had no problems with the songs – they were great... I invested two years of my life in that record, on and off, and it seemed to be going nowhere... They were spending a grand a day and producing nothing!'

Once the Roses fully realised how frustrated he was, there were a couple of last-ditch meetings that initially convinced Leckie temporarily to stay, but this amounted to him lasting just one more day. When he left, he jokingly suggested they got Led Zeppelin's John Paul Jones to produce. Whether they were tempted by this, or even appreciated the joke is not known, but at that point they gave up trying to persuade Leckie to stay and the engineer Paul Schroeder was promoted to fill the gap.

But a new 'producer' had no galvanising effect whatsoever, as they dallied in Rockfield Studios near Monmouth, where Queen had recorded "Bohemian Rhapsody". After listening to what had been recorded so far, they decided to ditch everything, using them only as demos, templates for the 'real' songs to be recorded later. But such recording was almost inevitably delayed: John became a devotee of mountain-bike riding (as well as, of all things, kite-flying). Soon the others were into it too and, alas, more time that could have been spent putting down the new interpretations of the tracks was wasted as they all disappeared off into the hills (literally!).

More often than not, they ended up in Monmouth, a market town where they became tolerably well-known at the Bull and Nag's Head pubs. Mani liked the place so much he married a local girl and settled down there, even playing football for the town's B-team. So this most dyed in the wool of city boys finally succumbed to the attractions of country living, along with his band mates.

Mani soon had a child with his new wife too, making all the Roses now fathers over this period, with the added commitments of family life no doubt contributing to the general lack of 'getting on with the job in hand'. Reni, John and Ian had all been in relationships with Manchester girls for some time. Ian's first son, Frankie, born in the middle of the year, was to be followed later by another boy Casey. Ian was, and continued to be a devoted father and has said that he would have as many as eleven children if he could.

If fatherhood was more than just a diversion to them though, it must be said that with Ian's varied interests, John's mountain biking, Reni's football (and so on) the Roses were extremely good at creating more, and when Mani started to show an interest in falconry, one is forced to ask whether they were in danger of running out of leisure pursuits to try out before the album got finished!

They were in no danger of making an album though. They reconvened in November 1993, but the same apathetic approach to the music re-emerged, while they threw themselves into partying with Lush, also in the studios at that time. In fact it took a curious visit from their press agent in December to actually turn their thoughts to the future.

Philip Hall had been used on many occasions by Gareth Evans during the Roses' career and had, indeed, won a prestigious PR award (the first of three) for his work on *The Stone Roses*. His company, Hall or Nothing, is one of the most successful and well-respected PR companies in the music business. A former *Record Mirror* writer, turned skilled PR campaigner, Hall had notable early success with the Pogues, though his most famous association was with the Manic Street Preachers.

Philip Hall was also one of the most well liked men in the music business and on hearing about his enthusiasm for their new songs, the Roses thought it an inspired idea to have him as their manager. Though obviously feeling they were well shot of Evans, it couldn't have escaped their notice that a major reason for their lack of productivity lay in the fact that there was no one to guide and direct them. When Hall agreed to the suggestion, the only mystery remaining was why no one had thought of the idea before.

But, tragically, it was not to be. This most popular of men in a cutthroat business had only weeks to live, suddenly succumbing to cancer. This was a terrible blow to many and Ian went on record with his feelings: 'Philip Hall was a diamond man. He'd have been good for us, no doubt. I don't think we'd have got into the messes we got in.'

Hall's tragic death had a sinister footnote indicating more troubled times ahead for the Roses and particularly the relationship between John and Ian. When John refused to go to Phillip Hall's funeral, he put another nail the coffin, in terms of his relationship with Ian, who took it very badly. To Ian it seemed to be yet another example of the cold, unyielding character of John Squire, one that could be added to Gareth Evans' condemnatory story about the Nazi videos. As Ian ominously related to *Uncut* later: 'The kid (Squire) wouldn't come to the funeral. I said "At least show his mother and his father that he meant something." No, he wouldn't come to the funeral. I knew there was something wrong with the kid then. I thought, "Little fucker."'

But there was little time to mourn Hall or to stoke up further tensions, because Geffen were finally running out of patience. They set a delivery date for the album – March 1994 – and there was talk of a single too. None of the songs could realistically be said to be finished, and, though there was *some* finished artwork, as 1993 closed, the pressure was on the Stone Roses – and in more ways than one.

XV

1994 was something of a landmark year in British music while an ultimately frustrating one for the Stone Roses. This was the year that saw Suede triumph at the *NME*'s *Brat* awards, walking off with the Best Group title. Commonly perceived, at the time, to be the 'Great White Hope of British Indie Music', and yet another heir to the Smiths, they were already building on a celebrated appearance on the *Brit* awards some months earlier when, at the eleventh hour, they'd been parachuted in as the token indie outfit, amongst the choreographed acts like Cher. Their brilliant performance of "Animal Nitrate" came across as nothing less than an invasion of the mainstream with *very* faint echoes of the advent of punk.

But, waiting in the wings were two groups who, like the Roses before them, were intent on achieving the kind of success that would become something so much more than a mere attack from the fringes. The first were Blur, who would produce their first and most commercial offering, *Parklife*, later that year (though the drive for major success would lose some appeal for them as they opted for a more 'off centre' approach in 1997's *Blur*, before going on to transform into something of an 'arthouse' band).

The second were, of course, Oasis, whose *Definitely Maybe* album was also an unashamedly commercial product, even though it held indie credentials with references to the likes of George Best and Burt Bacharach on the cover. The band they name-dropped most often was the Beatles, which spoke volumes about the deadly seriousness of their intentions to be a band with *mass* appeal. The other band they acknowledged was the Stone Roses, who, thanks largely to Ian, had blazed a trail with this kind of mindset, and whose deal with Geffen was the first real indication of what an indie band could do in terms of major mainstream success.

Though no one had a clue at this time of just how massive these bands would become, the Stone Roses must undoubtedly have felt the pressure of their emergence on the scene, even before they knew of their predilection to produce albums on a year-by-year basis. Mani has recalled the feelings of insecurity at that time: 'We knew that it had gone on too long. We knew someone might nip in and take over. We actually thought it might be Primal Scream, strangely enough.' Later he was to put it even more crudely: 'We opened the door, left it open and went to bed. Oasis got out of bed and said, "Right them cunts are asleep, let's get on with it." They snuck in – it's the tortoise and the hare.'

They re-addressed themselves to the problem of having no manager in January of 1994, flying to New York to meet Peter Leake, who was the manager of the Waterboys – but this came to nothing. Geffen applied more pressure by announcing a "Love Spreads" single for February, and then the new album, in April. To the amusement of many, it was to be called *The Second Coming*.

Unsurprisingly, those release dates would be scrapped and not before they lost another producer. Paul Schroeder stepped down because of family commitments, and the son of Rockfield Studios' owner, Simon Dawson, who had been in on every session, took over. The raw material generated through three producers and many, many months would make the basis for the album. Because of Geffen's pressure, the songs that they had built up, some of which they had since rejected, and many of which John Leckie had given up on, were now being worked on for inclusion on *The Second Coming*. In May, the *NME* sent Stuart Bailie out to find out what was going on. He reported on eighteen songs to feature on the album, now re-scheduled by Geffen for mid-September 1994.

It was a highly entertaining piece, one that clearly signalled something was *definitely* coming, but also retaining the spirit of wild speculation still surrounding the album. Dodgy's drummer, Matthew Priest is quoted in the article, also commenting on their pre album sessions thus: 'They had a huge bag of grass and were skinning up on an Aerosmith CD, so that gives you an idea where their heads were at.' Priest can also be credited with a nickname for Ian, which would stick with him. A reporter from the *Guardian* had been taken in by Priest when he said 'if you speak to Ian, you have to refer to him as King Monkey', a reference to the occasional simian look Ian had when pouting, dancing and, of course, swaggering on stage. Far from being offended, Ian was quite taken with the description and would go on to adopt it.

The 'Led Zeppelin sound' was noted as present by others who'd visited the studio, while Reni was marked absent by Bailie, said to be recovering from 'a mysterious illness.' Ian was reported as now owning 'a spectacularly 70s' Mercedes saloon in addition to hiring one of the Ford Fiestas – and there were also rumours of a benefit gig to come in a marquee. It's worth noting that the Gallagher brothers, who were about to release *Definitely Maybe*, were quoted throughout the Stuart Bailie article, while, on the opposite page, Blur's *Parklife* could be seen at the top of the UK albums.

On the news page of this edition of the *NME*, however, was another more serious reference to the Stone Roses: 'The Stone Roses are faced with the prospect of another long stint in court next year following the issue of a multi-million pound writ by their former manager Gareth Evans' it read. It would, in fact, be almost a year before any court appearances, but the generally positive thrust of Bailie's article would certainly have been marred when the band flicked the pages of the *NME*, only to find they were heading to court again.

No doubt the threat of a multi-million pound lawsuit spurred the Roses on in some way, as the album at last entered the final stage of completion, with remixer Paul Oakenfold also joining the studio team. A productive two-week session at Rockfield encouraged both the band and Geffen, who were employing a strategy which involved freely stoking the 'Led Zeppelin sound' rumours and were evidently happy to build up the album in any way they saw fit. John then deciding that he was going on a two-week mountain biking holiday may have dented their confidence, though, because in August it was reported in the *NME* that the album would not be released till 1995, the piece sarcastically putting inverted commas around 'shock' news and finishing with: 'Bookies are expected to take bets on which year – rather than which month – the record will eventually surface.'

In August, Oasis reached number one with *Definitely Maybe* and it would soon become the fastest selling debut album of all time. Where the Roses were reading cynical reports about them 'trying' to finish their album, the music press were showering their fellow Mancunians with the kind of press coverage they themselves had known when *The Stone Roses* was released. It was the cruellest of ironies.

Oasis were to combine the album's success with a now-legendary performance at Glastonbury, where Mani could be seen backstage, telling people that the album was nearly finished and speaking highly of it to boot. Just after this John Robb reports a strange incident. Two Stone Roses fans are said to have ventured down to Rockfield to see what was going on with the album for themselves, finding Ian disconsolately walking round the studio with an acoustic guitar, teaching himself to play Bob Marley songs. 'Speaking really slowly', he took the young fans under his wing, showing them where the recording had been going on and even playing them some tracks, before regaling them with stories of the Roses' immense stature, placing them alongside the Beatles, no less. According to this account, Ian was the only member anywhere near the recording equipment, Mani was watching TV, Reni somewhere else in the building and John 'probably cycling somewhere.'

Here Ian, for the first time, comes across almost as a 'Syd Barrett type figure' – a drifting shaman, miles away from his followers. Such a description of him by two devoted fans suggests he had lost his grip on reality and more than hints at the fact that drugs had actually got the better of Ian at this point. A rare drinker, Ian was far happier smoking weed, and it was much later that he admitted smoking *a lot*, post-'Madchester' – 'it turned my head to mush,' he said.

But Ian was going through much more than just a drugs haze. His long-term relationship with Mitch was breaking down and he was facing the prospect of a new life alone, and having to make do with weekly visits to Frankie and Casey. No wonder then, that he for one, wasn't as focused as perhaps he should have been.

Nevertheless, the fact that this was the very time when Ian and the band should have been putting the finishing touches to what was an extremely important album for them, is another strong indicator that *The Second Coming* was essentially doomed from start to finish. Whatever fine songs came out of it (and there were a few) it was produced amidst barely controlled chaos and, arguably, this was all too obvious in the finished product.

It certainly showed, for instance, when the band took the tapes they had into a London studio to be mixed by Bill Price, who had worked on the Clash's *Combat Rock*, and was known for salvaging albums. He waded through a morass of material dating back years from an assortment of sessions, and a multitude of John's guitar lines, whose influence on the album was sweeping, almost suffocating.

From all accounts of the time, easily the most isolated figure is Reni, the most naturally gifted musician of them all. Rumours of heavy drug use on his part persisted, as well as the 'mystery illness' story, but what is abundantly clear is that the relationship between him and John hit rock bottom. John's high-handedness towards Reni, first seen with the "Fools Gold" and "One Love" singles, continued and escalated over this period. If John really was as remorselessly cold, calculating and dictatorial (as Ian and even Gareth Evans had made him out to be), then Reni's presence, as the most naturally-gifted musician, must have threatened John's position as supreme leader. The ensuing power struggle between them – which John, of course, won hands down – was, almost certainly, a contributing factor to the breakdown of the group as a cohesive unit. With or without the influence of cocaine, John was ever keen to improve and widen his skills as an all-round guitarist, as he now swerved into the blues-rock terrain of his beloved Led Zeppelin, so he could claim musical dominance once Reni had caved in.

The cocaine factor, which, as we have already seen, was a huge part of John Squire's life at this time, is relevant to the group dynamic, in its infamy for instilling a steely, insular attitude in its user, cutting off and alienating friends. The gang mentality, so prevalent in the Roses' earlier days and so much a part of their strength, was unquestionably undermined, as John took on the age-old arrogance of a cocaine user.

Mani's well-documented easy-going nature, suggests that he was no more up for a power struggle than Reni. And anyway, inter-party conflicts were probably the last thing on his mind, since as well as recently getting married, in a short space of time, he also lost his father, his mother became seriously ill and he saw no less than fourteen of his friends die of heroin overdoses. With Mani and Reni out of the direct line of fire then, the most intriguing question is why a full-scale battle never took place between Ian and John, during this critical and long, drawn-out period in the band's history. Ian had always been the standard bearer for the group, but, despite his protests, the Zeppelin-ising of the band went ahead and Ian found it equally impossible to get John to recognise how damaging his cocaine intake was. Ian's enforced inferior musical role is confirmed when listening to an out-take of *The Second Coming*, where John clearly loses patience with Ian as he struggles with "Your Star Will Shine".

There's no doubt John was bringing most of the songs in, but evidently he no longer wanted to share the song-writing duties. This must have cut Ian to the quick. Here were two lifelong friends, who had created a seminal piece of work together in *The Stone Roses*. Growing up alongside each other, John had saved him from bullies at school, they'd exchanged boxes of Maltesers every Christmas – a tradition they carried on into manhood. But even if John had been aware of how hurt Ian was, the cocaine would surely have frozen him out, just as John Lennon's heroin habit froze out McCartney during the Let It Be sessions in 1969.

It was a rather dislocated group of individuals, then, who were finally able to inform Geffen that an album was ready, with the wheels set in motion for the comeback. They flew to Los Angeles with the finished tapes, impressing Geffen with their new rock sound, though with plenty of other releases due, and having waited so long, the company were not disposed to make it a huge priority title. Then a meeting was set up with Hall or Nothing to finalise the publicity campaign, which the band failed to turn up to. Nevertheless, they did rouse themselves eventually, becoming involved enough to insist on a Christmas release – a risky manoeuvre indeed. *The Second Coming* was to be trailered with the release of the single "Love Spreads" in November 1994, with the album itself due out in December. A bold move in the old Stone Roses style, they were confident that the anticipation built up around *The Second Coming* was enough to sustain a hit single, which would not be overshadowed by the slew of other Christmas releases.

They also went along with a Gareth Evans-type wheeze, of sending the "Love Spreads" single to Radio 1's Steve Lamacq in a security van, for its debut airing. In all honesty, the hard rock sound sharply contrasted with much on the playlist of Lamacq's prestigious and primarily indie show, but mercifully, the response was generally positive. The *NME* and *Melody Maker* both reviewed it well (the latter making it their Single Of The Week). There was also high praise from Primal Scream's Bobby Gillespie, a longtime fan, who called it 'the greatest comeback single ever.' It was a promising start at least.

However, tight secrecy surrounding the album was starting to annoy people, and the week after "Love Spreads" was released, the *NME* revealed that they had heard the coming album 'via a foreign source'. The 19th November issue carried a huge article, which proved a mixed blessing. Whilst in itself, great publicity for the album, the title ('What The World Has Been Waiting and Waiting and Waiting and Waiting For'), and the sidebars, depicting events from British history since the first album, smacked of sarcasm.

The Roses tried the patience of the press further when their first interview since 1990 was conducted with none other than *The Big Issue*, the homeless charity's magazine. Although a commendable gesture in many ways with Ian making it clear that the idea came from the band – 'Somebody's going to make money off us coming back, so it was the best thing to do. We thought let's put something back. If somebody gets a house just by the four of

155

us talking, then it's been worth it.' – it certainly hacked off the hacks!

To pull a stunt like this on the music press, however noble the cause, was more or less guaranteed to backfire on them. And they could only have themselves to blame if the reception to the music the journalists heard, once they had received their copies at the same time as everyone else, (also guaranteed to annoy) was anything less than sensational. They really *had* pushed their luck this time. *The Second Coming* would have to be as least as good, if not better, than *The Stone Roses*, to win over the press now.

The Second Coming was actually in the record shops before any journalists were able to play their copy let alone review it, and a fair number of fans, in London and Manchester, braved the cold, as the album was unveiled in selected stores, at midnight on a Sunday in December. Though it had been snapped up eagerly enough, there was a sense of unease, as the new and unfamiliar sounds from this legendary band filtered through the stores and homes, over the following weeks.

Truly, *The Second Coming* would have been quite an achievement for any band *other than* the Stone Roses. Over a decade after its release, it remains clear that it is a record of great power. Kicking off spectacularly with "Breaking Into Heaven" (despite its being eleven minutes long!) –as *The Stone Roses* had done with "I Wanna Be Adored" – it soon becomes clear that this is not a band effort. The overwhelming preponderance of John's guitar playing is indicated by the fact that "Ten Storey Love Song", for instance, contains a prelude of about a minute's worth of John running up and down his fretboard – something that would have been unthinkable on the first album. A second album of thirteen songs illustrates further the lack of judicious editing.

Ian's distinctive northern-accented vocals are now the only real indication that this is an English band's work, such is the wealth of American rock motifs on offer – the most jarring being Ian's northern accent intoning 'Well you ain't too young and pretty, And you sure as hell can't sing.'

Where the duties were split fairly evenly on the first album, much of *The Second Coming,* beyond his more obvious arsenal of guitar lines, is largely Squire's work also. For example the record features Squires lyrics almost exclusively, the only Ian Brown composition being the disappointing "Straight To The Man". Ian's comment on this was: 'He was constantly writing really good stuff so there was no point in me doing anything.' – suggesting another power struggle that John won, hands down, in the studio. The only song written jointly by Squire and Brown is "Begging You", an unusual track revealing another hitherto unknown influence – that of Public Image Limited.

As the world and his wife were already aware, the biggest influence overall was Led Zeppelin, apparent even on acoustic numbers such as "Tightrope". At times, John seems to be leading the band into some kind of Led Zeppelin parody, straying dangerously near to the signature riffs of "Stairway To Heaven" and "Whole Lotta Love" on "Tears" and "Driving South" respectively. Although coming in for a lot of criticism for these kinds of antics, it is on *The Second Coming,* as much as the first album, upon which John's giant reputation as a guitarist rests. While he may have alienated some fans and reviewers along the way, with this blues rock style, the second album provides a chance for him to explore his instrument further and on many tracks he succeeds spectacularly in displaying real mastery of the genres.

"Begging You" is the only track which reverts to the indie dance style of the Roses heyday, and Reni's drumming, although exemplary throughout, is often exploratory, as he tries out a range of fractured, breakbeat rhythms. Here he seems to be pulling against the no holds barred rock style of drumming – preferred by John no doubt – that was demanded by many of the songs.

There is a bewildering mixture of themes on the album. In "Daybreak", Ian invokes the name of Sister Rosa Lee Parks, a symbolic figure in the Civil Rights Movement and an inspiration to Martin Luther King, while there is a lot of religious imagery in John's lyrics for "Love Spreads", suggesting that Jesus should have been a black woman. Many of the songs rail against injustice of one kind or another, proving that the band still retained some of punk's revolutionary fervour.

The album's highpoint is also often claimed to be their greatest love song, "Ten Storey Love Song", easily the most luminous track on *The Second Coming*. The song's beautiful imagery, its rousing and heart-rending chorus, interlaced with Ian's piercing vocals, lift it far above anything else on the album and into that rarefied landscape from which "She Bangs The Drums" and "Made of Stone" arise. Probably no one, not even their greatest fans, wanted the Roses simply to repeat themselves with *The Second Coming*. But "Ten Storey Love Song" shines out from the album, with strong echoes of the band's former glories, in such a way that it must have left many fans wishing they could hear more of these kinds of parallels. It's worth noting, that this track exhibits John's most restrained guitar performance on the whole album, though even here he clearly couldn't resist a bit of noodling at the end, just before the segue into "Daybreak".

And what were the press to make of it? Like the album itself, response was mixed, with *Select* and *Melody Maker* being exceedingly generous, and *Vox* more than complimentary about John's guitar work. There was guarded praise from broadsheets *The Daily Telegraph* and *The Guardian*, while the sarcasm of the *NME* did not abate as they dubbed the Roses the 'Anti-climax blues band.'

In terms of reviews, the nadir was *Q* – a pretty serious issue for Geffen and the band if they were to ensure a runaway Christmas bestseller. The status of *Q* these days may be different, with greater competition in both *Mojo* and *Uncut*. But back in December 1994, *Uncut* was yet to exist, and *Mojo,* but a year old, was still finding its readership. *Q* was, at this time, in *the* prominent position of influence for CD buyers and, with its strong circulation in the US, would also have an important effect on the market for an album there.

One can assume Geffen and the band would have been hoping for four or five stars for the album, but Mat Snow was in no mood to oblige and under a headline 'Wonky' he laced his two stars with a sharp put-down or two. 'As often as they hit the much publicised Led Zeppelin button,' he said, 'they hit the ones marked Humble Pie and Robin Trower. *Second Coming* is just OK, which in itself is a disappointment.' With other reviewers still decrying the five-year wait for the album, it was clear that the bold promo campaign *had* backfired. It entered the charts at Number Four, rather than Number One and, though it had achieved platinum status by 1996, the Roses were a way off earning that 2.3 million advance.

The band themselves were disappointed with the response it got. Ian said: 'I was a bit shocked by the poor reaction to the album. I thought, and still think, it was a great album. I absolutely did not expect those bad reviews and I would be lying if I told you that they didn't hurt a bit.' Ian also admitted that the big plan, which had alienated much of the press, had been an error of judgement, while pointing out the vindictiveness of some: 'I remember one journalist writing a review that said the album was crap. And six months later he told me it was his album of the year. That just about sums it up.'

Even so, as 1994 came to a close, the band remained determined to bring the album to their audience, such as it was, in their first gigs since Glasgow Green in 1990. The comeback tour was being planned with their old gift for innovation and surprise, as they plotted to hold 'secret' gigs using a pseudonym and announcing them on the same day they were to be played – in effect, a large-scale variation of one of their warehouse gigs. They flew to the US to discuss dates for their first-ever shows there too, but if they thought at this point that they had put their jinxed years behind them with the release of *The Second Coming*, they were very much mistaken.

XVI

In January of 1995, there was a nucleus of Stone Roses fans who, it could safely be assumed were eagerly awaiting the return of the band, and who, in order to express their excitement, felt driven to desecrating public property in honour of their heroes. The "Love Spreads" single, still in the charts at this point in time, had featured a photograph of a cherub that was part of the decoration of a bridge in Newport, South Wales. A posse of fans ripped the cherubs off the bridge and, in what must have been a pleasant change from scanning hostile reviews, Ian found himself put on the spot by the *South Wales Echo* where he was cornered into criticising the Roses fans, saying 'People should have more respect for architecture.'

January was a busy month for the band as they remixed tracks from the "Love Spreads" sessions for future B-sides and carried on planning the coming tours. All of them were keen to get on the road, play their music and make contact with some of their eager fans. Reni said, pointedly, 'I'm sick of underachieving' while Mani was to admit, as Ian had done before him, that they were 'the laziest band in pop'.

In February, they were to be heard again on the Steve Lamacq show, with a special two-hour slot, where they played records in between fielding telephone calls from fans. But hard work and good intentions were inadvertently undone when John was suddenly taken ill. He contracted pneumonia (though some papers reported it as pleurisy) and all the dates that had been scheduled and announced in the *Melody Maker* earlier in the month were shelved. John started talking about his cocaine experiences as well around this time – just one of many extraneous utterances and events that overshadowed the Roses' 'comeback'.

In *The Face*, Ian, for some reason, let it be known that he was in possession of a melted-down machine gun. It was an Uzi, the preferred gun of the drug gangs in Los Angeles. A friend of his had retrieved it from a burned-out Malibu home and obligingly smuggled it through customs for Ian – since kept in an Adidas bag in his house. Whether the police were aware of this is unknown but when rumours began to filter back from Manchester to the band that Gareth Evans was gearing up to fight his case against the Roses, Ian would have had two reasons for thinking he might end up in court soon. Could these be omens that 1995 was not going to be a whole lot better than 1994?

The Stone Roses had, in fact, been steeling themselves for this fight in court. Evans had long argued that he was entitled to a proportion of their earnings after he had been unfairly sacked, based on the work that he had put into making them a success. With their lawyer, John Kennedy, the band drew up a large document, filled with testimonials from associates past and present (including Philip Hall and Lyndsey Reade) which was meant to attest to the general unreliability of Evans' management – implying therefore that the success of the Roses was less creditable to Evans than he argued.

This document has never been seen in court, but some of those who were witness to it (including Mick Middles) confirm that it was not as condemnatory as it could have been, suggesting, frustratingly for the band, that they were all too aware of his madcap managerial methods and implicitly at least, supported them. For Evans' part, he was also in possession of a document that held incontrovertible proof of his winning ways with the band. With Evans employing the renowned music lawyers, Harbottle and Lewis, it was clear that he was confident of winning the case, scheduled to start on 13th March.

But, in the end, there was no case to be heard as the Roses effectively threw in the towel. On March 12th, Evans received a fax from them saying they wanted to settle out of court. Knowing that they would have to pay Evans a huge sum, they must have been equally sure that they couldn't win the case to make such a decision. Evans had quoted the wildly optimistic sum of £10 million in his claim – but on the day was happy to settle for a cool million. This was not the last that they would hear of their former manager, however. Ironically, the *NME* would run an interview the week after this happened praising them: 'With the Silvertone case and the Revolver paint-throwing incident, they proved to the world that they would rather lose everything than be screwed.'

Perhaps now more than ever, the Roses saw the wisdom of getting themselves a proper manager – a real necessity that couldn't be masked by the cheeky invitations they had sent out to many respected figures asking them to 'attend auditions.'

Dan Goldstein, with the blessing of Geffen, arrived in Manchester from the States with a strange CV for the job of managing a band such as the Stone Roses, as his duties in this field in the US were with the other Roses – Guns N' Roses. The Stone variety wanted a real managerial presence, which they seemed to think they'd found in Goldstein, and by whom they were immediately charmed: 'He told us that we were a beautiful ocean liner without a captain,' said John, while, in the *NME*, Goldstein apparently referred to their infamous gang mentality as 'a cool system'. Their working relationship got off to a good start, the one tiny problem being that the partnership only lasted three months, as his continuing commitments to the other Roses made it impossible for him to remain in the UK on any lasting basis.

The band were stuttering now, a vintage interview 'performance' in the *NME*, published in March couldn't really disguise the fact that they were tottering from one mishap to another, sometimes of their own making, sometimes not. They had announced a string of dates for April, again summarily cancelled, but this time for the dubious reason that details of the six dates had been published in the music press.

A US radio tour, and part of Geffen's strategy to break them over there, was engulfed in controversy when Ian spoke out against the US army, telling them to 'stop killing babies.' Instead of the phone lines being warmed by the admiration of the budding Roses fanbase, they were red-hot and jammed with people offended by their anti-military stance – hardly what Geffen had been hoping for.

But much worse was round the corner, something that could have easily been predicted if one analyses events around the time.

Let's start with rumours of Reni's 'mysterious illness' at the tail end of the *Second Coming* sessions and soon after to be decoded as a serious drug problem and a combination of factors that had, for a while made Reni by far the most anonymous and elusive member of the Roses, almost as if he wasn't there at all.

Ironically, one of his last quotes as a member of the Roses in the *NME* concerned a Megadeth gig he'd been to – 'I went to see them and I was getting down with the metalheads.' –rather than any reference to his own band. And one only had to look back to the *NME* issue of two weeks earlier where the Roses had given that vintage interview to discover that Reni hadn't been involved in the recent "Ten Storey Love Song" video at all. Readers must also have noticed the pictures of Ian, John and Mani locked in a Clash gang-huddle, Reni nowhere to be seen and, throughout the interview, never mentioned, apart from the video reference. Later it transpired there had been a host of press and publicity commitments where Reni had been notable only by his absence.

As soon as the 'shock announcement' came in April ("Reni Quits!"), he seemed to be everywhere – celebrating. Seen in the bars all round Manchester, he was clearly relieved no longer to be part of this band, who were supposed to be conquering the world. His first utterance came in *City Life* magazine: 'It had died for me. I left. I was happy to be gone.' Although he justified his departure saying that he wanted to spend more time with his family, the drug rumours continued as well as talk of a resurgence of the old grievance that Ian and John were earning more money than him, now embellished with threats of legal action. Intriguingly, *Melody Maker* reported Reni's beef as being not only due to 'substantial' contributions going unrecognised but also related to Ian being 'largely absent for many of the sessions.'

As Reni was celebrating, the Roses were busy fending off questions about him, while preparing to enrol their new drummer, Robbie Maddix, in time for their first gig in over five years. Maddix was a fellow Manchester lad, slightly younger than the others, but with a wealth of experience already, having played with Terence Trent D'Arby and the Rebel MC. Even as they welcomed him into the fold, they must have been finding it hard not to dwell on the fact that they had just lost the greatest drummer of his generation.

A defiant new Roses line-up was promptly forced, by *Melody Maker*, to confront these feelings head-on: 'When the Roses exploded onto the scene in 1989, Reni's hypnotic drumbeats changed the sound of the rock rhythm overnight. Do the Stone Roses agree with the widely held belief that Reni is (or was) a percussive genius?' To which Ian tersely replied: 'The rhythm section set us apart from other bands, yeah.' With questions like this, Maddix must have wondered why he'd bothered to join at all. Elsewhere, he, John and Mani alternated from pointing the finger at Reni's lack of any dedicated interest over the past year, to vehemently defending him against the heroin rumours.

This tough kind of questioning – and from *Melody Maker* journalist, Dave Simpson, who had run a Stone Roses fanzine in the 'Madchester' era – speaks volumes in terms of lost patience, loyalty and faith in the Roses. Here were the remaining band members, valiantly struggling to prove that the comeback really was underway, on the back of *The Second Coming*. It must have been galling to say the least when their old friends Silvertone popped up the same month as this interview, with a compilation, entitled *The Complete Stone Roses*, a retrospective from their golden era.

From the point of Reni's leaving onwards, the Stone Roses story takes on an almost surreal quality. While the band persevered, everyone around them gradually seemed to realise that it was all but over if Reni was out. Robbie Maddix would prove to be a fine drummer *for* the Stone Roses, but he was never 'one of them'.

Nevertheless, they set out on their first world tour, kicking off in Oslo, with all kinds of points to prove. Reports were mixed to say the least. The *Melody Maker* gave them an ecstatic review in their exclusive live commentary from Oslo, while Norway's *Dabgladet* called the gig 'a disaster' and *VG* complained about Ian's singing as 'out of key almost all of the time.'

A few days later, in Copenhagen, John suddenly found himself alone on stage, as the rest of the band walked off and left him. Normally studied and thoughtful while playing live, John now proceeded to raise the guitar high above his head, before bringing it smashing down on to the stage. This was not guitar hero antics, however, but genuine frustration at the way the band were playing. Things got so bad that they cancelled interviews to allow for rehearsal space so that by the time they got to Paris, they were more like their old selves.

This refining of their live sound was timely, since they were due to play a very special gig that summer: Glastonbury. It was a measure of the standing that the band still carried that they had been handed the Saturday night headline slot. Oasis had, of course, delivered a towering performance there the previous year, heralding in the Britpop era, and as the Stone Roses moved towards the summer of 1995, they would have been all too aware that the UK was now fast approaching the high watermark of Britpop fervour, culminating in August's famous Blur/Oasis singles battle. But it wasn't all about these two bands, as the Glastonbury line up indicated a host of acts epitomising this new era, where the Roses had now come to symbolise an old one. The band would have to turn in an epic performance to justify their billing.

The press made a point of asking the Roses for their comments on all the young pretenders, Oasis included, to which Mani wearing his heart on his sleeve replied: 'Oasis are doing their thing. Fuckin' like 'em mate. They're the most exciting thing that's happened to English music in years.' Ian, sounding slightly more circumspect and protective of the Roses' own standing, while at the same time careful not to be too critical of Manchester's new favourite band, had this to add: 'If someone says to me they've started a band because of seeing mine, and they're good, I'm pleased about it. When Oasis started to come through, who did they have? Who was the competition?'

Behind this comment can surely be detected a hint of tension, which must have escalated as the Roses drew closer to headlining Glastonbury, although they had North America to tackle first. And what a lot of people weren't aware of at this time was that the tensions pervading the Roses camp went far beyond frustration or diffidence about live performances.

The Brown/Squire axis of the band was, in fact, falling apart. This US tour had all the rock star trappings, with tour buses and entourage, yet prophetically, Ian and John were now travelling separately from each other. Ian was reported to be smoking some very strong Mexican dope in his vehicle, while John's became the coke-mobile, and both were brimming with assorted hangers-on. Ian would say later: 'John just became the archetypal regular coked up spoilt brat guitarist.' Even Mani, though projecting his usual amiable persona, appeared not to want to be part of the gang any more, and one can only feel sorry for Maddix, who was still just trying to learn all the songs. Ian had finally split from Mitch, the mother of his children, and now, just when he might have needed him most, his best friend, John, seemed not to want to know him. All his performances must have been made with a heavy heart indeed. Weed seems to have been Ian's only solace and he admitted later that he 'monked it' on that tour – no doubt he could have called on groupies, but he was essentially mourning the end of two relationships.

With all this going on, it's a miracle that the North American concerts went ahead at all, let alone show any measure of success. And yet the only hitch of any significance occurred when the Roses cancelled a gig in Washington, on discovering they were to play to a seated area, which they felt to be at odds with their style. Actually, the irony was that now, just as the band's two key members were diverging, there were real signs of success awaiting them in the US and Canada. The hard rock flavours of *The Second Coming* were definitely appealing to the North American audiences, and far more so than other British bands about to try their luck there.

The success of the Roses in key places like L.A., where ticket sales were such that a larger venue had to be found, didn't go unnoticed. Oasis toured extensively trying to break America and failed, while Blur's attempt to find an audience was disastrous.

The huge success, at this time, of British band Bush (who were almost completely unknown in the UK) had depended on their adopting that US type rock appeal, and perhaps similar acclaim was now within the Roses' grasp, and if so Geffen could look towards earning some money off the band at long last.

But, typically, disaster struck yet again for the Stone Roses. As the band now reached San Francisco, the last stop in the US before carrying on the tour in Japan and Australia, John went out on a mountain bike ride over the Golden Gate Bridge and into Berkeley. Instead of coming back to report on an exhilarating excursion, he returned with his collarbone broken in four places and a fractured shoulder blade, after coming off the bike. Though immediately tended to by a wide variety of physiotherapists and remedial masseurs, the injuries were ominously serious.

As news started to filter back to the UK, the Roses camp was insistent that, first and foremost, the all-important night at Glastonbury would go ahead. The damage limitation exercise to quash rumours included a hilarious diagnosis and assessment of the 'innocuous looking tumble off his bike' from Mani in the *NME*: with John 'drifting in and out of consciousness' his last words to the band were, apparently 'Sorry about Japan, we'll have to pull it, but Glastonbury's still in the frame.'

An unlikely story perhaps, and one which was certainly made a mockery of when, only the next week, in the 24th June issue of the *NME* it was confirmed – Glastonbury was off. Not only was it a tragedy for the band and Geffen's promotion of *The Second Coming*, it was also a moment when Stone Roses fans everywhere made their feelings known through the new forum of internet postings, articulating what had been implied for a long time – that the band were well and truly jinxed.

Ian responded to this 'jinxed' label, as well as to the incensed phone calls from fans who had paid the full Glastonbury fare to see the Roses. 'It's just our way, innit? Things come and mess us up, it always happens. If we'd had our way we would have just motored on from '89 and never stopped. We keep getting kicked back. We just gotta keep going and cope with whatever gets in the way.' Though it was meant to reassure, it only reaffirmed the impression that Ian himself operated out of the mindset that the band were in fact jinxed, while reports from US radio stations that the they were splitting up anyway, John having already formed a new group, were not about to help.

Ian also pointedly remarked that he wouldn't be attending Glastonbury as a spectator (a festival that he's never actually been to). Sheffield band Pulp, were elevated to the Roses slot and in many ways it was a good job Ian had decided to absent himself, as Jarvis Cocker and Co. provided one of the highlights of the festival. The Roses did make a concessionary gesture to the Glastonbury organiser, Michael Eavis, by agreeing to play the tiny Pilton Festival. Pilton is the village nearest the Glastonbury site at whose festival some Glastonbury acts perform, the proceeds of which go to the village as an apology for the disruption it suffers every year.

John was in recovery for quite a few weeks, receiving treatment from Manchester United's own physio, John McGregor, but he was back on his feet in time for the Feile Festival in Cork, which proved an unexpected triumph. When they appeared at Pilton, it had been their first British gig since Glasgow Green, and they been billed alongside dodgy pet shows and a fruit and vegetable contest. At Pilton they'd played for 1,500 people, including the Gallagher brothers and Primal Scream's Bobby Gillespie. The show had been another successful one, the only black spot being the fact that John didn't condescend to socialise with the Festivalgoers afterwards as the others did, happily signing autographs.

And when they followed this run of success with an hysterically received set of shows in Japan and Australia, a renewed sense of confidence started to emerge from members of the band, and was reflected in their increasingly scathing comments about the music scene going on around them. Mani derided Blur, Oasis and Pulp, suggesting that the Stone Roses were the real article. Ian was imperious: 'I never feel we've been overtaken by anyone else. There's been a lull. We're here to bring things forward, do what we want. All these bands who want to sound like Ray Davies or Paul McCartney… that's just retro shit.'

The only sour note to this part of the tour came about as a result of Ian's involvment in an 'incident' with a drunken Australian tourist, which ended up with him having to have two front teeth extracted. With a swollen mouth and a black eye, he told the *Melody Maker*: 'I wanted to bottle him. He threw his drink on me so I threw one back. Then he punched me, been on painkillers and shit.' In the same interview Mani re-emphasised the band's fighting spirit: '*NME* will tell you that we're finished; the people on the street will tell you that we're definitely fucking not.'

"Begging You" was released as a single in October, in the same week as "Wonderwall" by Oasis. Oasis had come through the battle with Blur, which they were adjudged to have lost, only to go on to outstrip them – as well as most other bands – in terms of mass popularity. Their album *What's The Story (Morning Glory)* had received very average reviews but had been snapped up by the record-buying public in unprecedented numbers. Once again, it was someone else's year and the Roses' chequered recent history meant they couldn't hope to compete with the Oasis phenomenon.

Nevertheless, they put everything into the gigs around the UK that were, after all, meant to be a centrepiece of the comeback. Despite the fact that they had been all but written off in the UK by now, their huge effort won them back many admirers, and the shows had a much more intimate quality than the football terrace concerts of Oasis. Their disappearance for five years only added to the joyful sense of disbelief for diehard fans, now able, at last, to reunite with their heroes (albeit minus Reni), while also lending them an undeniable mystique for newer audiences. But those who had been along for the long and bumpy Stone Roses ride, noted the detachment of the core trio from each other, mirrored by rumours that backstage they each stood in opposite corners – gone was the 'gang' they had known.

Still, a smattering of concerts on this 19 date tour – starting at Bridlington Spa at the end of November and ending at Wembley

Arena – have gone down in Roses folklore, as some of the greatest ever, with a lot of attention being paid to John's guitar virtuosity. While Ian's tact was lamentably lacking at the Newport gig, where he was reported as wearing Cardiff City football shorts on stage, nearly causing a riot, more serious questions were raised at others, about his singing.

Their first London show since Alexandra Palace, at Brixton Academy, was played to ecstatic reviews; the next, at Leeds Town and Country club, saw Dave Simpson from *Melody Maker* reporting that tensions still remained within the band. It was here John told Simpson how it wasn't the same since Reni left and how the band weren't really speaking, just walking straight past each other in the corridor and so on. He then went on to admit that he and Ian had attempted to write something together on the tour bus 'but nothing came out of it'.

Ian was in a good mood at least when they played Liverpool Royal Court on 15th December, showing the Christmas spirit by donning a Santa Claus hat, while the Manchester Apollo, their homecoming gig, proved to be something truly special. There had been rumours circulating that Reni was going to guest on stage for a couple of songs, all false of course. Looking out into the audience, Ian spotted a banner that read 'Reni Lives'. There was tension in the air as he called for it to be brought to the stage, only to hold it aloft all the way through "Daybreak". The gig on home ground proved to be another triumph, again attended by the Gallagher brothers, and yet another where the audience came away awestruck by John's guitar playing. The Stone Roses went on to repeat this kind of triumphant performance at Wembley Arena – a gig which was to be memorable not only as victory for the Stone Roses, but also as the last to feature John Squire.

Ironically, looking back at the Manchester Apollo gig, Mick Middles wrote 'It was possible to stare long and hard into the eyes of Ian Brown, a man who appeared to be winning the battle gloriously'. But the writing was on the wall and soon there would be a new battle for him to fight.

XVII

Following the tour, the band took time off to recuperate, with a view, also, to working on some new material. Ian, Mani and Robbie met at the drummer's house, while John worked on his own, a mirror image of the tour arrangement. And while Mani and John saw each other at Old Trafford, there was no contact at all between Ian and John. Despite the favourable reception to the shows and general optimism expressed by the Roses, there was now the flimsiest quality to this band, who were no longer really a group, as such, and still without a manager, a source of seething frustration to John in particular. 'It's hard to get a unanimous decision out of this band,' he claimed, gruffly, at the time.

Despite his later comment –'there was no straw to break the camel's back' – it wasn't going to take much, at this point, for John to walk. And walk he did. As part of the Geffen empire, the Roses had plenty of access to lawyers, even if they didn't have a manager, and a lawyer's letter duly fell on John Squire's mat one day in March of 1996. But to his amazement this letter was not about contracts, royalties or fees, it was written in the name of his fellow band members and began: 'Positive noises are being made about the group going into the studio.'

For John it was a thunderbolt, the starkest reminder that he really was no longer a member of the band – if it had come to communicating through lawyers – and that the only thing left to do now, was actually and formally to quit. On the 21st he phoned the others and said he couldn't do it any longer. Revealingly, he later reflected that the conversation felt like the first he'd had with Ian in a good few years and that Ian, even then, didn't really understand what he was talking about. When he revealed his feelings fully, the band sought a meeting – the first of three – trying to persuade him to stay, and desperately attempting to salvage anything that might be left, but to no avail.

Despite recording Ian's initial mystification regarding the purpose of John's call, Mick Middles has suggested that he wasn't really shocked at all by John's announcement. This latter view does not seem to be borne out by later events. For one thing, it's reported Ian had been repeatedly trying to get hold of John, following work on the new songs with Mani and Robbie, in order to arrange for John to bring in his guitar skills, phoning him several times and leaving him long messages. 'I thought he was busy, but was he fuck,' he said later, 'he was busy sorting out the rest of his life.' This hardly sounds like someone in the know. In fact the way Ian handled the entire split doesn't suggest any prior knowledge.

Bizarrely, news of John's departure was leaked from members of the Roses road crew over to the Oasis crew, who had previously worked for the Roses. This led to an announcement on Jo Whiley's Radio One show, which in turn, led to an announcement from John to make it official. The remaining Roses' response to this – that they were 'disgusted', felt 'cheated' and vowed to carry on without him – was astonishing to say the least, especially in view of the previous meetings which had ensured all were in the know prior to announcements. The tirade also sharply contrasts with the almost serenely official comment, which had come from John.

With hindsight, the three-page spread which followed, featuring John's detailed dissection of the split, together with the fact that his new plans were put into action suspiciously quickly, inevitably leads one to wonder – as Ian obviously suspected from the content of the quote above – if John had been planning to leave for quite a while. John certainly would have been safe in the knowledge that he was the most important musician in the band – his departure would be a serious hindrance, if not a fatal blow, to any future attempts to create a viable Stone Roses line-up.

It was certainly assumed to be a fatal blow by the press, who were all too ready – despite statements to the contrary from Ian, Mani and Robbie – to report the Roses as dead and buried. General hostility was also directed towards the remaining three, especially Ian, with references to his singing as driving John away. A three-page retrospective on the Stone Roses in the *NME* read effectively as a farewell to them, as well as being hugely favourable to John at the expense of Ian, who was described as 'this cardboard cut-out of the Ian Brown of legend', principally because 'John Squire had clearly sucked Ian's charisma in through his fingertips and become twice the guitar hero he ever was.' This comment, though obviously a dig at Ian, was not really fair to either party, since John's continued rise in guitar prowess was down to sheer hard work and commitment, which resulted in his developing skills that could hardly have been transferred by osmosis from Ian.

It was just *two* weeks after this that John did his three-page spread for the *NME*. With what appears like unseemly haste he bore all the questions about the Roses but moved swiftly on to talk about his new band in the making. He must have known that many people would jump at the chance of working with him (and Geffen were more than happy to take him on their artist roster) and at this point he was already referring to two musicians, whom he had met 'quite by chance', as future band members. This article was followed by a full page in the June issue of *Q*, where he was good enough to comment 'I will deny any attempt to say that I left as a result of Ian's voice', only to go on to damn him with faint praise by concluding 'I knew he was doing his best.'

Meanwhile, the Stone Roses were silent about John's replacement, refusing to respond to rumours that the Verve's Nick McCabe would be joining them. It wasn't until June that they were heard from again, making the surprise announcement that they would be playing the Reading Festival – though, as far as anyone knew, they'd still to find a guitarist to fill John's place. It was, if anything, a typically defiant gesture.

In actual fact Robbie Maddix did have a friend who could, quite possibly, fill the guitar berth, someone who had been helping them out with the demos they'd been on the point of offering to John. The exotically named Aziz Ibrahim, also from Manchester, though of Pakstani extraction, appeared an engaging and interesting character, full of warmth. And perhaps just what the Stone Roses were looking for.

Since the age of eleven, Aziz had been playing guitar, developing into an all-rounder of some distinction, his cosmopolitan background influencing his interest in many styles including

Asian classical, soul, funk, fusion and rock. He'd played in a host of bands of all styles and built up such a reputation in Manchester that when Simply Red were looking for a touring guitarist he got the job even without an audition – his keen sense of style no doubt also helping his case.

The tour with Simply Red was a severe eye-opener for Aziz who had, at that point, yet to encounter an egomaniac on the scale of Mick Hucknall. He has recounted how Hucknall's suffocating dominance over the band drove him to his wit's end. Unable to stomach being in a band where each member was forced more or less to agree with everything their lead singer said, Aziz left as soon as he could, resuming his preferred pattern of playing in a range of outfits with varied musical styles, only punctuated by one other bizarre interlude, with progressive rock band, Asia.

When Aziz got a call from Robbie, though reluctant in general to join another band of this stature, the Stone Roses' reputation preceded them, and Aziz was certainly not about to turn an offer down lightly. When he met Ian an immediate rapport was established. Aziz interested Ian, especially in terms of his beliefs. If not a devout Muslim, then at least a committed one, Aziz, like many Muslims, had not been allowed to listen to Western music at an early age. However, once he had access, he was hooked, deciding to make it his life's work, but without adopting any of the rock 'n' roll lifestyle – and he remained strong in his faith. Ian's wide interests included Islam (he must have been one of the few people Aziz had met through his work, who had actually read and could discuss the Koran) and he was intrigued by the harmony that Aziz had created between his faith and rock music.

Aziz was chosen to play in place of John and rehearsals began almost immediately, not only for Reading, but for a preceding series of dates in Europe, a warm-up, in effect, for the Festival, where a Squire-less Roses were bound to face a critical reception. In June, even the band's own spokeswoman was to say 'it really is prove yourself time for the band right now.'

Meanwhile, as coverage for John's forthcoming outfit continued, by June the news was that all he needed was a drummer and an official statement of the launch of his new band was expected immanently. Rumours flew from both camps, from John's, that the new drummer was going to be none other than Reni and even more strangley, the *NME* reported from the Roses camp that the replacement for John was going to be in the form of Sylvan Richardson, an ex-guitarist for Simply Red alongside Aziz! Once word got out that any ex-Simply Red guitarist was in the band, the jokes started flying and now, even more pressure was on.

Incredibly, at this late stage, the Roses hit upon a suitable manager, appointing Lewis Kovacs to a role that had been unfilled for over half a decade.

The new Stone Roses that finally emerged from the rehearsal rooms in Salford, making their way to the Benicassim Festival in Spain for the first gig without John, were considered as a unit to sound 'astonishingly good' considering all that had happened. Aziz was found to have learnt John's guitar parts well and it was reported that the Roses music was going to be more dance-orientated – the dancing girls now appearing with them on stage presumably emphasised this, but left a lot of people bewildered.

Conflicting reports remain of the gigs played on this tour even now, but the most damaging press came in the form of rumours that the band were considering pulling out of Reading altogether, angrily denied by Lewis Kovacs at a press conference. Kovacs' assurance that they would definitely be there 'barring injury', was predictably met with quick retorts from the press gathered, asking if he would be preventing the band from riding mountain-bikes.

In retrospect, it was clear that the band were on the brink of disaster yet again, and to have pulled back from that brink would, at this point, perhaps have been the wisest thing to do, in order to avoid total humiliation. The pressure that had been felt before Glastonbury seemed as nothing in comparison, when you considered that Aziz had only played five gigs with the Roses to date, not to mention the stories of Ian's weak singing which were by no means totally fabricated. John Robb recounts a tale of another Manchester band rehearsing in rooms next door to what they described as 'a Roses cover band' pre-Reading. Of course, it *was* the Roses, such as they were now, attempting to ready themselves.

And surely adding to the pressure, as it had done at Glastonbury, was the quality of the bill they were playing with, including Shaun Ryder's new group, Black Grape. And beyond Reading, the Oasis phenomenon was still thriving. Prior to Reading, Oasis had played a series of gigs easily overshadowing anything that was happening on the festival circuit. Heading for venues such as Loch Lomond and Maine Road Football Stadium, the Oasis juggernaut was hurtling towards the UK's cities at breakneck speed and swamping them with thousands of fans.

The cornerstone of this gargantuan tour was their gig at Knebworth, one of the biggest events of its kind the country had ever seen. The band played in front of 250,000 people – over eight times the number of people who'd seen the Stone Roses at Spike Island. This was the pinnacle of the Oasis success story, and on the kind of grand scale that the Stone Roses had only been able to aspire to all those years ago.

And who should be guesting on guitar with Oasis at this pinnacle of their career to date? None other than John Squire from the Stone Roses. Walking out to a tumultuous reception and the obvious delight of the Gallagher brothers (who were effectively living out a daydream from their youth) here was John, effortlessly outclassing Noel Gallagher with his searing contributions to "I Am The Walrus" and "Champagne Supernova". With a new band being assembled and a record deal more than likely, there was absolutely no usurping of John Squire as he soaked up the applause.

And what a galling account for the Stone Roses to be hearing just before a festival appearance, which must have been beginning to feel like Custer's Last Stand. Why did they go through with it? Ian, indisputably, the leader of the group – although temporarily absenting himself from the role, during *The Second Coming* years – should perhaps have acted decisively and pulled everyone back, now more than ever before. But he was, and is, a proud man, and the news from Knebworth may well have spurred him on – to prove everyone wrong – rather than beckoning him to admit defeat.

Arriving at Reading on the Saturday, and due to appear the next day, Ian was reported as hanging around backstage, looking 'out of sorts', and often on his own. He was also said to be drifting into the crowd, trying to soak up some of the atmosphere. Meanwhile Mani was apparently shooting around, as confident as ever and the Roses management team were keeping to the line that they were going to pull it off. But Ian was not only acting out of character, he was clearly nervous and seeking out the guitar engineer Cressa, he proceeded to spend the night drinking and smoking dope.

The next day, Ian and the rest of the band would not exhibit any nerves as they calmly made their way towards the obligatory press conference. But if the Spike Island conference had been bad, it was a party in comparison to the one held before the Reading gig, as some of these exchanges show:

Q: Didn't John write most of the songs?
Ian: John wrote most of the songs on *Second Coming* because we let him do it. John's had his day and now he's gone.
Q: I heard that your gig in Portugal didn't go down too well. How did you feel about that?
Mani: It looked alright from where I was standing.
Q: It said in one of the papers that the audience was leaving.
Mani (*after an obviously forced laugh*) Ha ha ha. Bullshit. Do you believe everything you read in the press? I wipe my arse on it.
Q: Now John Squire is not around, do you feel you have to prove yourself all over again?
Ian: No, we just smile a lot more now. We're happy, can't you tell?
Q: Why do you think he wanted to leave the band all of a sudden?
Ian: Because he felt his power threatened. It was all a bit too much for him. He was on a power trip.
Q: But he is your main songwriter..

Robbie (*angrily*); No, you're not listening! He's your main song-writer. He's not our main songwriter. He's not here.

Q: Are any of you still friends with John?

Mani: He wouldn't even bother to phone my house if he heard that my mum, my dad and everyone who ever lived in my village was killed in a plane crash, because he couldn't be arsed to get out of bed.

And with that, the band left to prepare to go on stage. And as the three musicians made their way to face their audience and start the long intro for "I Wanna Be Adored", Ian hung back, as the music built up. Pumping himself with the old swagger once more, he strode confidently on to the stage and, unofficially, announced the end of the Stone Roses.

PART THREE

THE RESURRECTION

PROLOGUE

Prisoner BE9311, name of Brown, heard the cell door close behind him. He was now in Strangeways, his 'home' for the next four months. His 'pad mate' was a young kid addicted to heroin. In time he would share the cell with four other young men, all of them heroin addicts.

The 'Prisoner's Information Handbook for Male Prisoners and Young Offenders' was waiting for him on a table. This told him of his rights while incarcerated. Under volumetric control, he was allowed a radio, six newspapers, at least three books and sundry items such as a diary, writing and drawing materials, religious articles, a manual typewriter and personal toiletries. Even a birdcage was permissible, but the total amount of property for any prisoner must not exceed two boxes.

The handbook ran to 188 pages, with the whole range of prison life covered, from 'On Arrival' to the 'Leaving Prison' section. Offences that a prisoner could commit numbered twenty-five, one of which was to 'administer a controlled drug to themselves or fail to prevent the administration of a controlled drug to themselves by another person'. Prisoner BE9311 sniffed the air and recognised the marijuana fumes wafting all round B Wing.

He had entered the institution with face cream, his house keys and £80.00 in cash. These would be taken from him. The last time he had thought about life in Strangeways had been during riots in protest at living conditions, some years earlier – a cause with which he sympathised. Some of the inmates involved in those protests remained there still.

Those riots had taken place in 1990, when Prisoner BE9311 was at the height of his fame with the Stone Roses, the leading light of the 'Madchester' scene. In the past few months he had launched a successful solo career. He had been in New York, Paris, Sweden, Denmark and even Jamaica to promote his work. He had sold 200,000 albums already that year and that very month, a two-page article about him had been published in Q magazine. Now he was in prison.

Later, he said: 'I went into prison with no respect for authority, and came out with even less. It's done one thing for me, though. I used to be known as the singer of the Stone Roses. Now I'm Ian Brown'.

XIX

Fallout from the disastrous Reading Festival performance hit Ian harder than anyone. In the *NME* live review, for instance, generosity was extended to Aziz and Robbie and by default to Mani – by not mentioning him at all. But there was no let-off for Ian, who was mercilessly attacked, not only for his singing but also for his lack of stage presence. 'Instead of looking shamanic and sexy as he slides around the stage, he now resembles Peter Hooton of the Farm, it was difficult to tell whether the vicious comparison with Hooton, being the rather oik-ish leader of a lower division 'baggy' band, was more or less hurtful than the assessment of Ian's singing – 'utterly graceless, completely bereft of emotion, just a horrible, hollering moan.'

It would only get worse for Ian as the rumours about Mani leaving the band intensified. A fiercely loyal statement came from the bassist on 14th September in *NME*. 'To say that I have left the band is complete nonsense. I've got more bottle than to throw the towel in over a bit of bad press.' But this vote of confidence would have been cold comfort had Ian turned to the letters page to find even loyal fans begging him and Mani to call it a day.

As the national press ran in depth coverage of Oasis' dramatic abandonment of the US tour, following Noel and Liam Gallagher's spectacular falling-out, it might have struck Ian and Mani that outside of the music press a lot of people had stopped caring about them. And those journalists who did show an interest, were simply waiting to print the news that their band had ended.

In October it was confirmed by a Stone Roses spokesman that Mani had been asked to join Primal Scream, though no accompanying statement, at this point, revealed what his answer had been. Either way, Ian was now looking dangerously isolated, like the captain of a sinking ship whose crew was preparing to jump overboard. It was now just a question of waiting for Mani's statement which duly came in November, disclosing not only that he had been asked *long ago* to join the Scottish band, but also that he had been making moves, post-Reading, to start his own band, should the Primal Scream offer no longer be open. In addition, he apologised for his previous comments about John, wishing him luck and insisting that there was no lingering acrimony between any of the Stone Roses members.

Of course, this was not true. Ian had not spoken to John, or even attempted to and in fact one of the longest-running feuds in rock history was just about to reach its crescendo. While John was on the brink of unveiling his new band, fresh from his triumph at Knebworth, he was in an enviable position of strength, while Ian's situation now looked increasingly hopeless. And so it was Ian gave his statement announcing the end of the Roses, his humiliation complete as the last surviving member, clinging to the wreckage. Also, with no real individual song-writing experience, and no natural musicianship, it was the easiest and most natural thing to write off Ian Brown completely. Add to this his continued struggle with adjusting to living alone, without his children Frankie and Casey, one can only imagine the bitterness of Ian's feelings.

And when Geffen confirmed that they had dropped all the Stone Roses, except for John Squire, from the company roster it must have been like the tolling of a bell for Ian. Ian, Robbie, Aziz and keyboard player Nigel Ippinson had been rumoured to be working on the tracks meant for John Squire but the only comment from Ian at this point was both mysterious and detached: 'One day I'll tell everyone who's interested the real story behind the Stone Roses. All I wanna do is kick back and listen to the Audioweb LP.' And his position became even more ignominious as a demo tape of Ian's music with his new bandmates was offered to Geffen and promptly returned as unsuitable – and this, just as excitement built up around John's band, the Seahorses, who were to be signed to Geffen.

The attitude of Geffen shows that they did feel that they had really got their fingers burned with the Roses. Though generally a far-sighted company, as the signings of bands like Nirvana showed, their decision to support John displayed that they didn't really know their rock history. The chances of a guitar hero from a band like the Roses creating a new one and achieving the kind of success that they wanted were really pretty slim; there were too few precedents. But they'd made the decision to give John some powerful backing.

Geffen may well have been influenced by the press's keen interest in the Seahorses, and certainly the intention seemed to be to install them in the pantheon of Britpop bands. Squire's appearance at Knebworth obviously aided their positive perception, as, no doubt, did the revelation that he had written a song, "Love Me Or Leave Me" with Liam Gallagher.

Rock mythology has it that John changed the band's name to Seahorses rather than *The* Seahorses when he discovered that the latter was an anagram of 'He Hates Roses', although he poured cold water on this theory as he introduced his new band to the press. What was immediately noticeable during that introductory press conference was that two of his fellow musicians – singer and guitarist Chris Helme and bassist Stuart Fletcher – looked decidedly younger than he did. Reni having set a precedent as drummer supremo with the Roses, meant that the percussion auditions proved a very lengthy process, before John finally settled on Andy Watts. As they started to play live gigs, they gained some positive coverage as the Geffen machine started to build up anticipation for the album, due to be released in June 1997.

For Ian, the only option for now appeared to be to retreat from view, which he did in more ways than one. One of his new ports of call during the coming year was to be Morocco, which seemed a pretty good place to 'kick back', not least because of the plentiful supplies of strong weed easily obtained. But other aspects also inspired him there, especially witnessing the muezzin call to prayer, one of the most powerful expressions of Islam.

'It lifted me off my feet, like a Saturday afternoon when I was fourteen,' he said, 'it was so rough and raw echoing off the walls. The most uplifting thing I've heard for a long time.'

Such a comment typifies the mental leaps that Ian was more than capable of making. Comparing this experience with listening to Northern Soul or watching football, rather than being disrespectful to Islam, was an affirmation of his belief in the unifying force of music. This was a sentiment that he'd alluded to on stage many times and pithily referred to when asked about his Stone Roses 'stage act'. 'I'm not performing,' he explained, 'I'm partici-pating.' The rediscovery of such feelings in Morocco were made all the more powerful when mixed with the weed.

As we know, Ian had partaken of his fair share of drugs, but had always expressed the view that they should never be used for the purposes of oblivion. His 'You've got to stay conscious, stay awake' comment was, paradoxically, an exhortation to retain a cer-tain spirit of asceticism whilst taking drugs. For him, it should be viewed, like music, as a semi-religious experience, and he smoked weed – his only real 'drug vice' – in the same blissed-out way Ras-tafarians do, but without subscribing to the religion.

He criticised the bohemian hero William Burroughs, so be-loved of rock 'n' roll types such as David Bowie and Patti Smith, who had also spent a lot of time in North Africa. 'William Bur-roughs... He abused his life and he wrote a book about it. There's nothing more boring than hearing someone else's drug stories. But he's held up as some kind of literary great. For me, he was just a bum.' Ian actually had a point: in a numbed display of contempt for his own talent, Burroughs had spent an entire year in Tangiers taking heroin, and hardly stirring from his dishevelled home. Per-haps influenced by Aziz, Ian began to take a long hard look at the whole rock 'n' roll world and what it had to offer.

During his time in Morocco he is also said to have immersed himself in religious tracts. Writs served on him as the Roses' cheq-uered legal history unravelled, along with proof of the dishonesty of former employees, only served to heighten his anti-decadent feelings. 'I'd seriously considered gardening. Everything I'd be-lieved in was finished. John had left me. Me best mates were rob-bing money off me. I had summonses up to here. I didn't want to know any of it. Fuck it, I'll do gardening for old people.'

All of this suggests a long dark night of the soul for the singer, as *Second Coming*-style rumours began to swirl around him. Along with the religious readings, he was said to have grown an enormous beard, as he mixed his reading of the Koran with the

Bible, while also engaging in much 'therapeutic' gardening. The series of flings he has admitted to having during this time – post the break up with Mitch – show it was a period of some confusion for him. Then, suddenly, he met a person who was to change his life. Ian happened to be in New York and was predictably prowling through a series of parties looking for weed: ' I went into this apartment and there she was', he recalls, of Fabiola Quiroz, a Mexican model and actress. Fabiola had recently appeared in an acclaimed film called *Who The Hell Is Juliette?*, a powerful documentary contrasting her rather grand life as a model with that of a sixteen-year old prostitute. The couple fell head over heels in love and soon Ian was making regular trips to New York to visit the woman who he has always credited with finally bringing him luck.

Luck was just what he needed at that time: as a father of two he had to provide for his family but the grim truth was that there was a shocking disparity between the fortunes of Ian Brown and John Squire. While John had another advance from Geffen and could easily cover all his costs, Ian was not actually bringing anything regular in at this time (even in 1995 he was supposed to have only earned £9,000) and the house in Wales had eventually to be forsaken for a more modest abode, an ex-council house in Lymm, Cheshire. It must have been a sobering experience, then, when one of his children actually addressed the issue directly by asking 'When are you going to do something?'

But what Ian actually did do was to retreat even further – into his bedroom. Here he set about re-inventing himself from front man in a band to solo artist. 'I'm gonna stick in me room,' he told himself, 'put carpet up on the walls. I won't go out till I've got at least ten or twelve songs together.'

A remarkable vow when one considers that Ian had never really been a musician. His song writing duties with the Roses had amounted to writing lyrics and creating melodies, and with the Patrol he had hardly mastered the bass, if the truth were told. The only advances he had made musically were the result of a bit of self-tuition during the many fallow periods of *The Second Com-*

ing sessions. So as he locked himself away now it was with still only a rudimentary knowledge of music. He brought a Bob Marley songbook and a Blues anthology into his bedroom, along with a bass, a drum machine and an acoustic guitar – a present from Reni the year before, who had said prophetically, 'One day, you'll thank me for it.'

This retreat occurred as the winter of 1996 was drawing in. It was a tremendously brave thing to do and the old characteristics of self-discipline inspired by karate and that strong work ethic returned, which meant that he hardly stirred from home in the coming weeks, his sights firmly set on his goal. And there was barely a word about him in the press, excepting odd fanciful stories, such as the one that reported him as re-signing to his old label, Silvertone.

In contrast, there was considerable coverage of John and the Seahorses, who played again in the New Year and were praised mightily. Their debut album was being heavily trailed and they were included in the *NME*'s list of bands tipped for success in 1997.

Ian barely noticed as he toiled on alone, but then he had a catalysing visit from Aziz Ibrahim. For Aziz, it was almost as if everyone else had disappeared off the face of the earth after the Reading debacle. No one was contactable and the one visit he had made to his despondent former front man, prior to his leaving for Morocco, had culminated in Ian telling him that he was no longer interested in making music. So when Aziz made contact some months later, it was simply as a friend wanting to know what Ian had been up to.

Once he realised that Ian *had* actually been making music, he was able to join in instantly, for Aziz *always* had a guitar with him. In no time at all they were writing tunes together, the first time that Ian had written anything with someone else since the golden era of the Stone Roses first album. Very soon, they had moved the song writing out of Ian's bedroom and into a variety of studios, including the Rose Garden, the one that the last line-up of the band had bought with the Reading proceeds.

As Ian was taking his first tentative steps at recording in April 1997, John was releasing his first single with the Seahorses. "Love Is The Law" was an amazing success, entering the charts at number three – just missing the highest Stone Roses chart placing with "Love Spreads". The album, *Do It Yourself*, came out in May to mixed reviews, but the worst of these were balanced, and the best outshone by some of the live reviews the Seahorses were getting. John's guitar playing was naturally given high praise, but there was a bonus to be had in the pin-up quality of singer Chris Helme, who was even eliciting screams from parts of the audience. This kind of reception had been unknown with the Roses of course, and if it rankled with John, he certainly didn't show it. John and his Seahorses (for it was always, somehow, John Squire's Seahorses) were to go on to have a string of hit singles from the album. Geffen had seemingly made the right choice when they ran with John once the Roses split. The most curious thing about the album perhaps, is how it sounded so similar to the first Stone Roses album, (right up to and including Helme's Northern accented lyrics) with John seemingly well and truly out of his Led Zeppelin phase.

The other two former Roses had similarly contrasting fortunes to that of John and Ian at this time. Similarly to John Squire, Mani was poised for success with Primal Scream, who had always been fans of, and good friends with The Stone Roses but with only passing similarities in their music. When Mani joined them, they were intent on getting away from the Rolling Stones-flavoured music of their last album, in spite of its huge success. 1997's *Vanishing Point* was seen as a triumph and the ever-adaptable Mani provided a seamless transition. Bobby Gillespie would say more than once that it was as if Mani had always been a member of the band.

Like Ian, Reni had become an anonymous figure at this point. He was the only one of the original Roses still living in Manchester and Aziz often bumped into him at the A1 music shop, the very place where he had seen the 'drummer wanted' ad from the Stone Roses. Having been quoted as saying that he was going to give up drumming when he first left the Roses, Reni inevitably drifted back into music. In 1997, he was actually making music with Pete Garner, the first Stone Roses bassist, though playing guitar instead of drums. Reni met up with Ian in London that year, where they got up to their old waking-up-the-neighbourhood tricks. Walking through Soho, Ian spotted a paparazzi photographer taking their pictures from his car. After a short dialogue with the photographer, Ian kicked in his headlights and Reni climbed onto the roof of the car, jumping up and down while the photographer cowered beneath him. All in broad daylight in one of London's busiest areas! Reni and Ian still brought out the tearaway instinct in each other it seemed and, though they left this scene without attracting the police, Ian was soon after to be arrested for driving while banned.

But along with these relatively harmless spots of bother, were nastier incidents too. Between 1996 and 1998, Ian was badly beaten up three times. Firstly by an Australian bodybuilder in Tokyo, then, at a club in Warrington he'd gone to on his own, four doormen took exception to the attention (and free drinks) Ian was getting and decided to lay into him. He took about twenty kicks to the head in this brutal attack. Later, and also in Warrington, someone jumped out of a car with a metal bat and split his head open. At times like these Ian must surely have felt that nothing was going right for him since the Roses split.

Nevertheless, in the summer of 1997, Ian was putting finishing touches to the tracks that he had accumulated and adapted with Aziz and the other 'latter' Stone Roses. The songs included "Can't See Me" which dated from the *Second Coming* sessions, plus "Nah Nah" and "Ice Cold Cube" (this title referring to Reni's nickname for John Squire in the Roses days).

With 'no label, no lawyer, no manager' and a largely self-taught composer, Ian had produced a putative album within a year of the Roses splitting, having paid for the recording himself. But with the Reading fiasco still talked about in the press while John was still receiving vast amounts of positive coverage (the Seahorses had by now even appeared on *Top Of The Pops*), it would take a brave record company to take him on.

For one thing, Ian was just as intractable as ever and he submitted it to Polydor insisting that what he was offering was the finished article. He certainly wasn't going to tolerate a big-name producer coming in later to doll the album up, which he summed up thus: 'All it is is rhythms and tones and lyrics put together in a nice way.' With help from lawyer John Kennedy, Ian was able to convince them that he was worth an album deal. Polydor showed greater far-sightedness than Geffen had in accepting the terms: if they weren't embracing the album as it was, they were making a shrewd gamble on the name of Ian Brown carrying across into another audience. Or perhaps someone at the label had sensed that an era in British music was coming to an end, and that Ian – and his new music – would fit in perfectly with the one that was on its way.

Where 1996 saw the end of the Stone Roses, 1997 was to witness the sudden and irreversible decline of the Britpop era. In the summer, the Oasis 'magic touch' deserted them for good. The release of *Be Here Now*, their third album, carried with it so much press coverage it was difficult to imagine anyone on earth who hadn't heard of Oasis. But the ballyhoo wasn't worthy of an album that was within weeks, if not days, rightly perceived as a self-indulgent disaster. Where *The Second Coming* had as its main creative force a bit of a coke fiend, *Be Here Now* was, by the band's own admission, created in vast flurries of cocaine. And it showed.

The reality was that Oasis was no longer really a band anyway. Not only was it the last album for two of their members, the 'band' had by now become a beer-fags-coke-loadsamoney circus, distinguished less for the music than for the conspicuous consumption displayed by the band members and anyone closely connected. Noel and Liam now listed as personal 'assets' the obligatory airhead trophy 'wives'. Meg Mathews, Noel's partner, aroused appalled reactions in the music business later in the year when she started 'penning' an excruciating showbiz column called *Yeah!* in the *Sunday Times*. A highly dubious undertaking, Noel soon put a stop to it, though it wasn't soon enough to stop Mathews plumbing new depths of inanity for the genre.

Noel Gallagher looked up from all the binging to see the band's credibility was slipping from them as quickly as his wife slipped on her designer gear. He was reported to be totally enraged when his brother dedicated "Live Forever" to Princess Diana in concert not once, but twice – the second dedication presumably made to antagonise Noel further. Praise for such an establishment figure, whatever the circumstances, could cause untold damage to a band's rebel image and even Liam Gallagher's continued brawling couldn't counter-balance it as he was now simply boring people. All of this wouldn't have been so bad if their music wasn't being fiercely challenged as well. *Be Here Now* was trumped by Radiohead's wilfully strange and complex *OK Computer* – a potent symbol of the post-modern culture that made Oasis suddenly seem so dated.

And did this mean that the Seahorses were dated too, as they just happened to be supporting Oasis on the *Be Here Now* tour? Drummer Andy Watts was replaced in October of 1997 after he complained about the way that the band worked, with hints that John was being dictatorial; the replacement was in turn dispatched within a matter of weeks. Though they were being seen by a lot of people supporting Oasis and on the back of their own successful winter tour, all was not well in the Seahorses camp – the sands were seemingly shifting beneath them.

For Ian, as news began to filter out that a single and then an album were due for release, the scene could not have been set more beautifully. He revealed to the press that the forthcoming music, while displaying echoes of the Roses, was hardly in the traditionalist vein of his former band. 'There's all different kinds of stuff on there, from acoustic to more trippy and experimental stuff,' he disclosed, 'There is a real groove along the lines of the Roses but then there's a lot more different kinds of styles than the Roses ever had.' He added, pointedly: 'You get more understanding about how the Roses were written on this than you do by listening to the Seahorses.' It was a warning shot across the bows not only to John, but also to the press, that he was coming back as outspoken and independent as ever. 'I haven't got to watch anyone else's back' was the way he described the experience of being a solo artist.

The single "My Star" was scheduled for release in January, while the album was due to come out a month later. The album name was revealed as *Unfinished Monkey Business* with Ian smiling on his King Monkey nickname once more. When it came to his first major interview for well over a year, in the *NME*, the album title, along with the nickname, both of which could easily have been construed in the wrong way, were instantly transposed into something more seemly. From the beginning, it was as if the 'king of the jungle' that is the music business had walked back into everyone's lives.

'King Monkey pads into the vast lobby of Manchester's Palace Hotel, wearing a couple of day's worth of facial fuzz, a snorkel jacket and a broad grin. He's eating lunch: a banana. Tasty. Healthy. Easy. Quintessential King Monkey Cuisine.' From here, it was an effortless display of effortless cool. It was suddenly clear that in all those interviews as a member of the Stone Roses, while he was a leader of sorts, he had, in fact, been held back.

It was also obvious that Ian Brown was vastly more interesting than Liam Gallagher (or John Squire for that matter), and while he hadn't lost any of his self-confidence, he wasn't afraid to look at his own shortcomings, as illustrated by immediately confronting the topic of Reading 1996. But if he had shortcomings he had certainly begun to resurrect himself with this new project where – as the piece was quick to point out – he played bass, guitars, drums, harmonica and trumpet as well as doing the vocals. Also notable was the fact that he'd had a hand in designing the sleeve of *Unfinished Monkey Business*, featuring the extraordinary picture of his gaunt, but determined face staring out into the harsh realities of the post Stone Roses world. It was the defining portrait of King Monkey.

Noel Gallagher must have groaned at the *NME* piece, as Ian, in his first comment, gave 'thanks and praise' that he wasn't in the country when Princess Diana went. His subjects ranged from the hysteria that Diana's death generated, to religion, fox-hunting, Nelson Mandela, Oasis and then, of course, the Stone Roses and the Seahorses.

He wasn't damning about Oasis, whose derivative style – wildly celebrated only a few months before – was now being called into question. His comments suggested that he welcomed comparison in terms of independent bands achieving mainstream success, while also hinting that Oasis were imitators who fell far short of the artistic achievements made by the Stone Roses with just one album – 'For me, they've yet to live up to the name 'Oasis' he said. As for Liam Gallagher, he pointed out that his coked-up lifestyle was separating him from people: this had a Machiavellian quality to it, a whispering aside to his audience – one that said that Liam was the greatest imitator of them *all*.

Real scorn, pretty much, was reserved for John Squire though, as he went into the details of the Stone Roses break-up and discounted the music Squire was now making with the Seahorses ('They're just poor. Anaemic.'). John's ruthless streak re-surfaced once more through tales revealing that Ian had known nothing of John's dissatisfaction with the band and had gone to see him personally to talk about it, only to be turned away from the front door. Ian also described how John had driven past him in his Range Rover, avoiding his eye.

But the *coup de grace* at the end was the inference that John was just too flawed to be upholding the Stone Roses' legacy – 'I don't think the kid ever knew the love people did have for the Roses. Simple. I don't think he ever understood what the Roses were about.' This, preceded by the tales of John's 'cocaine bus' on the *Second Coming* tour and his undermining of not only Reni, but Mani as well, was the knockout blow. John, who was out working the circuit, was seen to be a jumped-up would-be superstar while Ian was still one of the people with a healthy dose of spleen.

The glaring inconsistency in Ian's thinking was obvious in parts too, but almost hilariously so, as he followed his 'John dia-tribes' with the assertion that 'If someone's wronged you and you keep that animosity, it's like a worm, you'll never release it.' What he seemed to be trying to say was that John, his boyhood friend, had wronged him and that he was not the one who should be apologising: the continued silence of John only helped Ian's cause.

XX

"My Star" and *Unfinished Monkey Business* were released in early 1998 to a surprised public. The guitar-led music that had been expected didn't materialise, it was almost a complete reversal of everyone's preconceptions about what an Ian Brown album would sound like: the strongest reminders of the Stone Roses were to be found in the lyrics rather than in the music.

The music itself was stunningly modern. Ian had always boasted the widest musical tastes of all the Roses, all too obvious here on an album which incorporated a range of songs to make an intriguing, sometimes fragmented, post-modern mélange. There was a blissful symbolism for Ian in the fact that some of the final mixing for the album had taken place at the ancient but still fully functioning Chiswick Reach Studios, where his beloved Trojan reggae singles had been recorded. In truth, the album reflected the ancient vibes, but expertly mixed with new music genres on this striking debut.

A track such as "Unfinished", which *is* unfinished, catches the spirit of the lo-fi music that was gaining ground around this time; the single "My Star" is, again, a rather slight song, but with a gorgeous "Dear Prudence"-like guitar hook, the space imagery in the lyrics making it a full-blown 'lo-fi psychedelia' blend of the ancient and the new. The Eastern-sounding lines concocted by Aziz, together with the tabla, give the listener a sensation of journeying, as do Ian's fleeting references to *Star Trek* in the lyrics. All this was accentuated by a promotional video to accompany the single, incorporating some of Ian's own NASA videos, space travel being yet another of Brown's interests. In one interview about the video, he decried the way that the space programme had been overtaken for military means, referenced in 'the new conquistadors' lyrics.

"Ice Cold Cube" has many psychedelic touches also, while Aziz lends it some Eastern flourishes, including an authentic Asiatic guitar solo that, though not perhaps to everyone's taste, demands to be heard. Acoustic guitars are to the fore on "Sunshine" which is a winsome, though not altogether winning track, probably the weakest song on the album, and showing up Ian's lack of singing strength. Most interesting in its striking similarity to later era Syd Barrett, this track sounds almost like an out-take from *The Madcap Laughs*.

In contrast "Corpses In The Mouth" is by far the catchiest song on the album, with a wonderful chorus, great 60s sounding guitars and punchy drums. It also has a wonderful 'dub' bridge with great blasts of harmonica all over it. The track carrying truest echoes of the Roses is "Can't See Me" which dates from the *Second Coming* sessions, but is another rather simplistic song. This was a funk-based tune that couldn't be countenanced by John, and there are striking similarities between it and "Fools Gold". It is fitting then, that Mani and Reni were not only happy to let Ian use it, but appeared on the track as well.

By far the most surprising track, is "Lions", a Rasta-inspired tune, where Ian relates being mystified by the fact that England use the imagery of lions in their flags and in Trafalgar Square, when there have never been any in the country. In one of his synaptic leaps, Ian then makes it into a protest song against the football anthem "Three Lions", despairing at 'grown men crying' at a game of football. The song had no discernible structure and could only be described as hip-hop for the terraces, with a crazy, endlessly repeated chorus.

Music aside, the messages to a former friend in the lyrics threatened to overshadow everything else, and of course, a lot of reviewers couldn't resist homing in on them. As "Ice Cold Cube" was John's old nickname, this song was dissected for John-references such as: 'I just ran into this ice cold cube, thought its ways could freeze me out.' Other gems include: 'What happened to ya, did you change your mind. What happened to ya, we were one of a kind' and 'I've seen you but you've never seen yourself.'

In spite of the lyrics forensics, the reviews were very generous indeed. It was clear that *Unfinished Monkey Business* was never meant to be a great artistic statement or taken as one, as it was presented in a very unpolished, under-produced way. But no one could deny that it was an honest statement by someone who had wiped the board clean and still had something to say. Many of the critics, as well as the public at large, seemed delighted by the unpredictability of Ian Brown producing such a record – and he would later prove to be unpredictable in ways other than music. This attitude was exemplified by the comment in the *NME*'s album review: 'Who'd have thought it? It's Ian Brown and not John Squire whose art emerges smelling of Roses after all. Round One to King Monkey.' In *Q*, the psychedelic tinges and wilful disorder of the album encouraged them to cast him as a latter-day Syd Barrett minus the drugs – 'when it's good, it's very, very good, and when it's bad, it still holds charm.'

In the round of interviews for the album Ian was as happy to look back as forward and he continued to lay the blame for the Roses' break-up at John's door, casting him in a poor light (as well as poking fun at the Seahorses singer Chris Helme for having a 'pseudo Manchester accent'). While he happily recounted the good old Stone Roses days and little else in *Record Collector*, he said a lot more in *Uncut*. Here he called John 'selfish and cowardly', and blamed him for some of his atrocious live singing, pleading that he could hardly hear himself with the guitar hero's amps turned up to 11, again casting shadows on John's version of why he left the band. Recalling the day he was turned away at John's front door, he said: 'Next day, he flies to London for a press conference. Suddenly, he's 'just found' a band, a management deal and a solo deal.' Instead of commenting on Ian's bitterness though, the article concludes by calling him 'The People's Prince' together with Fabiola's Mexican translation of Ian Brown as 'born winner'.

To John's credit, he didn't – and never really has – responded to these provocative comments. In fact, it was his singer Chris Helme who was irritated enough to defend John and himself in the press, wishing Ian would 'fuck off'. Of course, Ian wasn't about to do that, he was back with a vengeance and it wasn't only Squire and the Seahorses that came under attack or ridicule. Among the others he took stabs at were Tim Burgess of the Charlatans, who must have been delighted to read that the whole Brown family laughed about Burgess 'imitating him'; Oasis, who he summed up as 'babies pretending to be the Beatles' and the Verve were described as 'miserable.' Ian made most of these comments just before his first solo public appearance at London's Virgin Megastore, a unique little event during which Ian became store DJ for an hour, meeting people and signing autographs. Here he laughed about the Tim Burgess quote with fans before announcing that he would be playing Glastonbury in the summer, whilst making a careful note not only of the number of people who were there, but also the warmth that came from them.

Perhaps this sense of affection for Ian influenced his mood when interviewed by *Q* in February, as real warmth now seemed to be emanating from him too. Rather than an image of Ian with the simian look, the magazine carried a picture of him smiling broadly for the *Famous Last Words* feature on the back page and his responses conveyed not inconsiderable charm. His most unpleasant characteristic was summed up as 'I can't stop talking and it drives people mad. What can I do though?' before quoting William Blake, and some of the dialogue from *Citizen Kane*. He said he feared only God and spoke lovingly of Fabiola (whom he'd just sent flowers). He displayed his 'common touch' through relating a range of unassuming un-rock star ways such as his demeanor in hotels and in references to his emotions. There was no mention of John at all, unless you counted a passing condemnation of cocaine (no interview from this time seemed to end without Ian thundering against the drug).

Whether it was all planned or not, it worked beautifully and here miraculously, in the February of 1998, was Ian back in the public eye, undoubtedly a figure to be reckoned with, boasting a hit album and "My Star" the first of three solo hit singles. He was, above all, looking forwards. Meanwhile Liam and Noel Gallagher had topped the *NME* polls – as Dickheads Of The Year.

Ian's profile was further enhanced by his measured contribution to a debate about the still-young Labour government, solidifying his still-rock 'n' roll-rebel image. Tony Blair had relentlessly and cynically feted the music business (including a high-profile interview with the *NME*) prior to his election, proffering a youthful image that insidiously merged with the Britpop bands to create the chimera of 'Cool Britannia'. When his draconian policies revealed themselves the *NME* got their revenge in their fabled 'Ever Had The Feeling You've Been Cheated' issue. A host of rock luminaries were asked for a reaction to the new government – a host which included Ian but not, of course, the guest at one of Blair's parties, one N. Gallagher. Ian's reply made clear his sympathy for the young, poor and working people. He neatly dodged the Gallagher-baiting 'Should Pop Stars Be Going To Number 10?' question by invoking the name of Bob Marley, who, as Ian now pointedly reminded us, had let the politicians come to *him*.

A small report in the press relating Ian Brown's charge for a public order offence on February 13th showed he might just still have a knack for getting in the public eye for the wrong reasons, but overall media coverage was positive at this point. And besides, in comparison to Liam Gallagher, who seemed to be involved in antisocial behaviour of one form or another on a weekly basis, Ian's sporadic misdemeanours paled into insignificance.

In March, Ian played his first solo gig, following appearances on *TFI Friday* and *Top Of The Pops*, with the latter harking back to Ian's piss-taking appearance with the Roses during the publicity for "Fools Gold". This time around the antics amounted to the drummer playing a carton of eggs, which were then either smashed or thrown at a blown-up image of Ian. Brown had also been advertised as star DJ at the Blue Note club in London, a charity event for the *Big Issue*. The club-goers were reported to be astonished to see him appear with a four-piece band, playing "Can't See Me", "Corpses" and "My Star" as well as a cover of Jimi Hendrix's "Little Wing". It was a low-key return to live performance that worked well.

Throughout this time he was building up to Glastonbury, with festival gigs also now confirmed at T In The Park and V98, where, incidentally, the Seahorses were to join Ian and his band on the bill. In a faint echo of the Roses gigs of old, in the railway arches, five small shows were to be announced on Radio One, but only just prior to them taking place. He seemed happy to be playing Glastonbury and as he put it 'reaching people who've never heard of me'. His 'in touch with the people' image was seen to be intact when it was revealed that the third single release, the introductory track from *Unfinished Monkey Business*, "Under The Paving Stone", was to be a remixed version sent to Ian by a fan.

The air of frantic activity around the solo album suggests perhaps that Ian wanted to make up for all those wasted years of the *Second Coming* era, but he clearly hadn't yet learnt the lessons of diplomacy and reserve. In an April issue of *Melody Maker* he was installed as that week's singles reviewer. Among his cheery responses, he revealed that he'd taken up salsa with Fabiola and had spent five hours on the dance floor with her. All pretty harmless stuff, until he came up with a comment that caused a storm of protest.

Reviewing a single by Divine Comedy, taken from a tribute to renowned (and gay) songsmith Noël Coward by various artists, Ian stunned the *MM* journalist by seeming to criticise homosexuality, showing no sign of the firm grasp of history he usually displayed. Alluding, rather vaguely yet disparagingly to Noël Coward and Danny La Rue ('I don't trust that shit, me.') he was pounced on by the journalist and Ian burst out: 'Violence comes from Romans, Nazis, Greeks – they were all homosexual. And I've got gay friends that will back me up. I just think Noël Coward is an old tosser who got on with the Queen Mother... ' The rest of the thesis degenerated into strong men versus strong women dialectics, until the journalist moved things swiftly on, no doubt aware that this was going to cause great offence.

And it did. Neil Tennant (who had compiled the CD), Danny La Rue's producer and others went public with their anger, but more importantly, so did a lot of readers of who wrote in to complain. It was egg on the face time. Ian had *seemed* to let go of his grasp of history: he surely knew that the Nazis had persecuted homosexuals for a start! The terseness of the statement that came from his management suggested that he realised he'd got a bit carried away with his rantings, and in the same statement mentioned that he was generally tolerant and had gay friends himself. He also referred to his conspicuous support for the Anti-Clause 28 movement in the past, as well as letters he'd received from university professors backing him up by confirming that there had been homosexual power structures in all the civilisations he named.

He was probably relieved to have had a few trips abroad planned at this point, visiting Fabiola in New York, playing a couple of TV shows in France, and re-visiting Sweden and Denmark to do some warm-up gigs. There was a great response wherever he went, with Reni hats bobbing in front of him again; at one gig, Ian swapped his shades for a corduroy jacket belonging to a fan, prompting a shower of fashion items to cascade onto the stage for Ian to try on. There was also a trip to Jamaica covered by the *NME*, though this seemed to be little more than a mission to hang out with the locals and smoke the strongest weed possible.

At the end of May, he revealed his discovery that Reni *hadn't* been on the "Can't See Me" track at all: a mix-up of tapes meant it was breakbeat samples that Mani had used, not Reni playing as had been assumed. He was happy, however, for Reni to claim royalties, even though Ian was still in some financial difficulty himself – having made £70,000 from the album apparently, but owing the Inland Revenue £80,000. He also seemed to mellow a little towards John around this time, saying in one interview 'I wish him well'. Surprisingly it was Mani (who he'd always got on well with) that he had a slight falling-out with at this point, over the girl that Mani was seeing of whom, Ian said mysteriously, 'he had had some scene with.' While he was working hard – as he announced yet more music that he was working on – there were also signs that he was becoming unpredictable again.

The furore over Ian's comments on gays had still not quite blown itself out when he returned from his various trips, even reaching some of the national newspapers, and he was interviewed in the *Melody Maker* again in June, on this subject alone. He was described as 'worried, guarded and extremely paranoid' at the beginning of the article though he appeared to be anything but, as, instead of making a clear official-sounding statement, he talked discursively and openly about the whole issue. He argued that he had been talking about homosexual power structures recorded throughout history (which the *Melody Maker* confirmed) and not homosexuality *per se*. The furore was clearly on a par with David Bowie's 'Nazi' salute at Victoria Station (and Bowie had been 'flirting' with right-wing ideas – even discussing them with his black musicians) and in the end, the article seemed to be straining to say this-has-all-been-a-storm-in-a-teacup-really. In actual fact, Ian had considered suing the *Melody Maker* over the whole thing and this article was clearly the calling of a truce between the two: the pay-off was shown at the bottom of the page beneath the article: ' "Can't See Me" is out on June 8 on Polydor.'

But arguably Ian was lucky this didn't derail his career in some way. In early '97 the lead singer of Kula Shaker, Crispian Mills, found himself talking about the glamour of Nazism, stating: 'I'd love to have big flaming swastikas onstage.' This silly comment was one that Mills just couldn't shake off, with other bands almost universally deriding him, their second album proving a disaster and ultimately, their career was sabotaged by eighteen months of consistently bad press.

But, instead of having to continually defend himself, the summer climaxed for Ian with well-received appearances at three festivals; Glastonbury, V98 and T In The Park. Quite remarkably there were rapturous reactions to each appearance – and this, the man who'd had people shielding their ears at Reading two years earlier. The enthusiasm for Aziz Ibrahim, too, was gratifying for Ian, who was constantly praising the guitarist himself. At the latter gigs, where John and the Seahorses were also playing, there was plenty of speculation about the pair bumping into each other, even though they weren't playing on the same day. On these occasions Ian reverted to putting the boot in. 'He might be intimidated by me. I don't trust people that are intimidated by me. I want to know why they're intimidated. I love people. I always felt that way, and people get on his tits. That's the difference between us.' The tide was beginning to turn on John, however, with or without Ian's comments. One T In The Park reviewer dismissed the Seahorses by failing to mention John's guitar playing at all, merely wondering what he would have thought of the huge picture of Ian, clearly visible from the stage.

Also during this summer, Mick Middles records a curious incident where Ian encounters, of all people, Gareth Evans once again. Evans was now living in Knutsford, Cheshire, a location that often rings a bell with 'back-page' newspaper readers, being a popular area for Premiership footballers to buy their houses. Evans, now fittingly ensconced in the world of golf, was patronising a new course while also managing a hardcore Liverpool punk band.

With Middles in tow, Evans found himself transplanted to Lymm, Cheshire for a quick meeting with a builder. A resident of the town, one Ian Brown, was not out promoting his album and single, as might have been expected, but happened in fact, to be at home for a change. Spotting them from an upstairs window he knocked the glass a couple of times, Evans finally recognised him, and in no time at all, Ian was down the stairs and standing in front of the astonished pair, offering his hand and saying it was great to see Evans. According to the story, Ian was hardly looking like a pop star, but stood rather disconsolately in front of his ex-council house, saying the odd hello to neighbours walking by with their shopping. He talked about his new manager, Noel Walters, whom Evans knew well from the Manchester club circuit, and mentioned John Squire. He also disclosed, with some uneasiness, details of the dire financial straits that he had been in, thanks to the unfavourable Geffen deal that still hung over him like a dark cloud.

Middles describes here a character emanating bitterness and resentment, but, remarkably, none of it directed towards Evans. It was as if seeing an old face from his past had released certain feelings, as the pressures of a new fame built up around him. It seemed he was now feeling somehow a prisoner to his fame. And as abruptly as he had bounded down to see them, before they could make their exit, he turned on his heel and disappeared back into the house.

XXI

So, going into the autumn of 1998, the fortunes of Ian and John appeared to have well and truly reversed. Ian, having returned stronger than he had ever been, was revelling in his new position as a solo star. He had a settled band, and in Aziz, a much-valued (and now much-praised) guitarist as well as a great friend who was perfect for Ian: 'He doesn't drink, he doesn't take drugs and he chats.' Ian had played the festivals with shorter slots as he wasn't confident that he had a full set list, but after another bout of song-writing made the announcement of his first full-scale solo tour in November 1998.

As for the Seahorses, it was now horribly clear that they'd had only a short-term appeal and the link to Oasis, with whom John still hobnobbed, no longer held the kudos it had done initially. Despite supporting Oasis and the Manic Street Preachers, (who had themselves achieved public and critical acclaim after supporting an earlier Oasis tour) the Seahorses were clearly never going to become the same kind of headline act. The line-up had never really been settled – they were already on their third drummer – and cracks began to appear in the relationship between John and Chris Helme.

But Ian's time-honoured confidence, now displayed again wherever he went – on stage and in interviews – was hiding a significant worry. The tiny news item that had appeared in February alluding to a public order offence, that had taken place on a plane, and was not as trifling as might have been supposed. The incident, largely dismissed by Ian in interviews, had in fact been taken very seriously indeed by the powers that be, and despite three appeals by John Kennedy a date had been set for Ian's trial in October. The press had kept tabs on it, but the general impression given was that no one seemed to think Ian had any serious cause for concern.

Similar offences were committed by Liam Gallagher and Axl Rose at around the same time as Ian, all of which were part of a seemingly new phenomenon, exclusive to celebrities, and dubbed 'air rage'. Gallagher and his band (though he was the ringleader) were involved in a very ugly incident during which they threatened the crew and passengers on the flight. Liam was also charged with assault on a fan a few days later. Axl Rose didn't wait to get into the air to unleash his rage in a brawl with airport security guards. The attendant publicity around these events wasn't going to help Ian's case at all.

On Friday October 23rd, Ian stood at Manchester Magistrate's Court to hear his case, which involved a return BA flight to Manchester following a gruelling day in Paris, with Aziz and the rest of the band travelling first class. It appeared that an airhostess, Christine Cooper had come over to Ian thinking he needed serving. On realising that he didn't she motioned with her hand apologetically. Allegedly, Ian took offence at the gesture and became abusive. He was supposed to have said: 'Don't you wave your fucking hands at me. I will chop your fucking hands off.' She then called the captain to whom Ian was also apparently abusive, saying 'Piss off and have a shave.' Also, Ian was alleged to have approached the door of the flight deck as the plane was making its descent, banging on it loudly and causing the pilot to alert ground control at Manchester.

Ian's story was, of course, quite different. He told the court that he had asked her not to wave her hands in 'a dismissive gesture' and that she'd apologised. He did admit to saying 'If you do it again I will chop your hands off' – this was meant to be a joke he claimed, to which she 'smiled at me and kind of tutted and turned away and carried on pushing her trolley.' He also insisted that he had only seen the captain after he'd knocked on the door wanting to make a complaint.

As the testimonies of the airhostess and the captain were read out, complete with all the bad language, things began to look grim for Ian. The fact that he admitted to the threat of chopping off hands – however harmlessly meant – certainly wasn't going to sit well with any judge, and Ian's solicitors couldn't make any of his counter-claims stick. On the last day of the case, Ian's nerves began to show when he lunged for a photographer's camera and shouted: 'Take a picture and I'll take that fucking camera off you.'

This display hardly helped his case either. The tension rose as his lawyer asked the police, who had been waiting for him at Manchester Airport, to clarify the threatening and abusive behaviour that they described in their testimony. They would only say that 'it was his manner'.

When Mani was once asked what he would have been if he hadn't been a member of the Stone Roses he said, unhesitatingly, either a 'drug dealer or a car thief.' This was a not uncommon response for someone recalling a youth in Manchester that, for many, promised either unemployment or stultifying employment. The resulting tearaway spirit, as we have seen, was still very much a part of Ian, but it was nevertheless a fearful shock as the judge announced that he'd been found guilty of using threatening behaviour with intent to cause harassment, alarm or distress and was sentenced to be jailed for four months. Ian immediately asked for the sentence to be suspended for the sake of his two children, but this was refused, though an appeal hearing was granted – he left the court shouting 'I didn't do it' and was taken away in a police van.

A successful rock singer, aged thirty-five and a father of two, Ian must have thought he had avoided the destiny of so many wild Manchester teenagers, but here he was in a police van, possibly bound for Strangeways prison. His first stop was at Risley Remand Centre. In the holding rooms his assigned jailer greeted his arrival with: 'I can't jail him. I've seen him at the Hacienda, I've seen him at Blackpool.'

Ian was due back in court after the weekend to hear if his appeal had been successful, but for now he was locked up. Straight away he got himself into more trouble for refusing to use the 'sir' title and was promptly put in solitary confinement for 23 hours. On the Sunday night, there was a report of another air rage incident during which a passenger had hit an airhostess with a vodka bottle. There was hardly any point in him going to hear the appeal. Ian now knew he would be made an example of, and was definitely on his way to Strangeways.

In retrospect, it is difficult not to feel sympathy for Ian over the severity of the sentence. Whatever the truth of the hotly disputed words uttered, he had by no means been violent, as Liam Gallagher and Axl Rose had been. Gallagher, incidentally, had been merely banned by the airline while Rose 'fessed up and paid a fine'. The inconsistencies in dealing with such incidents is reinforced by the case of the normally mild-mannered Peter Buck of REM, allegedly possessed by air rage later on, in 2002. This colourfully reported and often unintentionally hilarious incident featured a rampaging ('I am REM!') Peter Buck in fights with two members of the cabin crew, and a yoghurt carton apparently wielded as a weapon, resulting in an upended breakfast trolley, which Buck had tried to insert a CD into. Leaving the comic aspect aside, it was an incident that could potentially have been extremely dangerous, while Ian's never really was. Moreover, Peter Buck's high-powered legal team not only wheeled on a host of star witnesses such as his fellow band members and Bono, they also rather ingeniously came up with 'non-insane automatism' as a reason for Buck's behaviour. Contrast this with Ian's turning up on his own at the Magistrate's Court, dressed in jeans and windcheater, with his pudding bowl haircut and cocky gait, trying to tell the court in his own words what really happened. Whatever the truth of it, Ian remains convinced, even today, that it was his ever-faithful 'attitude' that got him sent to prison.

When his conviction was confirmed, along with the cancellation of the November tour, Aziz spoke out against it, emphasising the opinion that Ian was 'being made an example of' in the light of the recent air rage incidents. He said: 'Ian didn't swear, he just told off the stewardess as your ma would say it. He was just being cheeky, 'cos he's always been a bit cheeky.' Asked how Ian would cope with prison, he said: 'He's a tough cookie with a strong mind. I dunno how it will affect him, but he's already been hard done by.'

Strangeways Prison in Southall Road had always been and remained a place that could inspire a chill, and the light-hearted headlines complete with Smiths references trotted out by the music press in their coverage ('Strangeways Here Ian Comes') wasn't going to make it any less grisly for Ian. Strangeways, built in the nineteenth century, is one of the ugliest of all the Victorian prisons, its Mordor-like tower dominating the Salford skyline and causing passers-by to shudder involuntarily. Strangeways is 'celebrated' as historically having had the most ruthlessly efficient 'executioners by hanging' among their staff – one pair killing an inmate within 7 seconds of being pitched out of his cell and on to the gallows. The executions had all taken place on B Wing and many of the guards have since reported the ghost of an executioner, one John Ellis, who had committed suicide in 1932, walking with his small briefcase towards his office. And B Wing was where Ian was headed, classed as a Category A prisoner, alongside lifers such as Dr Harold Shipman – who Ian claims to have spotted while there – and all for a verbal offence. His lawyer only later informed Ian that he should have been a Category D prisoner (meaning those who can reasonably be trusted in open conditions) and one can only speculate at the logic of such a ludicrous system where someone like Ian can be jailed alongside Category A prisoners – those whose escape would be highly dangerous to the public.

Ian had found it difficult enough to sleep at Risley, with the cold, rough blanket that made him itch and the moans that he heard from the other cells. Strangeways, however, was an altogether more intimidating place, with the inmates (and guards) potentially more threatening to a pop star than any other prisoner, through jealousy and/or contempt for his celebrity.

Some of the offenders, though, may well have remembered Ian speaking out in support of the protesters at Strangeways in 1990. Tension had been mounting steadily, in those days, over the appalling prison conditions – if overcrowding, intimidation and beatings by prison officers weren't bad enough, they were forced to live in what has been called a 'sewer'. After the beatings of two prisoners, one in full view of other inmates in the chapel, a protest spilled out onto the roof. Though *all* of the press reported hysterically in the first days, of kangaroo courts, castrations and hangings, (none of which was true) Ian saw the protest for what it really was and spoke loudly and clearly about it at the time. This outcry stood him in good stead now, bringing him allies beyond those who were simply Stone Roses fans.

His first two allies however were not in this vein. The first was the governor, who walked into his cell declaring that his nineteen-year-old son was a fan of *Unfinished Monkey Business*. He told him to get writing and ordered the guard to get him a pen, which, according to Ian, the guard threw at him. His second ally was a 'big Somalian kid' whom Ian had met in 1990 – he had given him two free tickets to the Spike Island concert. The Somalian said: 'Ian Brown, I owe you one. If anyone gives you any trouble, come and let me know.'

He had no real trouble after that, though the potential threat was always there. When he sat down for his first meal at Kirkham he had received abuse, but an ecstasy dealer that Ian knew from 1988 came to his defence there. In Strangeways, he was to find that the biggest threat to him came from the 'screws', who were all too conscious of who he was, tried to prejudice inmates against him and treated him shabbily. First of all, they said they'd lost his belongings: face cream, £80 and his house keys. When he questioned them, they said 'Are you saying we stole it, Brown?' He was strip-searched seven times in twenty-one days and claims he actually had more grief from them than other inmates, goading him to react and 'earn' more time inside. When, for example, he received his large amounts of mail they would loudly call out 'Brown, Brown, Brown, Brown' to wind up other inmates.

His prison mates were often a source of amusement, as well as gratifying him with their warmth, which included little presents of food, newspapers and so on. Ian's description of the general excitement at his arrival is hilarious: 'So I get to the jail and they all know I'm coming cos they've heard it on the radio. I get taken down to my cell and I know they're all craning for a look. Suddenly, the cell door opens and I'm like, having a piss. And I can here this lad shouting 'I can see his penis!' On one occasion, an inmate said 'you can't be in Strangways and not get stoned' and so, ever the rebel, Ian had a smoke of weed one day – even though he risked getting into serious trouble and extending his stay.

Ian had five 'pad mates', every one of them a 'smackhead'. Drugs were rife and Ian estimated that ninety per cent of the inmates were on heroin or crack. – 'I saw more heroin or crack in there than I've seen in the last ten years in the music business.' He was constantly offered both in prison – smoking heroin was renowned, he was told, for 'taking the walls away' – but instead Ian was one of those who helped carry the kids back to their beds after passing out. The desolation caused by hard drugs was not the only kind of grimness to be found in Strangeways, a notoriously violent place, even for a prison. Ian was to see or hear pool hall beatings and knife slashings, petty and major feuds all exploding within these walls.

'I saw a kid hit another kid in the ear with two pool balls in a sock, and his ear came up the size of a dinner plate. Through a crack in my cell door, I saw prison officers running down the wings with proper baseball bats to fill someone in... I saw a kid who'd beat an old lady up and her picture had been in the Evening News, and the screw put it on the table and pointed at him... They had him on the floor bouncing the door on his head, and he was just limp, and they dragged him off to the medical wing. It was genuinely sickening some of the violence I saw.'

Ian probably prided himself on being worldly-wise but he was certainly shocked out of any complacency here. One thing that struck him was the helplessness of so many of the convicts. 'The jails are full of kids from kids' homes. You're 16 years old and you're out on the street. How you going to fend for yourself at 16 if you've not had an education? You're going to turn to crime. There were kids in court with a vest and a pair of ripped tracksuit bottoms, and I'm thinking, "Fancy coming into court dressed like that". It's only when I'm locked up that I think that's all they've got. It's really sad because it's the same as it would have been 150 years ago.'

The daily regime, which had changed very little in 150 years, had been designed to produce some degree of corrective behaviour of course. At first, Ian spent 23 hours of the day locked up. Every morning the prisoners would be woken at 7.30 for breakfast and were allowed half an hour 'exercise time' in the yard and half an hour 'association time' during which they could take a shower, play pool or watch TV. Ian was happy to take up some of his time signing autographs for inmates and their girlfriends and he even rang some of the girlfriends while their partners stood excitedly beside him. With Christmas on the horizon, he also found himself signing Christmas cards for their mothers!

When Ian could get away from all the requests (in the first week his cell was always full of visitors), he developed a strict exercise regime in prison. Before he went inside, he had been doing 30 press-ups and 50 sit-ups a day. Within six weeks, he had worked this up to 500 sit-ups and 400 press-ups – the metal bed he had in his cell was perfect for sit-ups. He read voraciously and found particular inspiration in Marcus Garvey, the black activist. He also wrote lyrics, taking the governor's advice seriously, as well as writing to his loved ones. Ian was obliged to do some kind of work there too and was given the job of putting screws into electric components for cookers, and, while he refused to become a milk monitor at school, in prison he didn't have the luxury of choice and was made a bread monitor.

Ian quickly decided to 'convert to Islam' once he saw what was on offer in terms of food. It had been so bad that a present of an orange from one inmate was almost too much for him: he stared at the orange for half an hour 'as if it was a Christmas hamper.' The guards scoffed as he protested his new-found 'faith' but he was allowed to turn down the 'dog food pies' and had lentils, chickpeas and on Fridays, a chicken curry – with ' about two pieces of chicken in it.'

If the food didn't sustain him, plenty of other things did as he passed two months in Strangeways, at the end of which he would be eligible for parole. Among all the contact from his loved ones was a letter, regular as clockwork, every three days in fact, from Reni. Ian was also touched to receive a letter from Kevin Rowland of Dexy's Midnight Runners. Rowland had himself been convicted, of shoplifting, and had been shaken up by prison: though they'd never met, he sent a letter of support that Ian prized highly.

Deeper, older feelings were stirred though, when a package arrived for him one day in December. He opened it up to discover a box of Maltesers from John Squire, the present that they had sent each other every Christmas since they were young boys up until the Stone Roses split. One can only guess – though Ian has never elaborated – on the emotion he felt, with parole approaching, as he read John's tiny note: 'I still love you. I hope you're out before Christmas.' If ever an act belied the reputation of John as being cold and calculating this was it, the closest to a rapprochement that the two men had ever got. And yet, even then, Ian still couldn't quite forgive John, sending his thanks through a third party.

The week before Christmas, it was (erroneously) reported that Ian would be released on December 22nd. There had also been an announcement of a tour in February, but he sent a press release from his cell: 'Due to the fact that I'm being detained here at the Strangeways Hotel (bed and breakfast and evening meal not recommended) the November tour had been rescheduled without my knowledge. I don't wish to disappoint anybody, but upon release I intend to start working on a new album – at this stage tentatively titled 'From The Inside'... Thanks to everyone who has written to me here at Strangeways. Love and peace and joy for '99.'

Ian has said of his time in prison that 'all I ever got was love off the inmates. And hate was all I ever got from the screws.' When Ian's parole came through, the 'screws' had to stand back while he said goodbye to all the friends he had made, many of whom risked another twenty-one days inside by rushing up to Ian and hugging him. This more than anything, drove him to say later: 'the lads were beautiful, there's an honesty there. They were criminals but they were honest.'

It was Christmas Eve. All prison inmates are normally released before 8.45 a.m. To avoid press attention, the prison decided to let Ian go at 6 a.m. His belongings were given to him in a black bin-liner and as he stepped out on to Southall Road one lone photographer stood waiting outside. The release was so early that there was no one to meet him as he came out of prison either. He was determined to go for a walk and as he went on his way said to the photographer that he'd been waiting for the walk a long time, before stopping at a nearby newsagent that was just opening. The shopkeeper was surprised, no doubt, to see a photographer accompanying the man with the bin-liner, buying 20 Benson and Hedges cigarettes.

Ian set off on his walk, into the centre of town. As he had done when he returned from his travels, he got into the city centre just as it was waking up. He was back from perhaps his strangest journey of all. He had walked two miles by the time he got to Deansgate train station, and his feet ached, unused to such exercise after two months in prison. He boarded a train that took him to his parents' house in Cheshire, where he would soon be seeing his children, Frankie and Casey again. In the evening, he took his parents for a meal where, after the dodgy prison food he satisfied a constant craving he had been having for a large steak. Now, finally, he felt he was back.

XXII

Within a few days of his release, Ian was reunited with Fabiola. Less than a week after sharing his life with heroin and crack addicts in Strangeways, he was lying on a beach in Mexico with his girl, enjoying a short break before starting work on a new album. He had been coming up with ideas all the time he was inside and although he'd changed his mind about the 'From The Inside' title, he was keen to get moving after weeks of relative inactivity. Aziz had been very busy, spending the duration of Ian's sentence writing and producing the music for a Playstation game, as well as starting work on his solo album (which was to feature Mani) – but he was more than available to play for Ian!

Also, while Ian was incarcerated, the Happy Mondays had announced they were reforming, though without guitarist Mark Day. Nearly ten years on, the second leading 'Madchester' band had settled their differences – in other words, Shaun Ryder and Bez had reconciled – and this rather unlikely event raised a lot of the speculation as to whether Ian and John might do the same, resulting in a reincarnation of the Stone Roses.

These rumours were doubtless encouraged by the fact that John's Seahorses disbanded in the February following Brown's release. Even as the *Melody Maker* begged the question on their front page, as to whether Gay Dad were about to kickstart a Britpop revival (!) the Seahorses became yet another Britpop casualty, though their voluntary split spared them the ignominy of being dropped, as Menswear and many others had been. There had been rumblings of discontent for some time and the official statement – 'general divergence of musical directions' – was a dead giveaway to what everyone suspected – a major falling out between John Squire and Chris Helme.

Helme was mild-mannered about it at first, saying that John was 'particular about what he wants to write and who he wants to write with', but he later admitted to a significant 'personality clash' with some bitterness. The signs were that John had frozen out Helme, just as he had done Ian, but John, as usual, kept a stony silence while he began looking into other projects.

Meanwhile, as well as starting sessions for his new album, Ian was gradually moving out into the public eye again in his inimitable style. On January 24th, he made a surprise appearance at the London Astoria, joining in UNKLE's live show, after working with them on their "Be There" single. This was an entirely spontaneous decision: he was backstage, his voice came over the PA on tape at first, and then he strode out on to the stage to a rapturous reception. UNKLE mainman, James Lavelle, was effusive in his praise of Ian: 'I thought it went great. I was really happy. It's that kind of Ian Brown charm. He's an icon. There's something different, more than just music about him'.

This unassuming appearance may well have been the moment that Ian moved into his truly individual iconic stage, removed from the Stone Roses. The *NME* excitedly reported the low-key event as if Ian Brown had been on stage for hours. Brown also spoke up for the first time now, confiding his despair of Mani playing (if only for a very brief period) with a Stone Roses tribute band called 'The Complete Stone Roses', while celebrating the Happy Mondays reunion. He went on to make it clear that he was still most certainly the type to bear a grudge, not only against the people who put him away, but also against the *Melody Maker*, whom he accused of setting up an inflammatory situation over the homosexual furore. He said that he'd received a letter in prison 'from the kid who did that original interview' admitting it all, that 'he was told by his paper to write the piece as if there was a confrontation – y'know, do it this way, make out he's bad'. The 'kid' to whom he referred would have been Ian Watson, the Features Editor, who mentioned he didn't know what Brown was talking about: 'I didn't send him a letter. Maybe someone else did and he's getting mixed up, but it wasn't me.'

Ian was next seen sitting happily at the Brit awards where he was nominated in the Best British Male Solo Artist category – normally Ian wouldn't have been seen dead at such an event, but his new record company, Polydor, were keen for him to make an appearance, so he went along to thank the people that had worked hard for him. Though the award went to Robbie Williams, Ian was quite unbothered, especially as he got to see Stevie Wonder in the flesh! He revealed some new projects, including a collaboration with 808 State, who had left a tape for him to listen to at Strangeways Prison Reception. Showing he could airily forget grudges as well, Ian told his enemies of the week before at the *Melody Maker* that he was intending to write a book on his experiences in jail.

He planned to call it "Four Moons", symbolising the four months that he would have served, had he completed the full sentence: 'this book is my only chance to redress the bullshit that's been written about me, about prison and stuff. The things they said I did, and put me in jail for, I didn't do. And because I don't own my own national newspaper, there's nothing I can do except this.'

Just as he announced this intention, he heard that he was banned from British Airways for life. They even wrote to him to confirming and explaining their decision: 'We want to make it clear that we will not tolerate behaviour which puts the comfort and safety of our passengers and crew in danger.' This was a poser because Ian had been planning to reschedule his February tour – now that he had a criminal record, he would have to apply for special visas to play concerts in certain countries.

Ian was beginning to feel victimised. He told the *NME* directly: 'The *NME* and all these papers, they're supposed to be representing the youth which in turn is anti-establishment and all, yet these papers are calling me a hooligan and such. They're taking the words of the captain of the plane and using them against me.'

While Ian had a keen sense of injustice, the press were clearly not going to pay it that much attention. There was a sense that he was not being taken seriously and the good work that he had done with *Unfinished Monkey Business* was somewhat undermined by the loutish behaviour that led to the spell in jail. The *Melody Maker* put him in among their '50 Maddest People In Rock' while the *NME*, creating a putative football team for England – full of rock stars – had Ian down as a 'squad player' only.

The parlous state of British music at the time, post-Brit-pop and now post-Verve (the most recent indie band to have been championed by the press) meant that there was exaggerated interest in the reforming of the Happy Mondays – a pretty cynical and obvious exercise in money-making, hardly constituting the promise of overwhelming music. The first single release, predictably enough, turned out to be a version of Thin Lizzy's "The Boys Are Back In Town". Nevertheless, the Monday's release together with the totally unfounded rumours of the Stone Roses reforming, led the press to talk about a baggy revival – when only a few short weeks earlier they had spoken about a Britpop revival!

Though neither Ian nor John (nor the other Roses for that matter) had any interest at all in reforming the Stone Roses, there was however, an indication of some mellowing in Ian's attitude to John. In one interview, he said: 'John's a great guitar player. One of the greatest. I don't want John playing dull or flat songs. I don't associate his playing with those feelings. I'd like him to come out with a great record again.'

In March he announced his first 'official' live appearance since coming out of prison. One of the acts of the moment – Welsh band Catatonia – were taking a leaf out of the Stone Roses' book by putting on a huge show in their home area. Ian, bumping into lead singer Cerys Matthews in a bar, agreed to support her band at Port Talbot, in front of 30,000 people. 'I'm playing out of respect for Cerys and Catatonia,' he said, 'Putting on a show for 30,000 in your home area is something I can relate to.' Before that, though, was planned an impromptu gig in Osaka, Japan, the first recorded instance of Ian playing a Stone Roses song – an encore of the first Silvertone single "Sally Cinnamon" – while a solo star, and leaving the audience stunned.

March also saw Aziz premiering his first solo material at a fashion show in aid of the Stephen Lawrence Trust. Ian wasn't there, but Aziz's band included Andy Rourke and Mike Joyce from the Smiths, and the last song on the set was a version of Ian's "My Star". Though he was working with Ian throughout this period, the hyperactive Aziz still somehow found time for this new band, also to be called Aziz

Ian got together with Aziz to play some warm-up shows for the Catatonia support slot in Ireland. This mini-tour started off on a sour note in Cork where he noticed that a poster advertising the gigs had the silhouette of a plane over a picture of the singer, an unfortunate, though possibly unintentional reminder of the jail sentence over air rage.

Despite this, the show and all the others went very well: Ian shocked everyone first by including a version of Michael Jackson's "Thriller" in the set, and then amazed everyone still further by attempting to replicate some of Jackson's high notes. It was a choice of cover which one would have considered unthinkable for an ex-Stone Roses singer, but Ian was beginning to pull away from guitar band orthodoxies, as symbolised in the multi-talented, multi-cultural band that he had now assembled.

This consisted of Aziz, percussionist Inder Matheru (formerly of Fun^Da^Mental), bass player Sylvan Richardson and Simon Wolstencroft, last seen with the Fall, and now making his reappearance in Ian's story. Ian's eclectic tastes were perfectly reflected by this outfit and he was justly proud of Aziz, who was gathering a fearsome reputation with guitarists everywhere and had impressed everyone in Cork by playing the "Little Wing" solo with his teeth. Ian hinted that he was seeing new possibilities with this band, and if the press and public were expecting him to try and relive the old days, there was no suggestion at all of this in what he was saying: 'We're the untouchables. By the end of the year, nobody will come near us.'

As for the Catatonia gig, it soon became clear that it would have been wiser for Ian to have pulled out of that one altogether. Though the band were, at that time, receiving vast amounts of coverage, it was, frankly, arguable whether their rather limited talents really merited it. Significantly, the attention seemed to be mostly based around their feisty and glamorous lead singer, and when Ian turned up at the Port Talbort gig, dressed in a leopard skin style top, he almost looked as if he was trying to compete with Matthews in the glamour stakes! With Bjorn Again also play-ing, the gig was hardly a prestigious one to have been a part of, and Ian didn't stand a chance with the press either, who slated his performance while salivating over the headliners, for whom this was their 'Spike Island'.

Ian's next live appearance was at the V9 festival in Staf-fordshire, taking place in August. Here, rather than be billed with a guitar band, Ian chose to appear in the dance tent, supporting Orbital – a clear signal of the kind of direction he was taking. Though Orbital were the headliners, only fans shouting his name could be heard, ten minutes before he was due to go on. Then he went and surprised everyone by appearing not with a band at all, but with a DJ and percussionist, delivering a spirited set that led the *NME* to claim, 'the road to recovery starts here.'

At this point Tim Burgess of the Charlatans re-ignited a long-standing 'row' between him and Ian Brown. Burgess, still smarting over remarks Ian had made months before, now came out with a curious 'payback' comment, intimating that he knew for a fact Ian was 'desperate for the Roses to get back together' while on the other hand 'Squire doesn't want anything to do with him.' It seems unlikely that there was much truth in this, considering the direction Ian's music was going in, and as John Squire was appar-ently putting a new band together.

Ian's new musical direction was now being talked about, though it was never fully acknowledged that he was, arguably, a lot more in tune with what was going on in the music scene than most of the people who wrote about it. As the end of 1999 approached, Ian's sometime bete-noire, the *Melody Maker*, was experiencing a steep decline in sales, and this 'first paper of the popular music scene' was actually approaching its final year of publication.

When Ian had first gone into music the 'inkies' had been an integral part of the scene and the general consensus amongst them was that guitar-orientated music held a definite superiority over other forms of music. As the Millennium approached, with the internet widespread and music technology advancing at a rate of knots, the role of rock journalism began to change, undoubtedly losing some of its previously held power and influence. It seemed the music press could no longer talk up one guitar band after another in the opinion-forming way it had done for years, nor could it presume that the majority of music oriented kids wanted to hear guitars in their music.

While the inkies had gone from championing Oasis to the Verve right through to Richard Ashcroft, they chose almost completely to ignore a whole genre of music that was becoming increasingly influential and acquiring a huge fan base – dance music. This was the era of Ministry of Sound and superstar DJs like Jeff Mills, Carl Cox and Fatboy Slim, all of which had strong echoes of the baggy scene, with ecstasy back in fashion again. The coverage that dance music did get, often served to alienate their readership, and besides, the type of people who were into this kind of music weren't going to sit around reading about it in a paper anyway. And while the whole dance scene appeared to be taking over, there was a corresponding dwindling in popularity of the kind of indie guitar music from which Ian and the Stone Roses had originally sprung.

While it was noted in both the *NME* and *Melody Maker* that Ian's music was 'dance-orientated', he was most definitely not given credit for being the one artist in British music at that time who could claim not only to be bridging the gap between 'baggy' and the post-Millennium rave culture, but also to hold a genuine appeal for both the remaining indie crowd, to whom he was an icon, *as well as* the new breed, who appreciated his dance sensibilities. The inclusion of covers such as "Thriller" was a piece of post-modern irony that could only be classed as a bonus. What is surprising, in retrospect, is the fact that no one predicted just how successful the next Ian Brown album would be.

The build-up to the release began in October with a daring promotion in the form of a whirlwind one-*day* tour. With his percussionist, Inder Matheru and a DJ, the event started in the afternoon at Edinburgh's Liquid Rooms, where Brown premiered a couple of songs, "Love Like A Fountain" and "Getting High".

Using a plane to get from there to Bristol and cars thereafter, he also visited Newport, Cheltenham, Stoke and finally Manchester, at 12.30 am. The response to all the two-song sets was amazing and he was embraced by fans throughout the tour, which was, in fact, not exclusively promotional as proceeds went towards Youth Club UK, an organisation which helps provide facilities for young people.

As if not to be outdone by the attention Ian was getting, announcements from John Squire and Reni appeared simultaneously. John was putting a new band together with the ex-Verve bassist, Simon Jones, to be called, rather ominously, Reluctance, though this was an improvement on John's original suggestion of Skunk Works, after a Californian-based weapons systems plant where the U2 spy plane was developed. Reni had been working on a host of projects since leaving the Roses and, with a demo ready to take to a record company, he was looking for a 'clean-living band' with 'no dopers.'

In November, Ian returned fully to the spotlight, announcing a new single, "Love Like A Fountain" as well as the album, out on the 8th, the title of which was no longer 'From The Inside' but *Golden Greats*. His first solo London gig was to take place at the Conway Hall, acting as a warm-up for the tour, and 30,000 balloons bearing the album cover image were released at Old Trafford, just before the match between United and Leicester City. This was a shrewd piece of Manchester-linked marketing and one wonders whether John, a season-ticket holder, was attending that day.

At the same time, Ian gave his first full interview for nine months during which, as well as publicising Youth Club UK, he also seemed to want to make a point of reaffirming the way he identified with the kind of people he'd met in prison. 'People shouldn't be so quick to judge young gangsters. Maybe you're not born with a criminal mind, society gives you that criminal mind. There's nothing with more faith than a bad boy turned good.' While advancing a traditional liberal argument, culled from experience and his extensive reading, he was also making clear that his was still a 'bad boy' image, going right back to his roots and exemplified in the fact that he still hadn't made that much money. The only rock star trapping that Ian had in common with the Gallaghers was a bodyguard, which, with the many the unprovoked beatings he'd suffered, was now considered unavoidable rather than an extravagance. In the same article Ian also relates how it did occur to him once to buy a Rolls Royce, but since he knew that his mother would 'close the curtains on him' he'd given up the idea.

Ian claimed he was still being treated like a criminal as, more often than not, he was 'hassled' on his trips visiting Fabiola and his children. This is the Ian Brown, who apart from a fondness for weed (which was being declassified if not decriminalised anyway) had spoken publicly against drugs, now being subjected to the 'rubber glove' treatment *often* enough, but *always* being searched.

Ian was becoming an irresistible outlaw figure: having served a jail term, he had a genuine rebel status, of the kind that the likes of Liam Gallagher were desperate to simulate. About this time rock stars, even those on the 'indie' circuit, were beginning to feature regularly in celebrity magazines and were in the process of becoming as far removed from their audiences as they would ever get. Ian, however, was the one 'celebrity' with an authentic 'underclass aura' who touched ordinary music fans.

It wasn't that he *tried* to be one of the people: apart from the bodyguard and the trips to New York, he lived in much the same way as he always had, certainly in more or less the same financial position as he was before the Stone Roses took off, and his continued travails with the police (there were also alleged driving offences) made people feel he was one of them. He demonstrated his social conscience by having himself photographed with the money he'd raised for the youth charity, rather than conceding to the glamour shots that had become *de rigeur* in the press (the *Melody Maker* had by this time become little more than a glossy photo magazine).

At the Conway Hall he previewed a full set of songs from the new album, including the single "Love Like A Fountain". The mean stage persona was present, but now balanced with a playful one, evidenced by a deluge of pink balloons and another Michael Jackson cover, "Billie Jean" this time. The reception from both the public and the press to this key show augured well for *Golden Greats*.

XXIII

Once again, Ian was not afraid to use his own face on the cover of his album, but this was a vastly different one from the grainy, low-key 'documentary' look of Ian on *Unfinished Monkey Business*. The cover artist, Ian Wright, had sent Ian a striking painting of Mike Tyson in orange, green and yellow. Wright's painting provided a style slightly reminiscent of old boxing posters, but also with an iconic edge. His album cover shows Ian staring out sphinx-like, a pop star transplanted back to the age of the Pharaohs and the flight of Israel. During the infamous Noël Coward interview, when asked who his hero was, Ian had said: 'Moses. Follow the path of Moses and you can't go wrong.' Though some saw this admittedly messianic portrait as Ian aspiring to be Christ-like, it's tempting to imagine that it was Moses he had in mind when he approved the cover since, as with the music of *Golden Greats*, it was indeed as if he was delivering himself and his followers into a new land.

With *Golden Greats* it is possible to see for the first time how the Stone Roses might have evolved if they had inclined towards the style they'd created with "Fools Gold" instead of becoming enamoured with Led Zeppelin. Here the lo-fi approach of *Unfinished Monkey Business* is also rejected in favour of a production that is sometimes lush, making these two solo albums vastly different from each other.

The only real concession to guitar music is Aziz's "All Right Now" style riff on "Getting High", which comes after two beautiful pieces of his speciality Eastern-style guitar – which, with no offence meant, would be equally at home heard in an Indian restaurant. The whole arrangement was clearly a conscious effort on Ian's part to get the album off with a bang: 'It's the first track,' he said, ' I wanted it to sound definitive.' It was Ian's rockiest song so far in his solo career and Aziz's frantic but masterful playing is exceptional, complemented cleverly by a languid, laid-back vocal from Ian. This rock-out is a red herring for the listener, though, as the music veers off into more and more unusual territories.

With Aziz used far less for the rest of the album, Ian distils the essences of the wide range of music he's now listening to (hip hop, ragga and electronica as well as post Britpop) combining them with his own untutored, idiosyncratic style of song-writing to create a resolutely left-field, nervy and shadowy hybrid of music, probably best described as 'indie noir'. Much of this dark flavour is created through the overhanging pre and post prison theme – resentment at his jail sentence can, for example, almost be heard simmering in the odd but strangely compelling arrangement of "Babasonics", a thinly-veiled attack on the magistrate that sent him to jail.

There are plenty of jail lyrics on the album, including "Set My Baby Free", the title of which comes from a letter Ian had received from Fabiola, while in Strangeways. This is a very powerful song: a nagging, insistent keyboard line suggests Fabiola's urgent pleas as well as symbolising the walls that surround Ian. The haunting, claustrophobic feel is only heightened by the introduction of an incredibly sad flute, coming in towards the end.

"Free My Way" comes complete with prison sound effects and a jangling key intro. Ian's vocals on this track carry with them his anger, mixed together with the sympathy he feels for his fellow inmates, culminating in a devastating summation of the dark grind of prison life. It's a strange song with dramatic strings, eerily reminiscent of the Beatles from the White Album era and full of portent.

There is plenty of darkness around "So Many Soldiers" too, which carries an anti-militarism message, Ian intoning over a trip-hop background in his strongest accent, while the song winds down into a marching rhythm with the simplest of blues pickings – a brilliant coda, which recalls his prison experience.

The Biblical and religious overtones of the cover image are reflected in the lyrics as well as the music. Phrases like 'I cannot bear false witness' are heard alongside chanting in "Neptune" or "Set My Baby Free", while the oddball evolutionary theory of "Dolphins Were Monkeys", with its sub-tropical atmospheres, seems to transport the listener to the ancient Orient when people like Moses walked the earth. The chill-out sounds of "Neptune", with Ian breathily intoning 'Ladies and gentleman, on our left, we have Neptune", is an interesting song which seemed to anticipate the music of Groove Armada, who were still, at this point, to release their debut album.

There are plenty of funk workouts too, but they are very measured, as if Ian sent the guitar combo home after the first track and kept Aziz on call. The emphasis throughout seems to be on experimentation and the fact that Ian succeeds in making a highly accessible album amidst all the genre bending is no mean achievement. It certainly confirms his abilities as a song writer and adds to his credibility as the Stone Roses' co-composer; for, however off-the-wall his arrangements might be, his knack of coming up with a catchy tune, as on "Corpses In Their Mouths", is shown to be very much alive and well here too. Overall, Ian had produced a thrillingly modern and utterly hypnotic piece of work that was a significant advance on *Unfinished Monkey Business*.

Reception to the album came with surprisingly few of the references to his trials and tribulations that one might have expected – he was, in fact, granted new respect as the author of what was seen as a major work. In the *NME*, *Golden Greats* was classified as 'a magisterial comeback... the gods are smiling on Ian Brown again', while *Q* deemed it a significant improvement on *Unfinished Monkey Business* – 'Ian Brown's head is currently in a very interesting place.' Rather typically, *Mojo* didn't review the album at all, preferring to rewind and give a full page to Silvertone's latest Stone Roses release, ten years after its making. This anniversary special, with bonus material, discography, lyrics, quotes and, to round it off, a Pollocked 'Reni' hat, was undeniably worlds apart from *Golden Greats*.

And if this release was a source of irritation to Ian, he didn't let it show as he went on to play two triumphant gigs at the end of the year. With a stripped-down band (Aziz was in the audience on these occasions!) he played brilliant shows, first at the Manchester Apollo followed by a special New Year's Eve show, again in his hometown, organised by Manchester City Council. The latter concert took place at the 10,000 capacity Castlefield arena and tickets, instead of being distributed through Ticketmaster or the like, were to be obtained from either the ARC clothing shop, the Dry Bar or the Feed the 5,000 (another nice Biblical overtone) Sandwich Shop – in an effort to bring in revenue for small local businesses.

For Ian, the celebratory air of these two gigs was not only about reception of *Golden Greats*, as he'd finally tied the knot with Fabiola – who was also expecting their first (and his third) child – a few hours before jumping on stage to perform. One of his New Year resolutions was to learn Spanish properly as he wanted the child to be bilingual and because 'I don't want my girl and me baby talking about me in a year's time and I don't know what they're saying.'

But this resolution took on new 'Fabiola-inspired' dimensions as he started to think about re-recording old tracks in Spanish. 'I want to be the first kid from the UK to sing in Spanish in Spanish-speaking countries,' he said, 'I want to tour South America, singing my set in Spanish, I want to go to Spain singing in Spanish and I want to re-release some of my tunes in Spanish.'

He also spoke at this time about the book he was still planning to write, revealing that he had already written about one hundred pages and that he had been making notes while in prison: 'little notes in little spider writing of scenes that had happened, stories guys would tell me.' And in the midst of all this, he was already working on tracks for his third album.

Even with so many exciting and varied projects in the offing, it was still virtually impossible to escape the legacy of the Stone Roses. News filtered through that John was working on material for a debut album with Reluctance, while Reni was again reported to be working hard on new songs, but still having no luck in landing a recording deal. Bizarrely, he seemed to have lost interest entirely in the drums and was in fact playing guitar on the material, having 'trained' someone to play drums for him.

Ian bumped into Mani in New York, on tour at the time with Primal Scream. Over the last year, the press had mischievously suggested that there was an Ian/John style feud between Ian and

Mani, taking Ian's lack of enthusiasm for Roses tribute bands out of context. The friendship was, in actual fact, as strong as ever, the two men embracing as soon as they set eyes on each other.

Ian's thoughts would also have turned back to his ex-colleagues when he received word of the nominations for that year's *NME* Brat awards, voted for by the readers as well as writers. He was third in the Best Solo Artist category (it being still too early in his comeback to be winning such things!) but his old band featured strongly in three new awards that had been inaugurated. "Fools Gold" was sixth in the Best Single Ever category and it was an incredible achievement for the band to see their debut album named as the Best Ever, surpassing no less than three Beatles albums as well as all the more current bands like Radiohead and Manic Street Preachers, both of whom had a strong voting base in the *NME* readership. Perhaps even more notable was the fact that the Roses came fourth in the voting for Best Band Ever, beating the Rolling Stones, the Velvet Underground and, just behind them in fifth, the Smiths.

More live work continued at contrasting venues – all warm-ups for a 'Spring Collection' Easter Tour and a trip to the US –including a storming show at Brixton Academy and a secret gig at Northampton's Roadmenders Club. Also, "Dolphins Were Monkeys", accompanied by a crazy spy story video where Ian is killed and then resurrected, had become his best-selling single since "My Star", reaching number five.

Ian's profile was now as high as it had ever been with the Roses and having just settled in Bayswater with Fabiola and a new son, Emilio, an air of contentment exuded from him. He liked living in London: it was Fabiola's preferred choice and not originally his, but it was a good location from which to make regular visits to Frankie and Casey. He was used to living in a metropolis, of course, but he never felt at home in London, where people preferred not to talk to each other in bus queues. 'Before I came here,' he said, ' I thought I was cosmopolitan but now I think, I'm a proper northerner.'

His contentment was, as ever, mixed with lingering grudges. He revealed a new interest in astrology and spoke about his joy in waking in the morning and feeling free: 'I wake up in the morning and give thanks, and I feel happy that I've got a new day. The morning's a beautiful gift and when that's took off you in jail... '

His resentment about the court case was still very much there and the book was still a work in progress but there was also a residue of bitterness about the 'homophobic' rumours which, he said, had lost him a lot of work – 'I've gone right down in the UK... in terms of standing, about whether I could get any bigger, whether I could reach out to more people. (The album is) a definite good start.'

That it was indeed a good start was proved very quickly as it emerged that Ian had again been nominated for a Brit in the Best Male category. Saying 'you don't make music to get awards' he declined to go. More gratifying perhaps was the *Melody Maker*'s 50 Coolest People in Rock Poll where he was positioned at number 10 – having not been included at all the previous year. In a pretty inane Q & A with the top ten nominees, he distinguished himself by describing 'Joshua Ben Joseph, a.k.a. Jesus' as the coolest man of all time, while everyone else named rock legends or film stars.

The rest of 2000 was notable for some fine live performances, culminating in a New Year's Eve gig and including the Carling Weekend during August, in Leeds. One of the warm-ups for this was a trip to Japan for the Fuji Rock Festival. Throughout his career, Ian had been able to rely upon the unstinting support of Japanese fans and this hilarious gig was no exception.

He received a frenzied reception as he stepped on stage in a black singlet and army trousers, carrying a red plastic rod with silver grips, and looking like a slightly westernised, 21st century Samurai. Ian and the band built up amazing momentum with "Love Like A Fountain" and "Fisherman Song/Neptune", only for the sound to break down abruptly. Almost as if it was done accidentally on purpose, Ian instantly launched into a ten-minute routine of entertainment, and with a 'let me show you me kendo' he proceeded to show off his martial arts skills, twirling his rod around to whoops from the crowd. Then another prop of old, the plastic blow-up globe, was produced as Ian instigated a game of headers with Mani, who'd raced out from backstage, and was due on after him with Primal Scream. This was followed by a speech: 'I feel beautiful and I am beautiful, you know, and all those that are beautiful know that I am beautiful and they know themselves that they are beautiful and we're destroying the ugly by our beauty.'

While this kind of outburst might have left people scratching their heads in the north of England, it went down a storm in Japan. But in Leeds there were no sound problems and Ian delivered a powerful performance that was as cathartic for the crowd as it was for Ian himself, and an exorcism of old festival ghosts. The *NME* called him 'imperious and invincible... Adore him or deplore him, but ignore him at your peril.'

At the end of the Leeds Festival, a large party was thrown by Oasis. Here John Squire made his first public appearance in a long time, though it took a while for people to recognise him as he had become the third member of the ex-Stone Roses to grow a long beard. He was pictured with his arms round Mani looking happy enough, though there had been reports of him sacking the entire line up supposedly making up Reluctance. These reports probably led to yet another set of rumours about a possible Stone Roses reunion. Mani revealed that there had been an offer of big money for the band to reform, which they had unanimously declined. The rumours didn't quite make sense anyway as Ian and John still hadn't even spoken. And though Mani seemed to be keen on the idea when it was put to him, even he had to admit, 'I don't think Ian and John will get on again.'

However much he and the rest of the Roses disliked the idea of a reunion, Ian was not totally unconscious of the love that people felt for his old band. He demonstrated this when, having to pull out of an appearance at the Point in Dublin at short notice in October, he contacted Mani's Complete Stone Roses tribute band, so that rather than having to go home, the delighted crowd were treated to a full set of Stone Roses songs.

The next time Ian and Mani were to see each other was back at Alexandra Palace, where they had played together all those years ago. Ian supported Primal Scream at this end of year gig, where he gave what was essentially a greatest hits set, rounding off 2000 nicely. Earlier in the year he'd been saying that he would have an album ready to release, and he had been working hard on material, but he also had a new son and that took precedence. When the *NME* printed a round-up of what people were doing in 2001, Ian was conspicuous by his absence – it would seem the punters would have to wait a little longer than Ian had led them to believe for the follow-up to *Golden Greats*.

XXIV

Ian's stated plan to get the next album out by the end of 2000 had perhaps been somewhat ambitious what with setting up his new family home, and with a baby son to help look after. However, sessions towards the follow-up continued, while the independent music scene was going through some unique changes.

Melody Maker, the first UK popular music paper, first published in 1926, finally came to an end, right at the beginning of 2001. The paper's closure spoke volumes about the shrinkage in audience for bands that were visibly 'indie'. For some time, it had experimented with different designs and layouts, shrinking in size, looking increasingly garish, and in its death-throes even resorting to giving away posters – the final issue on the newsstands in December 2000 frankly might as well have been renamed *Smash Hits*. Also departing at the same time was the indie-centric *Select*, a kind of *Mojo*-Lite magazine. Ian had had his share of run-ins with both, and later in the year he was to remark sarcastically on their demise, unable to resist the smug observation that he had outlasted them: 'everyone who has slagged me off in the past like *Melody Maker* and *Select* aren't around any more. You can't curse the blessed – I'm so blessed.'

When Ian and the Roses were first starting out, four papers were available: *Melody Maker*, *NME*, *Sounds* and *Record Mirror*, all catering for a readership preference for guitar based bands. Now with only the *NME* left, anyone who harked back to the glory days of guitar music bands, intentionally or otherwise, was doing so at their peril. This was reassuring for Ian, whose music seemed to be constantly evolving, but less so for John Squire whose future in music could only realistically be built round his guitar. All reports coming through about John were making it increasingly clear that his place in the world was as the 'ex-Stone Roses guitarist'. He and Geffen had gambled wisely in the short term but it was Ian who had a long-term future.

Ian's exact place in the musical firmament remained tenuous however, for it was a very curious time musically. The *NME* had been suffering from schizophrenia for quite a while, encountering stiff competition from tabloids who now covered the n'eer-do-well antics of the likes of the Gallagher brothers. But they continued to run Oasis 'stories' for want of any other material and partly out of a habit, the nadir of which was still to come in 2002 when they printed four pages on Liam Gallagher losing two front teeth in yet another brawl. At the same time, they were moved to comment in depth about the break-ups of the Spice Girls and All Saints, and put Destiny's Child on the cover. An apparent desire to garner street cred could also now be gleaned from their featuring a hell of a lot of hip-hop bands. And when the May 2001 issue's first full page of news reported on the New York music scene, followed later by a lengthy interview with Janet Jackson, it was probably safe to assume that the *NME* had lost their grip on just what exactly was going on musically in the UK.

The increased competition from *all* newspapers, now covering 'their' music in depth was bound to have been *the* major cause for concern. And the success of a band such as the White Stripes, a bizarre yet highly talented outfit, is just one example of a record company's PR totally bypassing the *NME*, who found themselves championing the band at the same time as *The Guardian*, the *Daily Mirror* and even *The Sun*. All of which – one would have thought - might have led the paper to go for even more radical bands to promote, to corner a new market so to speak. But this didn't happen.

A new conservatism (which has remained to this day) started to creep in exemplified in 2001, for instance, by Travis being bestowed with the *NME* label of 'most popular band in Britain.' It seems almost incredible that the *NME* should champion a group who many deemed almost offensive in their inoffensiveness, (a relentlessly commonplace four-piece whose best-known song, "Why Does It Always Rain On Me?", arguably sounded like something that scouts would sing round a camp fire) alongside the White Stripes. (But far worse than Travis was to come soon).

It left Ian Brown, a dope-smoking egalitarian with fiercely held views, a pot pourri of musical styles and a criminal record to boot, as something of an anomaly. And generally speaking, he began to act, as well as being treated, like one, musically and otherwise. In February, he made his most unlikely television appearance to date – on *The Big Breakfast*. Normally a late riser, the last time Ian had seen the show was when he was in prison and being woken up at 7.30 – and now he found himself lying on a bed with its presenter, Donna Air.

The interview lasted just a few minutes, and included an airing for the "Dolphins Were Monkeys" video. He was asked quite a few questions about the Stone Roses and Air even referred to the story about him planning to take up gardening after the band split – 'I was lying', he retorted, to huge laughter around the studio. He went on to reveal that the band had been offered £2 million to reform but, however much Air talked up the Roses (even claiming that she had played the first album at her New Year's Eve party), Ian made it abundantly clear that, from his perspective at least, it wasn't going to happen. Air went on to ask about the forthcoming Brit awards and he poked fun at the 'old stars' that he'd been nominated alongside, including Tom Jones, the eventual winner. The mainstream nature of the programme was subverted momentarily when Donna asked what Ian would do if he won the award. If she'd been anticipating a response like a dedication to someone, she would have been disappointed as Ian quipped that he would 'raffle it for £2 a ticket' and spend the proceeds on 'kidney machines or the Third World. One of the two.' *The Big Breakfast* must have been relieved the interview was a short one.

Rumours about a Stone Roses reformation just wouldn't go away, fuelled, no doubt, by the appearance of a second tribute band, Fools Gold. Both were now regularly advertising gigs in the music press, although the Complete Stone Roses undoubtedly had the edge on Fools Gold, especially as Mani would often appear on the ads as guest bassist! It was even reported that they would be recording unreleased Stone Roses material as their first single: "Sun Still Shines", a track left over from the *Second Coming* sessions. The *NME* excitedly claimed that Ian and John were going to give permission for their impersonators to record a Brown/Squire original. But the generosity Ian had shown the Complete Stone Roses thus far, didn't extend to this and they were peremptorily knocked back in a terse statement from his manager: 'There's no way Ian Brown will give permission for this, for a so-called tribute band.'

At the beginning of 2001, Ian had refused to be involved with a Nestlé promotion, along with Pulp and Dodgy, in the light of the food manufacturer's famously dubious methods of commerce in Africa. The deodorant makers Lynx, however, were apparently more PC as Ian did appear at a tiny gig-cum-Lynx-PR-event, in London, at Acton's Black Island Studios. This acted as a warm-up for events later in the year, including a 'Very Special Guest slot with the Manic Street Preachers', with whom he was also collaborating at the time. With only three people in his band, Ian spent a lot of time at the studio recreating a dub vibe. His band went on to play a secret gig in Reykjavik as additional warm-up for the Manics and his manager revealed that he was going to be directing the video for his next single – 'all about wanting to ride Icelandic horses.'

Ian's first major appearance of the year was at the V2001 festival on a bill with Tricky and Sparklehorse. He took to the stage riding a bike (an old gimmick of Tom Waits) climbing back on it a number of times during the set to the bemusement of the audience. Ian thundered from the stage about the evils of cocaine while Aziz treated the audience to another display of Hendrix-like playing, complete with use of his teeth. Just as they had been with his gig in Acton, the *NME* were vitriolic in their review and rude about his singing, suggesting he'd outstayed his welcome on the music scene and concluding that the success of his first two albums had been an anomaly, just like him.

An important and distinctly un-conservative band of the time that the *NME* did support, the Manic Street Preachers, were only slightly more strident in their politics than Ian. They followed their much-publicised trip to Cuba with a single, "Let Robeson Sing", for which Ian contributed a remixed version. Paul Robeson was an attractive figure for Ian and he was keen to pay tribute. This popular black American singer of the 30s and 40s, with a heart-warming and unforgettable bass voice, is most famous for his timeless rendition of "Old Man River". Robeson's popularity extended far beyond the U.S. and on his trips abroad he discovered that racism was far more pronounced at home: in London, for example, he would receive a feted reception at the front door wherever he went, whereas most places he went in the US, he entered through the back door marked 'Negro.' What the title of the single referred to was his indictment at the House Committee of Un-American Activities after speaking out against racism in his homeland – a show trial that effectively ruined his career. Ian's spirited remix of the Manics' tribute to Paul Robeson's life had him contributing backing vocals with Aziz on guitar.

Ian was now also 'author' to a new CD titled *Planetgroove: Ian Brown*, the third in a series of 'bad-lad mix albums' from the Beechwood Planet label – the previous two having come from Shaun Ryder and Huey from the Fun Lovin' Criminals. Ian's included an eclectic mix of tracks that would have had many an indie kid recoiling in horror: hip-hop from Public Enemy, dancehall from Sizzla and even Randy Crawford.

This project was closely followed by single and new album releases. It was as if Ian was loath to return to any inactivity after the nightmare of *The Second Coming*, for he was working at a furious rate and "F.E.A.R.", the new single, was indeed a ferocious record. Described in one review as 'Massive Attack trying to make a pop record', it may also have been Ian's best-ever single. With powerful strings and a driving beat, the potent concoction that is "F.E.A.R." is rounded out by the conceit of having each line of the verse spell out the title – 'For each a road, For everyman a religion' and so on, leading up to the chorus 'F.E.A.R. (you've got the fear)'.

As a single it was difficult to ignore and it was justly met with huge acclaim. On the other hand, when the ads started appearing for the new album, a lot of people were left scratching their heads. The 'trailer' in the music press went something like this: 'It seemed to the Pythagoreans that the distances between the planets would have the same ratios as produced harmonious sounds in a plucked string. To them, the solar system consisted of ten spheres revolving in circles about a central fire, each sphere giving off a sound the way a projectile missile makes a sound as it swishes through the air: the closer spheres gave lower tones while the farther moved faster and gave higher pitched sounds. All combined into a beautiful harmony, the music of the spheres.'

For a pop album to take its inspiration from a medieval philosophical concept, as *Music Of The Spheres* did is, to say the least, highly unusual, even if it is a typical Ian Brown thing to do. With his interest in space travel and astrology, the Pythagoreans' concept of music as *pure* mathematics involving the planets was probably just irresistible to Ian. The press preferred to treat him as a space cadet however, with the *NME* pointedly choosing to give Kylie Minogue the lead review the week Ian's album came out, while bemoaning the 'erratic path' that he had taken.

Ian Brown was in danger – though this he probably would not have minded – of being cast out into the margins of music along with the Julian Copes of this world (who by now was enjoying a twin career of musician and 'writer on prehistory'). If there wasn't out and out derision, then there was certainly a weariness in the tone of some reviewers: *Q*, for instance, implied that Ian had just simply had too much ganga and christened it '4am Learning Zone Esoterica' while *Mojo* summarised it thus: 'Self-mocking simian and notorious aircrew upsetter comes back more cosmic than before.' His first two albums were always going to be seen as transitional and people were so unprepared for the sheer scope of *Music Of The Spheres* it was perhaps all too easy to categorise Ian as having lost the plot entirely.

But, just as Julian Cope's 'mad' ventures had been warmly received by the public, in general, likewise was *Music Of The Spheres*. His third album of 'esoterica' proved the journalists out of touch by soaring into the top three and, by the end of the year, there had been enough interest to warrant release of a companion album, *Remixes Of The Spheres*. But is *Music Of The Spheres* any good? The most important point to make about this third album is that people felt the full force of Ian's ambition as a solo artist as he turned in a bewildering, often intoxicating set of songs – when it succeeded, it did so spectacularly, but there were a at least a couple of near-misses in "Stardust" and "Hear No See No".

The surge of strings on the first track, "F.E.A.R.", makes for an uplifting 'blast-off' while emphasising the album's commercial appeal. *Music Of The Spheres* is further demonstration of Ian's gift for strong melody and there is a rejection of some of the dissonant sounds we heard previously on *Golden Greats* (which were largely a reflection of his travails). Happily married and with his prison sentence well behind him, Ian now seems to be back in celebratory mood throughout most of the songs. One notable exception is "The Gravy Train" which bears a resemblance to the dark sounds of Tricky, with fractured, intricate rhythms and a return to the well-worn theme of the evils of cocaine.

It has to be acknowledged that Ian does indeed often seem to be on some kind of 'space trip' with lyrics such as 'I landed from Mars, made my way through the Milky Way' ("Bubbles") and 'I'm Made From Stardust' ("Stardust") combined with the astral sounds of tunes like "Northern Lights", creating a kind of '70s lounge psychedelic sound. But there are all kinds of other nuances on the record too (funk, rock, folk, chill-out and so on) and a breathtaking variety of sounds produced, while some of the strings used, as for example on the second single "Whispers", are absolutely captivating. Ian had assembled an adventurous group of musicians who helped him stretch the sounds as much as possible and Ian even made his promised foray into Spanish vocals on "El Mundo Pequěno".

At a time when Radiohead were still commonly being perceived as by far the most adventurous rock group of the new millennium (and their position as such was pretty much unassailable), it seems a little unfair that the fearlessness shown by Ian and his band in creating such an individual, leftfield album wasn't more fully recognised. They may not have been as successful, but they were, at the very least, thinking as laterally as Radiohead, or for that matter, anyone else making music at the time. When the *NME* set out their best albums of the year, the *retrogressive* sounds of the heavily-plugged Strokes were deemed to be top of the pile – while the *progressive* quality of *Music Of The Spheres* didn't even make it into the top 50.

Two months after virtually writing off Ian's last album, the *NME* was nevertheless recommending that people go to see an artist 'in just about the best form of his career' as he embarked on a nationwide tour. And they were right, at least, in promoting his live work, for Ian produced an electrifying series of shows, the highlight probably being the one at Brixton Academy in December, which was sold out weeks before the performance. If *Music Of The Spheres* was a celebratory album, this end-of-year show was practically a party, with the band playing illuminated instruments to get in the festive mood. Ian now had a guaranteed audience that was spread across the age groups, and not exclusively male by any means. Many of the women at Brixton made their presence felt by hurling their bras at Ian throughout the show. During one song, Ian wore a bra strapped across one of his shoulders and a hat, also thrown in from the audience, before passing the bra to the keyboard player, who in turn put it on for the next song. Ian then went on to reveal his skill on the mouth organ for the first time on "Corpses In Their Mouths" and received huge cheers. The party mood was such that the band may or may not have forgotten that they played "Stardust" early on in the show, because they went through the whole thing again when they came out for an encore.

And the tour carried on well into the next year. Constantly working and touring (when he wasn't travelling) Ian the artist was becoming increasingly difficult to ignore or marginalize. As he began to work on *Remixes Of The Spheres* it seemed that his eye was persistently fixed on reaching people, even if the eyes of others weren't initially always turned towards what he was doing. The striking cover image for *Spheres*, with one of Ian's dark brown eyes staring out at his audience, served as a potent symbol of this.

In February 2002, *The Guardian* featured an interview with Ian titled 'The Unsinkable Ian Brown' and, for the first time, it seemed like the emphasis was going to be on what he was *doing*, rather than what he *had done* with the Roses. It was a portrait of a forward-thinking artist in his own right, and it also saw Ian, for the first time, as at least half-dismissive of what the Roses had done, wryly commenting of their heyday: 'People wore flares for a year or two, d'ya know what I mean? That's all we did.' But he also acknowledged and appeared to feel, quite keenly, the waste of the Roses, as he commented – 'We George Bested it, for sure.' The interview was peppered with pithy quotes from Ian on familiar subjects. On the advantages of dope-smoking, for example he expounded: 'You get locked into something different - what's going on isn't in the width of your trousers, it's what's blowing in the wind', while lambasting, as usual, the use of cocaine, but this time adding alcohol, and finally heroin to his list of disapproved of substances, concluding: 'I've seen people turn into a bag of dirty washing in half an hour.'

Inevitably, he was asked about the Stone Roses split and regarding John, he spoke of 'absolute betrayal.' But the emphasis was generally on the life that Ian lived now and he articulated winningly and uncompromisingly about the advantages of a rock star life that doesn't involve excess. He predictably viewed his one vice, dope-smoking, as a healthy pursuit ('it's medicine, innit'). And though he lived well, he claimed he refused to be a spendthrift in the style of the Gallaghers, describing, in contrast, a life that was built around music, travel and reading, which he said he now pursued more widely and voraciously than ever – including continued obsessive reading of the Bible, although exclusively in this case 'for the stories.' Most of all, he created a picture of a life centred round his wife, whom he was in love with more than ever. He made it clear that he despised the 'lad' culture which he had often been accused of being indirectly responsible for, and it was certainly surprising and refreshing to read an assertion like 'men are 90% babies' from someone like him. His interviewer did slyly hint at the sanctimonious air about him, a touch of the Messiah complex, given credence by revelations from Ian, such as the content of his recurring dream where he was to be found sitting under a tree with a golden crown on his head, a lion and a lioness under each arm. Using the same kind of language as Julian Cope, Ian punctured this by saying: 'I do feel righteous - because I live a righteous life.'

The overwhelming impression coming from the article is that of Ian having *arrived* at last, as a solo artist and with many of the hangovers from the Roses era at last disappearing. His money worries were certainly behind him now: he'd bought a second home in Wales and was able to live 'a life that my grandfather could never have dreamt about.' Financial security also enabled him to take his travelling to new dimensions, exploring, more than ever before, a wealth of obscure destinations and different cultures. His recent trips abroad at this point included a dream exploration of Japan, where he immersed himself in the culture of the Shogun warriors. He also made more extensive trips to Mexico where his taste for peyote often produced spectacular results: on one occasion, he claimed to have seen the colours of the planets, felt the heat of Jamaica coming across the sea and heard the jaguars growling in the jungle!

And Ian did allow himself one trip down memory lane, as he for once broke the rule of not appearing at showbiz events, by going to the premiere of *24 Hour Party People* – the 'film of Madchester.' Though not a classic by any means, this is undoubtedly better than your average rock 'n' roll movie, having been made by the acclaimed director Michael Winterbottom. With Steve Coogan playing Tony Wilson, it tells the story of Factory Records from the end of the 70s up until the nineties. The Roses were, of course, peripheral to the Factory story and it was more significant for Mondays fans than anyone. On the DVD's 'Deleted Scenes', however, there is a cocky character making fun of Tony Wilson, thought to be Ian Brown or Ian Curtis – no one has ever been able to find out for certain. On being asked yet again about a Roses reunion, Ian reiterated his view by quipping 'never return to a lit firework'. But, during the remainder of 2002, he was going to be reminded of the Stone Roses more than once.

XXV

The *NME* celebrated 50 years of publishing in April of 2002 and marked the occasion, rather unimaginatively, with a list. List making passing for journalism (both in the press and on T.V.) was a concept just gathering momentum at the time, and the genre has gone on to become something of a dinosaur since. But *NME*'s 50 Greatest Artists of All Time, as a fairly early prototype of the form, was fairly entertaining and featured the Roses at no 3, just behind the Beatles and the Smiths, showing that their reputation held firm.

Meanwhile, with an editorial policy that made a virtue out of casting backwards glances, it was inevitable that *Mojo* magazine would one day jump forwards into the 80s and 90s to examine the legacy of the Stone Roses. This was done in some style a month after the *NME*'s celebration issue, with an eleven-page article, including an appreciation of the first album from Bob Stanley. Though it was advertised as a look back on the early years, it nevertheless had some bearing on the present and the future.

Ian was contacted along with the other members and asked if he would like to speak to *Mojo*'s John McCready. Through his management, Ian told McCready he had absolutely no interest in looking back at the Roses. McCready had had more luck with the others though: John had agreed straight away and since Mani still had a taste for jumping on stage with Roses imitators he was hardly likely to say no. Even Reni, who had been making quiet progress with his new band, the Rub (which also featured Pete Garner), finally decided to break his long silence. McCready, a Mancunian like the Roses, was in no way faint-hearted, and in an attempt to smoke Ian out, he faxed a super-persuasive message, which included a reminder that they used to live two streets away from each other and that Ian had had a romance with McCready's current next door neighbour. Delighted by the fax, Ian arranged a phone interview the same day.

Reni, meanwhile, provided his answers by fax, John emerged out of hiding to meet McCready in a coffee shop in Manchester, and Mani dragged the *Mojo* man into a pub. The multi-voiced, split Q & A session is a fascinating document that goes into far more depth than simply a resumé of the early years: it is Reni, the first member of the band to leave, whose voice seems most tinged with regret, though clearly retaining his sense of humour, while Mani is full of exuberance, pride and some emotion. The continuing division between Ian and John can be detected in their answers, markedly contrasting with two pictures from the early years on show, both of which have the pair sitting together, shoulder to shoulder. In his answers, it is Ian, surprisingly, who appears happy to talk about their former closeness, while there remains no comment at all from John on the subject.

According to McCready, Ian 'burned' through his questions, and it became clear that he was, naturally, the one least prone to bouts of nostalgia. He made a point of emphasising the faith that he had in his new band while eulogising the old: 'I can't say I miss it. I loved it and what I do now is a different thing. I'm still working with great lads, they're great players.' This in response to by far the most direct question from McCready; 'Do you miss it?' Revealingly, only John implies a feeling that he does.

While Ian, with three successful solo albums under his belt, had to be charmed into talking to McCready, it was probably a more necessary and expedient move for John, who was preparing to release his first solo album. John had endured a frustrating time trying to get the Reluctance project off the ground with ex-Verve bassist, Simon Jones. Finally, he decided to go it alone, trying out his own vocal cords, rather than casting about looking for a singer.

In July, John came out with an announcement regarding his new album, in the same week that the Complete Stone Roses finally released their first single "Tell Me More", though thankfully he did nothing to encourage the 'Stone Roses to reform' rumour mill. The money offered for a reunion gig was now half-way to a seven figure amount and Reni's manager had even received an offer for the Roses to play the opening of the Commonwealth Games. But John wasn't having it, blaming the breakdown of his relationship with Ian – 'because we wrote together, we knew each other for the longest, (it) hurt the deepest.'

At first he seemed to be at pains to put the Roses behind him and his first interviews were full of purgative comments dating back to the *Second Coming* era, such as: 'I realised the person inside Ian wasn't the person I loved. I couldn't find him. I looked into his eyes and it was a different person. It was a frightening experience.' While he admitted he did miss Ian and a meeting between them was 'long overdue', his response to the idea of a Roses reunion was 'I'd rather remove my liver with a teaspoon.'

It was something of a surprise, then, to hear that John's album, entitled *Do It Yourself*, was 'a nostalgia trip' looking back at the early days of the Roses as well as his first long-term relationship. There were indeed specific references to the Roses and Ian to be found, as John acknowledged later in the song "I Miss You" and less explicitly but more tartly, the 'that crown of thorns suits, ya' lyric in "15 Days". When *Do It Yourself* appeared in September, its good reception was marred by the guitar god references ('Zeus of riffs') and identifications with 'traditional' music – 'classic '70s bardic rock... strong enough to compete with and instruct the Ashcrofts and Gallaghers.' These kind of responses weren't going to help John rival Ian in any way, as a progressive artist with a future in the post-millennial music scene.

But it honestly appeared as if John didn't care *that* much, his argument being that he had simply wanted to make a musical statement. But then he amazed many by playing Stone Roses songs at gigs to promote the new album – even starting a couple of shows with "I Am The Resurrection", as well as regularly playing "She Bangs The Drums" and "Waterfall", at the expense of his new songs which were frequently raced through on stage.

In later interviews, a groundswell of feelings about Ian and the Roses was detectable. In November for example, he succumbed to *Q*'s *Cash For Questions*, as Ian had done before him. Where Ian, even back in 1997, had shown he had plenty of other things to talk about (and be asked about), the same old familiar subjects were just inescapable for John. He was easily drawn out on the possibility of reforming and *now* he seemed to think it was pretty much inevitable. When asked yet again about his 'relationship' with Ian too, he now seemed to think that they would get back together, following up this turnaround view with the curious comment that he'd heard Ian was 'back to his old self.'

Ian would only have had a passing awareness of the coverage for John, because he was keeping up his furious work rate, which would have left little time for reading the music press. The promotional tour for *Music Of The Spheres*, supposedly concluding in April of 2002, effectively rumbled on regardless. The man who had signed himself on as 'the laziest man in showbusiness' was now arguably doing everything in his power, and more, to become the exact opposite: he played gigs in every single month in 2002 and worked on another track with UNKLE, before concentrating on *Remixes Of The Spheres* which came out on November 4 – ironically, on the very same day as the *Very Best Of The Stone Roses*. Ian liked the *Remixes* project a great deal and he did show some signs of warming towards the *idea*, at least, of what his old band represented musically. He said that he'd thought of the Stone Roses directly in his approach to the tracks on *Remixes*, and he wanted to re-make them 'in the classic style' of his former band.

His live gigs varied wildly in quality, and there were reports of below par singing once again – only to be expected really, considering his gruelling schedule of playing practically every week. By all accounts he was superb at Glastonbury, which was becoming a lucky venue for him, and there were continued spates of bra throwing at a number of other gigs. Probably the worst effort was at Move 2002 where he was held up from going on to stage for fifteen minutes because of technical difficulties that continued throughout. The highlight for this audience was a mere snippet of "Fools Gold" which appeared during "Love Like A Fountain".

Another more notable gig was V2002, where he put his support behind the charity Sight Savers who had secured a presence at the festival. Sight Savers were trying to draw attention to the plight of many Africans who were losing their sight needlessly through cataracts when the operation could cost as little as £15 in

English money. Ian posed for pictures and had his hand printed for auction by Sight Savers. He then held a lengthy press conference where he charged journalists £15 for every question asked. True to form, Ian got fairly carried away in his answers, railing against the social injustices that existed. Presumably, Ian contributed something himself, and this, together with his impassioned (and, as usual, foul-mouthed) display meant Ian was good value for Sight Savers. 'No one gives a shit about the people in the Third World,' he said, 'Society is structured so that we don't give a fuck about the poor. Poverty's deliberate.' He even found a way to promote the cause while simultaneously making reference to one of his pet hates: '£15 will pay for a cataract operation in the Third World – a gram of coke's about £60, I think.'

One could be forgiven for thinking that Ian was developing a bit of an obsession with the evils of cocaine. He had been railing against it regularly ever since the Stone Roses split and when he stepped up to receive an accolade at the Muso awards in September he was at it again. The short-lived Musos consisted of tributes voted for by fellow musicians, making it marginally 'un- showbiz enough' for Ian to consent to be at the ceremony. Held at the Ocean club in Hackney where, instead of white tablecloths and footmen, the organisers recreated a mock festival backstage area, and many of the winners were given a merry heckling, instead of mechanical applause. Other winners that year included Badly Drawn Boy and PJ Harvey but Ian got the biggest laugh when, after saying thanks for the Best Single award for "F.E.A.R." he shouted out 'Stay off the coke!'

He rounded off the year with another set of gigs supporting the Manic Street Preachers who were promoting their *Forever Delayed* greatest hits collection. Though Ian was faced every night with the famously partisan Manics fans, he always got something positive from them, and his now perfect version of Michael Jackson's "Billie Jean", in particular, invariably drew an enthusiastic response.

In 2003, the punishing live schedule was put on hold for the time being, as Ian started thinking about a new album. The first speculation as to what Ian would be up to next was about as un-believable as a Stone Roses reunion. In January, the *Manchester Evening News* ran a story alleging that Ian was going to be taking a role in the film *Harry Potter and The Prisoner of Azkaban*. This, at the time seemingly dubious story, was related in the paper just as they were interviewing John, who was still touring, and he was invited to comment. 'People have to find a new hobby when they are approaching middle age,' he retorted, 'but more seriously I hated the first two films – but I would definitely see the third if Ian was in it.' The tone of this response shows how seriously the Evening News – and John – thought the rumour to be. The whole idea that a Manc lad like Ian would even consider appearing in a luvvie-fest such as a *Harry Potter* film was after all pretty far-fetched.

But the source of this rumour was more reliable than one might suppose. The director of the third *Potter* was a Mexican filmmaker, Alfonso Cuaran, who just happened to be an old friend of Fabiola's. Cuaran had been approached to do *Potter* after the success of his film *A Little Princess*, from the Frances Hodgson Burnett book – the story of a young girl who is relegated to ser-vitude at a boarding school when her father goes missing and is presumed dead.

When Ian met Cuaran, he found him an appealing character. Cuaran's ambition, other than being a film director, was to be an astronaut and he and Ian shared an interest in politics as well as space travel – one of Cuaran's pet projects being a film on the violent student's revolt in Mexico in 1968. He had already had a galvanising effect on the young stars of the *Potter* movie, which was at the time in preparation and Cuaran was generally highly regarded in the industry.

Then, one night over dinner, Cuaran told Ian that he could have a role for him in *The Prisoner of Azkaban*. Ian had always loved film and was very knowledgeable – from an early age, his favourite director had been the 'director's director', Orson Welles. Even so, he'd never indulged any of the hankerings for film star-dom that have seized many a rock luminary. He liked JK Rowling, admiring her for the fact that she 'wrote the book in a café when she was on the dole, and now she's richer than the Queen', and he also liked the books, as did his kids. Accordingly, he deferred to them when he realised that Cuaran was deadly serious about giving him the role. "Go for it!" they had said.

It would have been fun to have encountered Ian's northern vowels amongst the likes of Alan Rickman and Dame Maggie Smith and he did in fact have a screen test for a speaking role, but in the end his part was a lot less demanding, so small that it actually went uncredited and largely slipped past the attention of the press at the time. Quite a few of his fans would indeed leave the cinema having missed him, or having assumed that it was just somebody who looked like him. Ian doesn't speak but is seen dressed as a wizard in the Leaky Cauldron pub, reading a copy of Stephen Hawking's *A Brief History Of Time*. Those big dark eyes stare out from under his headgear, he has gold teeth and his finger hovers over a cup of tea, which then begins to stir itself. Ian only spent one day on the set and saw it as a kind of *Jim'll Fix It* experience – 'it was good to be a film star for a day – to have a trailer and a golf cart and all that.'

There was also more serious business to attend to. With storm clouds gathering in the Middle East as the US and the U.K. prepared to invade Iraq, Ian was among many artists who lent their support to the Stop The War coalition. At first, he was scheduled to appear with UNKLE at the huge demonstration to be held in March at Hyde Park. This proved to be too tricky to organise, so a gig was re-scheduled for the Fabric club late in March, as part of the wider effort to stop the war. Ian and UNKLE playing two tracks on an emotional evening, which also included Jarvis Cocker on the DJ decks.

Ian was also continuing to come up with ideas for the next album and he was actually toying with the thought of doing an album with a girl singer: he was most keen on using someone with an unusual voice such as Sinead O'Connor, and preferably someone who, like him, was 'a bit of a rebel.' Ian's only other gig in 2003 was at the St Austell Eden Project in August, a concert he agreed to on the spur of the moment, in order to make contact with fans in a part of the world he didn't often get to.

Ian 'authored' another CD towards the end of the year with the second of the *Under The Influence* CDs. The first of these 'compilations-chosen-by-stars' had been put together by Morrissey with selections as far ranging as New York Dolls and Diana Dors, and Ian was a clever second choice as their tastes hardly converged at all. The recent death of Joe Strummer may have influenced Ian's choice of the Clash's "White Man In Hammersmith Palais", but Clash would always mean a great deal to him. He also chose the Sex Pistols' little-known "Submission", but the remaining tracks were rap (Public Enemy once more), reggae (Sizzla) or soul (Edwin Starr, Bobby Womack) influenced. It was a good, eclectic list that contrasted hugely with Morrissey's, and suggested, frankly, that Ian had his finger on the pulse far more than Morrissey did. This was only re-emphasised by the covers for each album: Morrissey looking solemnly heavenwards outside a pub called 'The Grace Maurice'; Ian staring directly at the camera in one of his trademark monkeyman poses, wearing a sweatshirt carrying a Rastafarian image – and looking rather cool.

Speaking of cool, the *NME* ran its second 'Cool List' in November 2003. Another of the 'list passing for journalism' scams, this one had been ominously foreshadowed in the pages of the defunct *Melody Maker* – and the *NME* was also now giving away posters as the *Maker* had done. The *NME* had, in fact, become a kind of musical version of *The Sun*, full of glossy, usually inane photos and trashy gossip masquerading as news.

The latest in their carousel of sleazy iconography centred round the exploits of *nouveau* punks the Libertines and Pete Doherty, a front man who seemed determined to out-Liam Liam Gallagher. Doherty's prison sentence for burgling his former bandmate in late 2003 had papers drawing parallels between him and Ian. The burglary certainly made Ian's feud with John pale in comparison – but it was a lazy comparison. Doherty's exhaustively catalogued drug/drink problems and highly publicised relationship with model Kate Moss constituted a lifestyle that was undermining his talent and probably shortening his life.

By contrast, Ian was moving into 2004 with his appetite for life – his 'righteous life' – undimmed and his appetite for work after a fairly quiet year, pretty much insatiable again. Coupled with that, his exploits in the next two years would bring him his biggest audience yet and explode all notions of cool so loosely applied by the *NME* and other music commentators. Where the careers of Doherty, the Gallaghers et al were stifled and imprisoned by media coverage as much as they were furthered, Ian's appearances in the press were, if anything, becoming even more rare. He had been building up and nurturing an audience for years, in his own inimitable style – an audience with whom he felt a direct bond, in many ways harking back to the participatory 'Madchester' style of old. Seemingly laid back about the media as well as his rivals (most of the time, anyway) he was, if only they had known it, rapidly outflanking everyone – soon the resurrection would be complete and he would be a new and energizing icon for the modern times.

XXVI

Aziz Ibrahim had come to appear increasingly peripheral to Ian's career as he was used less and less with each new album. Personally the two were in fact, if anything, closer than ever and Aziz, for one, thought of Ian as his best friend. Aziz had been busy with his own band and had set up a label called Indus, specialising in his Asiatic sounds. He was also involved in arts projects in Manchester and Birmingham as well as performing regularly with an amazing tabla player, Dal, whom he'd met in South Africa – they nicknamed themselves the 'Bombay White Stripes'. In short Aziz was a true match for Ian creatively – just as prolific and driven. Ian and Aziz would always find time to write tunes and jam together, and the guitarist was now integral to Ian's plans for the new work that he was developing, which he wanted to be more guitar-heavy and more melodic. He was warming again – actually in a fiery way – to the Stone Roses legacy, having had reports from fans that he met that John Squire had been delivering rather ropey versions of their great songs.

John seemed to have acquired a renewed work ethic of his own, and was actually preparing to release his second solo album. There had, over the years, undoubtedly been something of a reversal of fortunes: John, now in his forties like his former songwriting partner, had a comfortable home with his partner, three children and ten guitars, but the days of record company largesse were gone – in summary, he *had* to go out there and continue to make a living, where Ian was in a different place altogether. This dichotomy is painfully obvious when one looks at a gig guide from 2003, where Ian is listed headlining at the Eden festival, while John is to be found as just one of the supporting acts behind R.E.M. He was also trying to make money from his art for the first time with an exhibition of Stone Roses cover designs (amongst other things) being held at the I.C.A. in London.

Reni, meanwhile, had retreated to the shadows once more after failing to make an impact with the Rub and Mani was working his way round to making a new album with Primal Scream

– though they liked to take their time with these things. In one interlude between work commitments, he hit upon the idea of challenging Peter Hook and Andy Rourke to a three-way bass duel. After the trio locked themselves away for a barmy few days, Mani finally emerged to tell the *Manchester Evening News* that it was he who held the crown as Manchester's greatest bass player of all time.

Meanwhile, Ian's work ethic naturally inclined him towards completing the fullest possible tour to promote the album, which was rapidly taking shape, and announcements were made for the tour to start in August. With four albums' worth of material to choose from, deciding what to play was now something of a dilemma. 'It's like a Bruce Springsteen set,' he said, 'it's cutting it down that's the problem.' But this problem was only intensified when someone happened to put a tape of one of John's solo gigs into his hands. Hearing the versions of songs like "Waterfall" and "She Bangs The Drums" that John was playing, Ian became incensed and decided that *he* was going to start playing Stone Roses songs as well. Of the tracks he was party to, he said later: 'Man, it was poor... and I thought "That was out of order" – if he ain't got the respect then I'm not gonna have none no more so I'm gonna play them myself now.'

To the impartial observer, such a decision would seem to guarantee the feud between Ian and John entering an even stranger phase, but Ian was, of course, quite unbothered. In March, he announced details of two warm-up gigs for a 2004-2005 tour to support the forthcoming album. He quietly booked members of Fools Gold to play with him and only a select group of people knew what was in store. Meanwhile, the profound legacy of the Roses was confirmed once more when a huge poll in the *Observer Music Monthly* saw *The Stone Roses* named as the greatest British album ever, the first time in any of these lists that the band had eclipsed the Beatles.

By now, Ian, Aziz and the band were working hard to finish the new album, to be called *Solarized,* and scheduled for release in September. Aziz had said in an interview that it would be 'fresh and different' and an indication of the guitar-led direction the album was taking was given by the fact that Ian was collaborating on a song, called "Keep What Ya Got" with Noel Gallagher. Now well into his thirties, Gallagher was becoming something of an elder statesman in British rock. He had always maintained a certain sense of gravitas, lacking in Liam (though he didn't mind having the odd pop at other bands like Coldplay) and there was a mutual respect between him and Ian. Also acting as guest on the album was Groove Armada's Tim Hutton.

As sessions drew to a close Ian played the first of two warm-up gigs, at a tiny club in Dublin on July 23rd. This was less noteworthy for Ian including Roses songs than it was for a little fracas that ensued: while he was singing he saw the guard trying to deal with one of the audience in a way that he objected to. Ian walked over with his mike and hit the guard over the head with it – the crack against his skull was heard clearly over the PA system and a huge row ensued which overshadowed the whole evening.

The atmosphere was likely to be more sedate at the next gig two days later, a benefit in aid of the National Trust, of which Ian was a great supporter. It was held in the very un-rock 'n' roll-like Claremont Landscape Gardens in Esher, Surrey. Claremont, dating from the time of Queen Anne, includes a house and gardens that have been major attractions for years but it is also notable for the three acre turf amphitheatre in its grounds, the last surviving example of such a structure in Europe. The stage for Ian's second warm up gig was constructed in front of this.

News of the Dublin fiasco had only filtered through to a few people so, for many, there was a sense of something unexpected in the air when Aziz played a short acoustic set and walked off stage, mysteriously declaring that he wouldn't be around for the next part of the evening. Very soon, Ian appeared on stage with an unfamiliar group of people.

Close to 5,000 fans listened in disbelief and awe as a frighteningly familiar bass rumble came from the band. Could it be "I Wanna Be Adored" that they were hearing? It was, and Ian was singing it – this time perfectly – for the first time since that shocking day in Reading. The response to that one song was amazing, but there followed, incredibly, a full hour of Stone Roses songs for the fans who were later described as being 'delirious with joy' with 'many actually in tears'. All the classic tunes were played as well as songs like "Mersey Paradise" and "Sally Cinnamon" which hadn't been heard live since before the first album came out. And this catalogue of Roses greats was followed by just a couple of solo Ian Brown songs – all in all an unforgettable evening in unforgettable surroundings.

Very soon Ian was back on the front page of the *NME*, being asked if the Stone Roses reformation was now at last immanent. And perhaps it was more forgivable for them to be asking now, as they could have argued that things come along in threes – there had recently been a band-approved DVD set, an interview with Reni and Mani which didn't discourage any rumour, and now this. But Ian used the opportunity, as ever, to take a swipe at John, this time complaining about his poor coverage of the Roses songs and sneering at his playing "Fools Gold" at all, rekindling an age-old grudge: 'He's got no respect, because we had to beg (Squire) to play "Fools Gold". We only played it three times. So, I thought, in that case, I'll bring it back to the people.'

With the album to be completed soon after this, Ian got back to talking about his solo career at the beginning of September, when the promotion started for *Solarized*. This included an appearance on Jo Whiley's Radio 1 show, with Noel Gallagher as 'guest' in Ian's band. Released on the 13th, it was soon clear that Ian was developing incredibly as an artist: if anyone had entertained fears that his astonishing work rate would mean a decrease in quality, they were quickly allayed, as, if anything, he was fast approaching a time when he would be making classics of his own to rank with *The Stone Roses*. *Solarized* represented a huge leap forwards: where it could justifiably have been said of the previous albums, that there had been a slightness to the songs or the singing, *Solarized* is, overwhelmingly, an album of strength.

The emphatic opening in "Longsight M13", reflects a fully assured and accomplished performer and composer from the kick-off. Longsight is an area in Manchester, Aziz's home area, which had sported "Free Ian Brown" graffiti all over the walls of buildings at the time of Ian's imprisonment. The graffiti is there to this day and Ian has been along to see it for himself. This song is a tribute to those graffiti artists in particular and his fans who have sustained him in general – whilst having a dig at 'ex-friends in a frenzy, green with envy-jealous eyes'. There is a startling intro of looping guitars and keyboard sounds created by Ian and the band, before a driving rhythm builds up for one of the most rousing choruses ever written by Ian, easily on a par with "Made Of Stone".

The brass player, Groove Armada's Tim Hutton, is an important presence on *Solarized*, especially notable on "Time Is My Everything" which somehow manages to combine Latin flavours with echoes of the *Coronation Street* theme music! The song written by Ian and Noel Gallagher is another fine collaboration. The strong chorus bears Gallagher's influence, while the song as a whole avoids the usual Oasis-style end-of-song disjointed paroxysms. The lyrics also cleverly emphasise the contrasting views of the pair, with lines like 'no-one's gonna notice if you're never right or wrong' suggesting Ian's moral certitude was chiding Gallagher for his equivocal responses to issues like the war in Iraq (which was receiving a lot of coverage at this time). In fact, this is Ian's most overtly political album to date, with "Kiss Ya Lips" a direct attack on the mooted introduction of identity cards by the government, and "Upside Down" littered with Ian's speechifying with phrases such as 'seven per cent own eighty-four per cent of all the wealth on Earth.'

The rock bias of the album is most emphatically revealed in "Destiny Of Circumstances" where it is Ian himself who is playing the weighty power chords in what is ostensibly a spiritual song – 'is it destiny or circumstance that leads you to the Lord of The Dance?' Meanwhile he is at his most romantic on "The Sweet Fantastic".

One of the greatest joys of *Solarized*, though, is the return to prominence of Aziz, who co-wrote the majority of the tracks with Ian and contributes some of his most stunning guitar playing yet. With his inimitable Asiatic style, he is as recognisable now as John Squire ever was, and here, apparent more than before, is his genuine talent for 'getting inside' a style: on the final track "One Way Ticket To Paradise" he produces a gripping series of fuzz-toned riffs and shifting rhythms, a devastating 'Eastern hard rock' hybrid.

But perhaps the most outstanding track of all on the album is Ian's and Aziz's "Solarized". Beginning with a beguiling series of chimes from Aziz, it suddenly explodes into life, driven by incredibly heavy bass, and spinning rhythms with keyboards appearing like great shafts of light, in keeping with the album's title. The haunting overall sound creates the feeling of a search-light tilting in and out of the song, even in parts reminding one of the 'Mysterons' motif used in *Captain Scarlet*. It is, in fact, a love song, a dark, masterpiece of a love song where Ian acknowledges the devil inside him – 'the light that she lives for in the dark she'll always find.'

Solarized is also by far the most commercial of Ian's solo albums and this time round there was no danger at all of him being treated as a space cadet in reviews. But the daring nature of the music and the breadth of his themes nevertheless made him difficult to pin down. Perhaps Ian would have been deemed avant-garde if it wasn't for the plain speaking in his lyrics *and* the heavy Northern accent. The *NME* gave him his due in coining him 'that increasingly rare beast: a songwriter who takes an interest in sound' and rather than welcoming the collaboration with Gallagher they now felt they had to point out that Noel wasn't even 'working in the same league' as Ian. Likewise, the *Guardian* couldn't resist the rival comparisons in their review: though they called it 'too mystical by half', they also felt obliged to acknowledge that it was 'streets ahead of John Squire's plain-Jane rock.'

Though strange that the *Guardian* called this, his most commercial effort, 'too mystical', it was a comment that hinted at a special status held by Ian. Now having had a longer recording career as a solo artist than he had had with the Stone Roses, Ian's reinvention was truly complete. King Monkey had taken an evolutionary step from being an 'alternative artist'. He could now clearly be seen as a *populist* mystic working in music, even as an indie icon. He had started out as one of a crowd – albeit a very prestigious one that included Shaun Ryder and Noel Gallagher, and of course John Squire – but now he was truly one of a kind. His political outspokenness, sympathy for the oppressed, close identification with his audience, personal quest for enlightenment, emerging romanticism and apparently daffy prejudices (pro-weed, vehemently anti-coke and now, anti-pork) all combined with his fearless explorations in music to mark him as a true original in his field.

Moreover, that close identification with his audience, which he'd cultivated and nurtured through punishing live schedules, had resulted in one of the most intensely loyal fanbases in music. The live tour that went with *Solarized* was the most successful he'd ever had. But did all this stop people speculating on a Stone Roses reunion? It seems not. And Ian hardly discouraged it by continuing to play renditions of Roses songs. Speculation steadily began to mount in October as he played these reworkings in Manchester for the first time, only to be joined on stage by Mani. Around this time, Ian was offered £1 million, for him alone, if he'd agree to a Stone Roses reunion – but he again declined. It was commonly believed that it was Ian who was stalling, that the others were in principle agreeable, and that a reunion was, in any case, inevitable.

Then, all of a sudden, it was John who scuppered the idea. The acclaim for Ian may or may not have got to him (for he had never really gone on an all-out attack before now), but Squire launched into an astonishing tirade in the December 2004 issue of *Q* that started out as a denial that his problems with coke had ruined *The Second Coming*. Though he later claimed that he was quoted out of context, he was alleged to have said that it was Ian who was stoned throughout the second album's sessions and 'at best, he was a tuneless knob, at worst, he was a paranoid mess.'

By contrast, Ian was in a cheerful mood in October, talking about the old days to the *Independent*. This was brought on by a

BBC3 documentary series *Blood On The Turntables* that focused on rock band's business wrangles. Gareth Evans turned in a stellar performance on this, showing off his golf course and giving the impression that he had been somehow the fifth member of the band. 'When it came on,' Ian said, 'I thought I was gonna be, like, blazing by the end of it, but I was laughing.'

For the time being, Ian said nothing in response to John's acerbic comments. In December, when the interview with John had been published, he was in the middle of his tour, at the same time busily helping to launch one of his altruistic endeavours. On the 11th, he became a patron of James Watt College in Greenock, one of the most deprived areas in Europe, which had opened a state-of-the-art recording studio. Ian helped launch the facility with a gig and revealed that he would be taking an active role, holding musical workshops and recording sessions regularly: 'It's a major honour,' he said, 'the guys have put a lot of work into this place, a lot of love.'

But, in an interview in January, Ian hit back at John and the rumours that the Roses were reforming once again – whilst also taking the opportunity to mention that his own greatest hits album was coming. For many, this was the first that they had heard of a greatest hits album and it was an indication, in itself, of how far Ian had come in his solo career – whereas John's had, by now, effectively stalled. Ian was already working on a new track to include on this compilation as well as making his first major foray to the United States, now interested to see if there was an audience for his music in America, rather than launch an all-out attack on the market. Because of contractual difficulties, only *Golden Greats* had been released in the US thus far, so this was something of a debut. A series of shows there in the spring did go down very well – only marred by an attack on Ian from a fan coming out of the audience. For a couple of days, the headlines seemed to be trying to suggest that Ian was somehow back to his 'bad old ways' when it was reported that he was arrested, but it was actually a minor incident with no repercussions.

In May, a mellower interview with John appeared in *Time Out*, causing the rumours of a Roses reunion to start up yet again. In this one, John said that his immediate plans were to record 'a ferocious guitar album' and then 'to get the Roses back together.' Then, he, Mani and Reni were all seen together in a Manchester club and Reni also suggested in an interview that they would all play together again.

Though he must have felt he was hitting an exercise ball in a boxing gym that came back at him all the time, Ian issued yet another rejection of the idea ('there's more chance of me reforming the Happy Mondays than the Stone Roses') – even though the personal offer he had received to reform was now hiked up to £1.8 million. Some band reunions were big business now. One of the notable stories in 2005 was of the reforming of the Pixies, a much-missed band that had reunited when a couple of the members had fallen on hard times – they all achieved financial security with this one tour.

If Ian was becoming bored with it, Mani was becoming exasperated with Ian and John: 'They're both over 40 now and it's getting undignified,' he said, 'I'm determined to orchestrate the pair of them being in the same room together without the other knowing.'

But Ian was as difficult as ever to keep up with. Fresh from the States he announced more festival dates, including T In The Park, Glastonbury, V2005 and another unusual choice of venue in Thetford Forest. He also issued a statement in time for the General Election that year, outlining a set of strident political lyrics. Though it wasn't really taken seriously and it may even have been ill advised, he was making a serious point about the lack of any real difference between the three main political parties. His anti-Establishment stance remained unchanged, despite his wealth. And he was also using his wealth to help others: at one extreme, playing a benefit gig for the victims of war in Kosovo and at the other, sponsoring a tiny local football team, and getting involved with his community in London.

There was a community spirit for the gig at Thetford too, Ian's fans having to walk deep into a forest in summer to get to see him. It turned out to be an atmospheric communion with his hardcore followers, whom Ian spent a long time chatting with and signing autographs for either side of the gig, before disappearing into the trees. By contrast, the T In The Park show was plagued by technical problems and a less partisan crowd made their feelings known. Ian responded angrily, embarking on a series of rows and even taking the band off the stage at one point.

Glastonbury was still good for him though he wasn't happy about the organiser, Michael Eavis, trying to get him to reform the Roses as a special event for the gig and, in contrast to a lot of people, he hated the idea of someone like Kylie Minogue appearing at the 'alternative' festival. His show, especially now it included so many Roses tunes, was one of the best received at Glastonbury, which was still considered a 'lucky' place by him. At V2005, Ian seemed to attract the most comment from sporting a bright pink tracksuit. And the gigs could be summed up in one sentence by Ian: 'I've got white whiskers, but the crowds just keep getting bigger.'

Following the festival run Ian was soon announcing yet more gigs to come as well as firm news of the greatest hit compilation. The retrospective included two new songs that Ian had been working on: "All Ablaze" and "Return Of The Fisherman", both strong tunes in the style of the numbers on *Solarized*. The decision to call the compilation *The Greatest*, after his old hero Muhammad Ali, may rank as him at his most immodest ever, but it nevertheless somehow held a certain charm. The rather *un*glamorous, grainy black and white image of Ian, now starting to appear all over the UK, showed a forty-two year old artist staring out confidently – it contrasted sharply with the *Monkey Business* photo of yesteryear, where the story of the album had made its start.

As interviews came round for *The Greatest*, it became clear that the accent was still on forward thinking, further emphasised by the video for the "All Ablaze" single, which featured Ian throwing images of the Roses in the fire. And its iconoclasm didn't end there. Written on the day that Pope John Paul II died, it was a song about 'how the organised churches have stolen God from the people in an attempt to sell him back.' And the hacks kept drawing him to comment on John and the Roses, though in the *NME*, he was as emphatic as he could be on the reunion idea: 'Definitely not. It won't happen. No way.' As for alluding to John, he twisted the knife in this time, highlighting the contrast in fortunes between the pair: 'If it were me and I'd left and formed the Seahorses and hit a brick wall, while John was releasing his greatest hits, do you think he'd be thinking about reforming the Stone Roses? I don't think so.'

The *NME* article, prefaced with 'Why we need him more than ever', was an irony considering that they had never really taken him seriously up to this point, but with the ritual of the Roses questions over, this interview presented a clear insight into the man as he stood in 2005. His essential non-conformism was more firmly held than ever. He was still going on marches and poured scorn on Tony Blair as well as the Pope. Perhaps more interestingly (especially as this was printed on the pages of the *NME* circa 2005), he spoke about a moral code, how money was unimportant and how 'music should only be about expression and connecting with people.' This interview, incidentally, took place soon after the Live 8 concert, which the *NME* had backed: Ian had predictably been amongst the tiny minority with (serious) criticisms about the event – 'the end result is to up the profile of the bands, sell records. Who do these people think they are, thinking they're saving the Africans? It's the same attitude we had 100 years ago. "Let's educate the savages." It's patronising.'

The *NME* was unquestionably right: a rock star in his forties, releasing a greatest hits compilation, and unafraid to deliver an uncomfortable message like this was worth having indeed.

There followed another major interview in *The Guardian* expounding more of the same kind of thing, but this piece made particularly fascinating reading as the journalist zoomed in on the bitter feud with John Squire in greater depth than the subject had been tackled before. The questions weren't so heavily geared around a Stone Roses reunion in this instance, acknowledging for once, the full emotional impact of the Ian/John feud over the years. It was possible, the piece argued, to see the dark and light in Ian's character, already suggested by Ian himself in 'the light that she lives for in the dark she'll always find.'

It was equally clear that Ian had demonised John in his mind ('he didn't give a fuck,' he said of the split), and John had got under his skin. With someone of such moral certitude, the devil 'already in me' was John, if it was anyone: one could suggest that this continued resentment was spurring Ian on in his great success, and the warmth from audiences that he always responded to with genuine love – his light side – counterbalanced any hate that he might have felt for John – his dark side. Ian mentioned to The *Guardian* journalist how John had said he still loved him in the message that he'd received in prison. The journalist shot back: 'Do you still love John?' The answer came back 'No.' 'But', continued the journalist, 'I'm not convinced'.

He may be right, but as the end of 2005 looms in sight, with Ian Brown's *The Greatest* a resounding success, more gigs in the offing (including a planned concert in China) and a new deal for two albums, which Ian has already started working on, there's one thing you can be sure of: the ongoing feud between Ian and John is alive and well. It is one of the most fascinating, most mysterious feuds in rock history. The one between Waters and Gilmour may have recently been laid to rest at Live 8, but the one between Lennon and McCartney lasted even longer and was never resolved before Lennon's death.

Looking at Ian Brown today, it is the shadow of his feud that looms largest over him, as well his former band. After years of struggle, Ian is a major figure in rock in his own right now. Any reunion of the Stone Roses, however fondly they are remembered, would somehow dent the prestige of Ian's incredible achievements as a solo artist – and ever since he came out of prison he has made it clear he meant to be remembered as Ian Brown and not Ian Brown of the Stone Roses. But a reunion is dependent on some kind of rapprochement between Ian and John.

It may never happen, just like Lennon and McCartney – and with such things, rock myths can only thrive. It is this author's guess that a rapprochement, and thus a reunion, will *never* happen. If so, Ian Brown may find himself in a unique position. With his phenomenal work rate and musical daring, all the signs are that the best is yet to come: his resurrection has already ensured his major status as an artist, and so – alone among all his peers – he seems destined to become a musical legend. With the Stone Roses, *and* without them.

EPILOGUE

Why We Need Ian Brown More Than Ever

The object of *Already In Me* was to provide a detailed history of the life and career of Ian Brown, with and without the Stone Roses. It's probably worth pointing out that, ultimately, the most significant purpose in writing such a book is not to provide an exhaustive and painstaking list of all the music that has been made or the gigs that have gone down, (that's what the internet is there for) but to chart the unique *trajectory* of Ian Brown's career.

There are few people – and even fewer rock stars – who have achieved the kind of personal and professional rebirth that is central to Ian Brown's story, and it is certainly all too easy to forget that Ian was *the* member of the Stone Roses whose reputation was in complete tatters, following their split. But, he was also the one who proved *every* commentator wrong when he came back from the dead.

At the age of forty-two, his career has spanned quite a few eras in British music: Indie, 'Madchester', Britpop and so on. Of all the artists of the post-punk era, Ian Brown is one of the very few –alongside Morrissey, for example – to achieve solo success after being in a celebrated band: the likes of Bernard Butler, Richard Ashcroft and, yes, John Squire have all fallen by the wayside. And with his continuing development as a musician and composer, Ian probably even has an edge on Morrissey who, in any case, seems to drift back on to the circuit merely to 'remind' people of his iconic status. Somehow, Ian *always* seems to be there now as a major British rock icon of the 21st century.

His appeal is undoubtedly rooted in the fact that he is now very much a *multi-dimensional* rock artist. Though he has never come up with any formal credo, his humanity, egalitarianism, sense of political injustice and morality are all evinced in his proclamations – in interview, political statements, activism, lyrics *and* music. He's a long way from walking the land in sackcloth and ashes, but even so, it is almost impossible not to see him as an Old

Testament figure transplanted to the 21st century: whether he is leading the ever-increasing crowds in 'communion' at a concert, tilling the soil, alighting on another good cause to promote, exalting the 'righteous life' or simply thundering against cocaine and alcohol. In this age of conformity, all this makes for an inspirational figure – even though it lays him wide open to accusations of having a messiah complex.

As for his place in the musical landscape, it really depends on how you prefer to look at these things. If you were to see him, as it were, on the horizon, he would seem to be walking along with his monkey gait, sometimes walking tall, at other times stumbling along, and occasionally (spectacularly) dropping from view – but he picks himself up and just keeps on walking. Or, if you prefer to look at it from a birds eye view, he has really been bobbing and weaving all along, ducking and taking the blows– just like his hero, Ali. And now he has reached the higher ground.

In his life and in his music, tramping through all the haphazard events that have defined him, it surely wouldn't be going overboard to say that he has emerged as a great Englishman with, and in common with all great Englishmen, a serious worldview. In short, Ian Brown is a man for all seasons.

APPENDIXES

I

An Ian Brown Bibliography

As we have seen, the books in Ian's Brown life have inspired him just as much as the music. As he has already provided a view of his favourite music on the *Planetgroove and Under The Influence* compilations, a short digest of 'Ian Brown' books seemed to be in order. While it isn't suggested that he has read every single one of these books, all of them reflect his interests or bear reference while considering his work – and are vital in any understanding of the artist and the man.

The Bible - Exodus
The book of Exodus recounts the delivery of the Israelites from Egypt, the giving of the law at Mount Sinai and the creation of the tabernacle (or sanctuary) for worship. The central figure is, of course, Moses. Ian is a regular reader of the Bible 'for the stories' but the stern, often unyielding, brave and righteous Moses is far and away his favourite character.

Bruce Lee: Fighting Spirit – Bruce Thomas
Curiously, there are only a couple of English-language books on Lee but this one, written by Elvis Costello's former bassist, is generally considered to be the best.

The Citizen Kane Book – Pauline Kael
Citizen Kane is Ian's favourite film by a long way – he once watched it continuously at a Manchester cinema from 11 a.m. to past midnight and can quote huge chunks of dialogue. This book is the distinguished American film critic's controversial story of the film.

Collected Poems - William Blake
A visionary poet and artist, William Blake is also one of England's most celebrated mystics and oddballs. An even more intense devotee of the Bible than Ian (it is said that he broke down in tears every time he read the story of 'The Prodigal Son'), Blake, like Ian, saw visions, – though presumably peyote was pretty thin on the ground in 18th century London. Ian's favourite poem of Blake's is "Tyger, Tyger".

Grafters – Colin Blaney
This constituted some of Ian's more lightweight reading in 2005, the recollections of journeying football hooligans.

Harry Potter and The Prisoner Of Azkaban – JK Rowling
Bedtime reading for Ian and his son Emilio, the third in the series of *Potter* books has the thirteen-year old wizard take on a maniacal mass murderer.

Here I Stand – Paul Robeson
Paul Robeson published *Here I Stand* in 1958, when his career was practically in ruins. With America still in the grip of McCarthyism, it was a bold, unflinching riposte to the people who had blacklisted him. Though it didn't resurrect his career, it is a moving autobiography as well as proud testament to the Black struggle in America

The Koran
The Holy Book of Islam, Ian was given the Koran as a present by his sister. It has been an inspiration to him just as much as the Bible and, in recent years, he has often sought to point out its essential message of peace and love to all peoples – including non-Muslims.

Muhammad Ali: His Life And Times – Thomas Hauser
This is the definitive account of the life and career of Ian's foremost hero.

Music Of The Spheres: A Nature Lover's Astronomy – Florence Armstrong Grondal
Ian's interest in astronomy extends beyond NASA videos, and this book, published in 1926, is an accessible and wacky almanac (with chapter headings like 'Behold The Stars!') that nevertheless studies in depth the Pythagorean theory of *musica univeralis*: the music of the spheres.

The 1932 Kinder Trespass – Benny Rothman
Published in 1982 by Willow Publishing in Ian's hometown, Timperley, this is the definitive account from Rothman himself fifty years later. This protest against the upper classes' seizure of common land led to Rothman's wrongful imprisonment, but it was a milestone in the campaign to eventual victory for public access to the moors and mountains.

The Rise & Fall of The Third Reich – William L Shirer
Shirer was an American ambassador to Berlin in the 1930s and he saw the rise of Nazism at firsthand. This is his account of those days, but it also provides a history and explanation of the homosexual power structures of Ancient Greece and Rome (as well as Nazi Germany) – and helps clear Ian of any taint of homophobia in his *Melody Maker* comments.

Soul On Ice – Eldridge Cleaver
This is probably the most important book that Ian read while in prison. Cleaver, who went on to form the Black Panther movement, wrote it while he was in Folsom Prison: and it is a potent, highly recommended mix of confession, history, politics and boxing stories – including the legendary fight between Muhammad Ali and Floyd Patterson.

The Scramble For Africa – Thomas Pakenham
A gripping and often shocking history, this explains the 'dark continent' and its systematic rape by Europe, who sent over explorers, politicians, evangelists, mercenaries, journalists and tycoons

in the vicious scramble for loot, markets and slaves. It also tells how the former colonial powers still dominate the economies of the African nations, most of which are under one-party or dictatorial rule.

II

Second Coming Apocrypha

The crazy 'interlude' between *The Stone Roses* and *The Second Coming* has provided a wealth of outlandish stories as people speculated on just what it is that the Stone Roses were doing in and around all those studios – when they were supposed to be recording their second album. Here, in no particular order, are the ten best stories to emerge from those wacky days.

1 While based in Wales, the band saw that they were surrounded by golf courses, a new game to all of them: they soon joined the local club and became addicts, often playing dozens of holes in one day.

2 When Ian met Noel and Liam Gallagher in Monmouth, he discovered that they were recording nearby and invited them over. Their regular visits in the dead of night led to a series of moonlit tractor races between the two bands.

3 Having joined a local football team in Monmouth, Mani had a chequered debut in the first game: he scored three goals (three brilliant individual efforts) but accidentally hit a fan's dog with one shot that went astray and got sent off – all in the first half.

4 All four members of the band became obsessed with Ford Fiestas when they first hit the countryside, and hired a fleet of them to race around in.

5 Early on in the sessions, John Squire once watched the video of Led Zeppelin's *The Song Remains The Same* continuously for twenty-three hours.

6 Ian drastically put on weight during the sessions, going up to eighteen stone.

7 In the first month of the sessions, the band insisted on eating take-away pizzas every night for their evening meal.

8 In one burst of activity, and itching to get on stage again, the band rehearsed a twenty-minute version of KC & The Sunshine Band's "That's The Way I Like It" for their live show.

9 As Ian had now become quite a skilful gardener, he entered some of his roses in a local flower show – he came in at third behind a retired colonel and an eighty-one year old lady who wrote Mills & Boon novels.

10 When the band learned that the *NME* were sending yet another journalist up to the studio to see what was going on, they had an eight-foot 'Reni' hat made. It was placed in one of the fields just next to the studio and, as the Roses huddled together underneath, the journalist walked past, thinking it was a capsized tent.

III

Discographies

These short discographies are really only intended to detail the main and original versions of Ian's and the Roses' work. It's with a small measure of resentment that one includes the overwhelmingly cynical later singles releases from Silvertone - and contentment that the equally cynical albums are excluded!

For a really exhaustive list of everything, complete with exact dates, cover images, full commentaries etc, readers are directed to www.ianbrownwhisper.co.uk which is linked to the official Ian Brown site at www.ianbrown.co.uk . For the Roses, the best site is www.thestoneroses.co.uk

Stone Roses Discography

Albums

The Stone Roses (1989) ORELP502 Silvertone
Track listing: I Wanna Be Adored, She Bangs The Drums, Water-
fall, Don't Stop, Bye Bye Badman, Elizabeth My Dear, (Song for
my) Sugar Spun Sister, Made Of Stone, Shoot You Down, This Is
The One, I Am The Resurrection
N.B.: The tenth anniversary edition also included the following:
Fools Gold, What The World Is Waiting For, Elephant Stone,
Where Angels Play. The second disc included an enhanced por-
tion with music videos, a discography, lyrics and a photo gallery.

The Second Coming (1994) CD GED 24503 2xLP GEF-24503
Geffen
Track listing: Breaking Into Heaven, Driving South, Ten Storey
Love Song, Daybreak, Your Star Will Shine, Straight To The
Man, Begging You, Tightrope, Good Times, Tears, How Do You
Sleep, Love Spreads, The Foz

Singles

So Young/Tell Me (1,200 issued) 12 Thin 001 Thin Line
Sally Cinnamon/Here It Comes 7 Black REV 36 Revolver
Elephant Stone/The Hardest Thing In The World 7 ORE 1 Silver-
tone
Made Of Stone/Going Down 7 ORE 2 Silvertone
She Bangs The Drums/Standing Here 7 ORE 6 Silvertone
Fools Gold/What The World Is Waiting For 7 ORE 13 Silvertone
One Love/Something's Burning 7 ORE 17 Silvertone
I Wanna Be Adored/Where Angels Play 7 ORE 31 Silvertone
Waterfall/One Love 7 ORE 35 Silvertone
I Am The Resurrection (Pan and Scan Radio Version)/I Am The
Resurrection (Highly Resurrected Dub) 7 ORE 40 Silvertone

Love Spreads/Your Star Will Shine 7 GFS 84 Geffen
Ten Storey Love Song/Ride On 7 GFS 84 Geffen
Fools Gold, Fools Gold (The Tall Paul Remix)/Fools Gold
(Cricklewood Ballroom Mix) 12 ORE T 71 Silvertone
Begging You (album version)/Begging You (chic mix)/Begging
You (cox's ultimatum mix)/Begging You (stone corporation vox)
12 GEFST 22060 Geffen

Ian Brown Discography

Albums

Unfinished Monkey Business (1998) 539 916-1 Polydor
Track listing: Intro - Under The Paving Stone: The Beach, My
Star, You Can't See Me, Ice Cold Cube, Sunshine, Lions, Corps-
es In The Mouths, What Happened To Ya Part 1, What Happened
To Ya, Part II, Nah Nah, Deep Pile Dreams, Unfinished Monkey
Business

Golden Greats (2000) 543141-2 Polydor
Track listing: Getting High, Love Like A Fountain, Free My Way,
Set My Baby Free, So Many Soldiers, Golden Gaze, Dolphins
Were Monkeys, Neptune, First World, Babasonicos

Music Of The Sphere (2001) B0000784XR Polydor
Track listing: F.E.A.R., Stardust, The Gravy Train, Bubbles, Hear
No See No, Northern Lights, Whispers, El Mundo Pequeno, For-
ever And A Day, Shadow Of A Saint

Remixes Of The Spheres (2002) B0000784XR Polydor
Track listing: F.E.A.R. (UNKLE Mix), Northern Lights (The
Freelance Hellraiser Mix), The Gravy Train (N.O.W. Mix),
Forever And A Day (Cedarblue Mix), Shadow Of A Saint (The

Boy Bierton Mix), Hear No See No Speak No (Album Version), Cokane In My Brain (DJ Mark Nuremburg Scratch Mix), The Gravy Train (N.O.W. Instrumental), Stardust (Instrumental), El Mundo Pequeno (Live Acoustic Version),
F.E.A.R. (UNKLE Instrumental)

Solarized (2004) B0002QCBFO Polydor
Longsight M13, Time Is My Everything, Destiny Of Circumstance, Upside Down, Solarized, The Sweet Fantastic, Keep What Ya Got, Home Is Where The Heart Is, One Way Ticket To Paradise, Kiss Ya Lips (No I.D.). Happy Ever After

The Greatest (2005) B000A0BC02 Polydor
My Star (Album Version), Corpses In Their Mouths (Album Version), Can't See Me (Bacon & Quarmby Remix), Be There (collaboration with UNKLE), Love Like A Fountain (Single Version), Dolphins Were Monkeys (Single Version), Golden Gaze (Single Version) F.E.A.R. (Album Version), Whispers (Album Version) Forever And A Day (New Version), Keep What Ya Got (Album Version), Time Is My Everything (Album Version) , Longsight M13 (Album Version), Reign (Album Version, collaboration with UNKLE) Lovebug (New Version), All Ablaze, Return Of The Fisherman

Singles*

My Star/See The Dawn 571986-7 Polydor
Corpses/Jesus On The Move/Come Again (Part 1) 569 654-7 Polydor
Can't See Me/Can't See Me (Vocal Dub) 657092-7 Polydor
Love Like A Fountain/The Fisherman 561516-7 Polydor
Dolphins Were Monkeys/Corpses 561637-7 Polydor
Golden Gaze/Sunshine 561844-7 Polydor
Thriller/Billie Jean 561908-1 Polydor
F.E.A.R./ F.E.A.R. (Instrumental) 587284-7 Polydor
Whispers/El Mundo Pequeno 570538-7 Polydor

Keep What Ya Got/Love Bug 986777-4 Polydor
Time Is My Everything/Where Angels Play 987000-7 Polydor
All Ablaze/Destiny Or Circumstance 987325-3 Polydor

* all original 7" releases, other versions exist in different formats

Singles With Other Artists

Be There – with UNKLE MW108CD1 A&M
Let Robeson Song – with Manic Street Preachers 671 7735 Sony
R.E.I.G.N. – with UNKLE GUSIN007CD A&M
Desire – with Gus Gus H2O036CD Underwater

Ian Brown As Compiler

Planet Groove Presents Ian Brown (March 2001) Planet CD03
Planet Groove
Track Listing: Love Is The Answer – Garnet Silk, No, No, No
(World A Respect Mix) – Dawn Penn Ft. Bounty Killer, Dennis
Brown and Ken Boothe, One Way – Sizzla, Queen Elizabeth –
Eek-A-Mouse, The Stopper – Cutty Ranks, Complaint and Buju
Banton, Roadrunner – Junior Walker And The All Stars, Talkin'
Loud Sayin' Nothin' – James Brown, Love Child – Diana Ross
And The Supremes, Just Don't Mean A Thing – Funk Inc., Check
Your Bucke – Eddie Bo, Are You With Me? – Son Of Bazerk,
Devil Made Me Do IT – Paris, Basic Instructions Before Leaving Earth – Genius/GZA, The 900 Number – 45 King, Gangsters
Paradise – Coolio, Paid In Full (Coldcut Mix) – Eric B & Rakim,
The Fug – Cymande, Dreams Of Santa Anna – Orange Lemon,
Stars – Mr Fingers

Under The Influence – Ian Brown (September 2003) UTICD002
DMC

Track listing: Liquid Swords – Gza/Genius, Meaning Of The 5% - Brand Nubian, Man In The Hills – Burning Spear, Fade Away – Junior Byles, Complaint – Buju Banton, (White Man) In Hammersmith Palais – The Clash, Mi God Mi King – Papa Levi, No Other Like Jah – Sizzla, The Fug and Cymande, T.I.M.E. – Edwin Starr, Take Some Time Out For Love – Isley Bros., War On The Bulllshit – Osiris, Too Late – Larry Williams, Across 110th St – Bobby Womack, Lover – The De-Lites, 99½ – Dorothy Love Coates

A WORD ABOUT THE AUTHOR

Michael O'Connell has worked in publishing and, in particular, music books for well over a decade, being one of the 'founder members' of the world's only music specific book shop. His fascination and admiration for the Stone Roses generally, and their erstwhile lead singer in particular, began when he caught a very early show by the band in a tiny Manchester club, attended by less than thirty people.

O'Connell has written for a number of periodicals over the years, including several fanzines, and has had his essays on the Stone Roses and connected subjects published all over the world.

Michael O'Connell lives in West London. Ian Brown - Already In Me - With And Without The Roses *is his first book.*

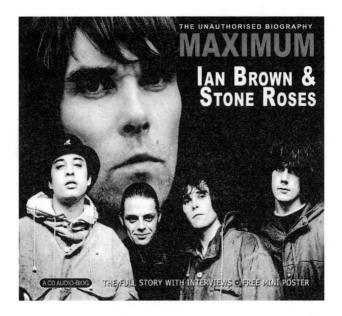

Maximum Ian Brown & The Stone Roses

The Unauthorised Biography
Cat: ABCD217

A 60-minute spoken word biography of Ian Brown and The Stone Roses featuring interview clips throughout and covering the extraordinary life and career of The Roses and their unconventional frontman. This limited edition package is a must for fans and collectors alike.

Comes in deluxe packaging with outer slipcase, 8-page illustrated booklet with rare photographs and free fold out poster.

Available from all good record stores, online at Amazon and other good sites and from ***www.chromedreams.co.uk***

INDEX